SoHo

Charles R. Simpson

SoHo: The Artist in the City

The University of Chicago Press
Chicago and London

CHARLES R. SIMPSON is assistant professor of sociology at the State University of New York at Plattsburgh.

The University of Chicago Press, Chicago 60637
The University of Chicago Press, Ltd., London

88 87 86 85 84 83 82 81   5 4 3 2 1

Library of Congress Cataloging in Publication Data

Simpson, Charles R
    SoHo, the artist in the city.

    Bibliography: p.
    Includes index.
    1. Avant-garde (Aesthetics)—New York (City)
2. Artists—New York (City)—Socio-economic status.
3. SoHo, New York (City)—Description. I. Title.
N6535.N5S53   306′.4   80-27083
ISBN 0-226-75937-7

Maps by Jonathan Williams
Photographs by Woody Goldberg

For Anita

Contents

	Illustrations	viii
	Acknowledgments	ix
1.	Introduction: Art and Cultural Renovation	1
2.	The Structure of the SoHo Art Market	15
3.	The Dealer: Gatekeeper to the Art World	31
4.	The Unsuccessful SoHo Artist: The Social Psychology of an Occupation	53
5.	The Successful Artist in the SoHo Market	73
6.	The Integration of the Status Community	97
7.	The South Houston Industrial District in Transition	111
8.	SoHo and the Politics of Urban Planning	129
9.	The Achievement of Territorial Community	153
10.	Family Life in SoHo	189
11.	The Evolution of SoHo as a Real-Estate Market	219
	Appendix 1: Methods	245
	Appendix 2: Tables	247
	Notes	251
	Index	267

Illustrations

Maps

Southern Manhattan   x
SoHo   xi

Photographs, following page 152

The SoHo "valley"
Galleries along West Broadway
A SoHo gallery interior
Selling art alfresco
Street life in SoHo
Moving art into a loft studio
A painter's loft
Artist, son, and assistant in the studio
The SoHo Center

Acknowledgments

Research which involves participation in the life of a community generates a debt which is too extensive to adequately acknowledge. I wish to try to recognize that debt, however, by expressing my gratitude to each resident and observer of SoHo with whom I had the pleasure of speaking. They generously took time from their own tasks to give me the benefit of their insights during lengthy interviews and informal conversations, answering more questions than I had thought to ask.

This study began as a doctoral dissertation at the Graduate Faculty, the New School for Social Research. Both while I was a student and thereafter I have been fortunate in having the advice and commentary of Stanford M. Lyman, Jeffrey C. Goldfarb, and Arthur J. Vidich. I am in debt to Arthur J. Vidich in particular for numerous suggestions from which this manuscript benefited. I would like to thank Anita Rapone for her continuous objectivity and criticism in reading each version of this manuscript. She is to be credited for preventing at least some of my errors from finding their way into print, and her personal support was invaluable. I would also like to thank Rosanne Martorella for her suggestions and encouragement.

I would like to express my gratitude to the U.S. Department of Housing and Urban Development for their dissertation grant, number H-5076, which helped support me while conducting much of this research.

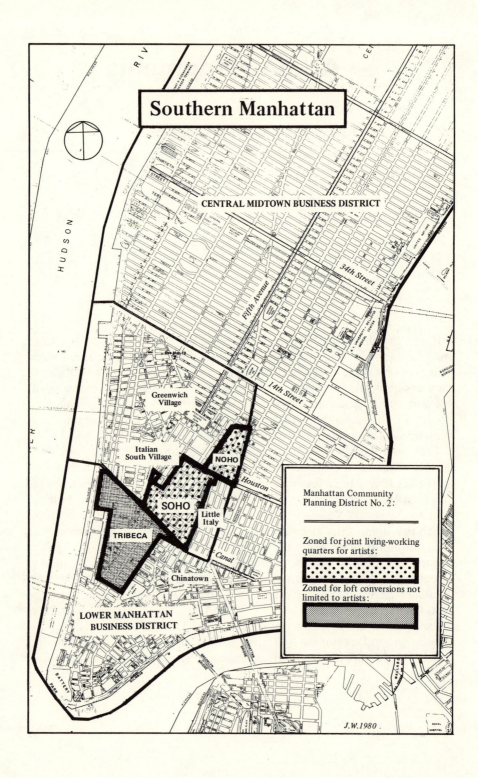

Southern Manhattan

CENTRAL MIDTOWN BUSINESS DISTRICT

34th Street

HUDSON

Fifth Avenue

14th Street

Greenwich Village

Italian South Village

NOHO

Houston

SOHO

Little Italy

TRIBECA

Canal

Chinatown

Manhattan Community
Planning District No. 2:

Zoned for joint living-working
quarters for artists:

Zoned for loft conversions not
limited to artists:

LOWER MANHATTAN
BUSINESS DISTRICT

J.W.1980.

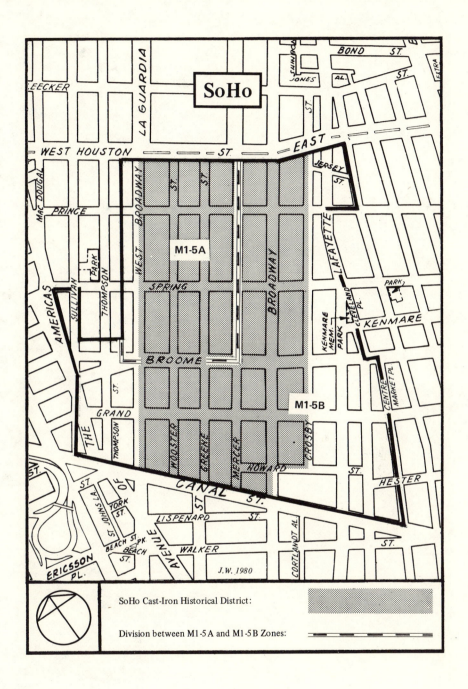

SoHo Cast-Iron Historical District:

Division between M1-5A and M1-5B Zones:

1 Introduction
Art and Cultural Renovation

Cultural Layering and the SoHo Community

To the observer standing on an abandoned Hudson River pier at Hoboken, New Jersey, the Manhattan skyline appears as two sky-scraper ridges separated by a valley. These ridges are, of course, the commercial buildings in the midtown office area and in the financial district at the southern tip of the island. During the period of rapid construction of office towers which began in the late 1950s and ended with a glutted market for commercial space in the early 1970s, these clusters of skyscrapers thrust up and outward toward each other. But they did not meet. Nor has the renewed office construction of the late 1970s obliterated the valley between them. Contrary to the vision of Manhattan guiding the actions of the public planners and private developers, the valley area had remained a low-rise and low-density exception to the general pattern of land use in Manhattan.[1]

A visitor walking the streets of this valley encounters at its center the forty-three block district known as "SoHo," a term originating with urban planners who as late as 1962 referred to this area as the South Houston Industrial District. The acronym designates the structurally intact but now socially transformed district where most of New York's and much of the nation's visual art is created and marketed. A residential population of approximately forty-five hundred people, predominantly artists and their families, work and live in renovated factory lofts. They have created a community whose economic foundation rests on

1

the demand for contemporary fine art and whose cultural identity is rooted in the dynamics and contradictions of the American middle class.

The artists of SoHo first drifted into the district in the late 1950s. They were a shadow presence in a zone of least resistance to un- authorized dwelling. The artists settled into the segments of industrial decay which ribboned through what was then a zone of doll makers and dress manufacturers, rag balers and waste-paper processors. Painters, sculptors, and dancers found that deserted factory lofts were uniquely adaptable to their needs for unrestricted space. Landlords found artists to be useful scavengers of otherwise unmarketable upper floors in poorly maintained buildings. They were occupants who improved the lofts they inhabited and who were legally in no position to ask for anything but to be left alone, beneath the notice of the law in their interstitial niche. A symbiotic contract was struck. Landlords received a modest rent and could count on leaky roofs being fixed by the tenant; artists in search of cheap but ample studios found space here on a scale commensurate to the widest sweep of artistic expression.

In the decade of the 1960s SoHo's population of artists grew. The industrial base of the area declined and, simultaneously, more and more middle-class youth set out on an artistic trek which led them inevitably to New York City, the nation's center for art education, museums, and art sales. Having perfected the techniques of coping with life in lofts, and finding that more of the district's spaces were losing their attraction for manufacturing tenants, painters and sculptors formed cooperative asso- ciations to occupy and remodel entire factory buildings for studio and residential purposes. The "art world," the urban subculture to which artists belong by virtue of their shared commitments and common in- stitutional focuses, was augmented by a new basis of interaction: finding, renovating, and collectively financing loft studios in SoHo.

The extent of the growing renovation brought the artists new prob- lems. At first they had only to supplant the established rat population and provide heat and hot water in buildings with coal furnaces long rusted into uselessness. But as greater numbers of artists copied the success of the "pioneers," open confrontation with the city became the artists' most pressing difficulty. In the early period, fire and building inspectors had been third parties to the illegal housing accommodation between artist and building owner. The inspectors took their tithe in petty graft or simply attended to higher priorities elsewhere in the city, thus informally licensing the residency. The increasing numbers of art- ists and the growing publicity surrounding their residency inevitably made their occupancy a political issue. An illegal expedient had grown into a de facto urban design. Parties with an interest in the course of urban change—the planners protecting their professional prerogatives, the developers, the urban reformers of varied stripe, and elected officials—generated opposition which made the place of artists in the city an explicit issue.

The SoHo artists, trading on the patron relationship between art and its sponsors, won legal sanction of their residency in SoHo by 1971 in a contest which reveals much about the position of the artist in urban society and national culture. The humanistic prestige of art was hammered into an administrative code of protections.[2]

The artists had won a political struggle to defeat demolition schemes and to secure a residential monopoly in what was otherwise a manufacturing zone, and SoHo subsequently became an attractive location for art dealers. The gallery display technique and the storage of art require extensive but modestly priced space. This is especially true when, as with contemporary art, much of the dealers' inventory is speculative in value and executed on the large scale established by abstract expressionism. SoHo offered the dealers more space for their money than was available in the established gallery district along Manhattan's Fifty-seventh Street. More important, the surrounding artist community facilitated interaction between artist, dealer, and client, generating an ambiance which lured clients away from the more fashionable uptown art neighborhood with the prospect of investing in new trends at their very source, a concept promoted by the garment industry in their use of the Manhattan "factory showroom."[3] During the 1970s new galleries opened in SoHo, and the contemporary-art operations of many established uptown dealers were relocated among the artists' lofts, making the area the focus of the city's trade in the work of living artists.

The galleries, in their turn, attracted art lovers and the "culture-curious" from among the professional and managerial populations of Manhattan which were growing with the completion of each new office tower. Having established themselves as a part of the urban design, however, the artists discovered that complete control of the area was beyond their economic and political resources. The middle class exacted a tribute in return for its sponsorship.

SoHo was rapidly becoming known as a quaint ramble for which architectural guidebooks and historical tours were quickly provided. To exploit the pedestrian traffic into galleries and through the district, entrepreneurs opened sophisticated Japanese, Chinese, and French restaurants. These all but displaced an earlier generation of laborers' cafeterias and inexpensive health-food eating places; the remnant of these thrive by studiously ignoring the transformation around them and supplying the new clientele with industrial or bohemian authenticity. Boutiques with designer clothes and their own coffee bars, wine restaurants, and cabarets have materialized in the spaces between the galleries along the main streets of the SoHo district. The continuing manufacturing operations—a boiler repairshop spilling out onto the sidewalk, an industrial blade sharpener, paper warehouses, a commercial bakery—have acquired a picturesque prominence. They provide a patina of authenticity to much-photographed sights, as does the commercial lobster dock in a New England harbor otherwise given over to pleasure boats.

The new SoHo "industry," besides the essentially unseen creation of art works and the surviving manufacturing activity, is the servicing of the gallery crowds—those students, suburbanites, and camera-carrying lawyers who undertake urban excursions in search of the excitement of art and of the artistic life-style. Some of these tourists in the realm of the aesthetic, typically professionals with Manhattan offices and substantial buying power, have purchased lofts in the district. Though a few have set up medical, architectural, legal, or academic offices in their residences, their renovations have on the whole modified the notion of the loft studio away from production toward stylized consumption. The presence of these nonartists and their families has complicated SoHo's occupational and community structure, just as the recent organization of non-art-related small businesses into a chamber of commerce has complicated the business structure of this art market. SoHo is still an artist community. Treading up a wooden staircase worn smooth by the feet of garment workers and hatmakers for over seventy years, the SoHo artist returning home is likely to hear dancers overhead or smell paint and turpentine. But he is also likely to pass the lofts of newer neighbors, a college professor working at a desk, or a lawyer relaxing in his California hot tub.

Art, including avant-garde art, is finding a growing market among the culturally sophisticated middle class who are returning to urban residence in search of a varied and individuated life-style unavailable in the suburbs. This same middle class now supports new, developer-initiated loft renovation taking place not only in SoHo, but in the financial district of Manhattan, in Washington, D.C., along the Boston waterfront—wherever obsolete warehouse and factory districts are juxtaposed to an expanding core of government or corporate offices. SoHo "gentrification" is being underwritten by a national and international corporate headquarters sector whose expansion in Manhattan is facilitated by tax breaks and planning policies.[4] A growing class of executives and professionals, in step with a trend toward corporate patronage of the arts and influenced by their desire to escape bureaucratization of the soul, are comprising a new market for contemporary fine art.

But a paradox will soon become evident in SoHo's process of gentrification, should its embrace by the middle class continue unchecked by administrative or political restraints. The housing investment being

made there by the middle class, artist and nonartist alike, will create a
real estate market too expensive for the remaining industrial operators
and too expensive for most, if not all, artists just beginning their careers.
By escalating the real estate market, the nonartists have set in motion a
process of community change which could leave them in the kind of
homogeneous community characteristic of the suburbs from which they
fled. The particularly urban qualities of diversity, the vitality of numerous subcultures, and proximity to an artistic avant-garde may well become priced out of the area. The artists remaining in SoHo could become limited to the small minority with high incomes, or a residue of
aging co-opers, their studios rather than their careers having become their
wealth, socially marooned in a rising tide of property values.[5] The vital
artistic community will have been displaced. With luck, it will regroup in
and transform another area of urban decay. But SoHo as a vital community supporting avant-garde art will have been destroyed; a territorial
base essential to the concentration and independence of critical artistic
activity will be gone. But such a prospect remains some years in the
future, as the existing artist residents struggle to incorporate change
without destroying the artistic nature of the community.

The Artist Figure as a Conception of the Middle Class

The existence of SoHo and, by implication, avant-garde art in
America cannot be understood in sociological terms without an explora-
tion of the relationship between the artist and the bureaucratized middle
class from which the avant-garde artist distinguishes himself yet upon
which he depends for economic, political, and ideological sponsorship.
In Weberian terminology, the avant-garde artist claims a status which
depends most immediately upon the middle class for recognition and for
conversion into political power or economic position.[6]

The artist, nourished by a subordinate theme in middle-class socialization, makes, in his choice of an art career, a conscious move to realize
a position incomparable to the commercial or bureaucratized professions. Art is something of a "sacred" profession in a secular society.
It is different—admired and disparaged—because it is seen as striving to
create something of universal and permanent value. Neither the shop-
keeper nor the office worker, however exalted, can get away with such
a claim to emancipation from the mundane. Indeed, as bureaucrats they
are at best custodians and rationalizers of the mundane; the artist claims
transcendence toward questions of ultimate value. In contrast to the
usual tasks of the middle level in a society of markets and managers,

where performances are judged by criteria of efficacy and efficiency, the fine artist can hope to carve out a piece of absolute value; or so the middle class, artists and audience, understand the undertaking.

Artists see themselves, and are seen by their supportive audiences, as not simply adding to a boneyard of art history, but as renewing the vision of civilization and revitalizing the present society. The art community, producers and informed audiences, believes that aesthetically successful new imagery pushes the horizons of reality away from us all, expanding civilized consciousness. Should the process of creating new vision cease, should the fine art challenge go unmet, then the world would become visually finite. An anticipation of sameness and routine would crush the modern spirit. It would be as if civilization, having trod a path inscribing reality, were to confront again its own footprints and the realization of the closed nature of that reality. Such is, I believe, the metaphysic supporting the avant-garde artist in SoHo, a world view which unifies the art community, motivates individuals to launch art careers, and can be transformed into an ideology in the service of artists.[7]

Of course the process by which a work of art is credited with extending visual reality is a social process, largely in the control of nonartists. Exalted as the artist's heroic claims may be (claims prudently muffled, for the most part, to escape the derision of the unenlightened), the artist is revealed by the art market to be dependent upon others: whimsical dealers, emotional and financial patrons, art editorializers, museum keepers, and government grant agencies. These are the parties whose touch imparts social existence to a particular work of art and another season of life to the struggling artist. The art career begins with a perception of the insufficiency of the middle-class careers of parents and neighbors, and so must make a relatively exalted claim to be sufficiently motivating and defensible. Art as one-of-a-kind carpentry, as political cartooning, as an advertising lubricant—such "art-of-the-world" would be inferior to the professions for which it acted as a mere lady-in-waiting. No such mundane conception of art could overcome the political and economic disadvantages which follow the decision to be an artist in this society. Instead, it has come to be perceived as a rebellion in the name of exceptional values and the assertion of an exceptional identity.

Much of the cultural meaning of the artist's occupation in the SoHo community is derived from artistic values harbored within the middle class which act on that class as both a self-reproach and a self-defense. The modern artist figure is a liberation dream born out of the fear of incorporation into a routinized and bureaucratically entrenched lifestyle. It is a negation of the values underlying the career success of those buyers and patrons upon whom artists will ultimately be dependent.[8]

The artist, as well as his sympathetic audience, sharing as they do the art community's outlook, define the creative artist and the routine world of business, finance, bureaucracy, and professional practice, to be in mutual tension. Whereas nonartistic work is seen to be motivated by extrinsic considerations such as salary, advancement, and security, the artist finds intrinsic satisfaction in the creative experience itself. This creative work is usually performed under economic subsidy from the artist's other occupations, interpreted as a sign of imbalance in the economic order rather than lack of talent in the artist. Nonartistic work pursues economic growth or social domination for its own sake rather than for the satisfaction of human needs. Nonartistic work disrupts the unity of the self, divorcing rationality from emotional satisfaction in the individual. Creative work, on the other hand, encourages personal growth and the unity of reason and emotion in the artistic expressive act.

Nonartistic work is portrayed by the adherents of the artistic subculture as frequently stultifying the imagination with routine and leading to psychological depression. Artistic work is pictured as a personally risky journey to the frontier of social presupposition, stressful but heroic in its implications. As compensation for this strain, the artist can rightfully claim some exemption from competing and mundane social demands.

The nonartistic work available in this particular society of market coercions and bureaucratic logistics is seen as blinding the individual to the reality of persons and concrete things with a rulebook and cash-register method of perception. The routinized organizations in control of society inherently manipulate those people whose behavior they coordinate. Restrictions crush the spontaneity of workers and citizens, and the dominant instrumental outlook of the economy makes creativity a fugitive. By contrast, artistic work reawakens performer and viewer to an awareness of the emotional and visual texture of persons and environments. It is inherently sharable and uplifting. It liberates because it proceeds by self-definition of the task and self-regulation of the means employed in its accomplishment.

Those who share the perspective of the artistic subculture are aware that nonartistic work is socially necessary. It is credited with consolidating the gains made by creative individuals, unburdening them of custodial and maintenance chores. But such work is considered essentially derivative and unworthy of claiming the highest prestige. The creative work of artists is understood to be of primary importance for the welfare of society because it renews both perception and the perceiver, preventing the onset of spiritual atrophy.

Business, government, and helpful individuals are assigned the role of promoting the aesthetic vitality of society by sponsoring and assisting artists without obstructing or seeking to control their work. Artists seek social space within their control as individuals, not a revolution in the social order. The provision of unrestricted grants and commissions is considered the ideal method by which the routinized structures of society can support creative individuals. Artists, in their turn, should realistically be willing to seek out and accept the support of government and business and to employ marketing agents and self-advertising where necessary, setting aside any childish delusions of self-sufficiency or any impulses to make a bohemian display of their opposition to the mundane order of society. Such display is not understood to be the mark of irreconcilable genius so much as it is the smoke screen for creative failure.

The conception of the artist which these attitudes support is that of a figure whose labor fulfills a longing for individuality born out of resistance to bureaucratized mass organizations. In maintaining the identity of "artist" as an open possibility, society refuses to regard the world of meaning and objects as simply an administered or market system, beyond control or imprint by the individual, which it so often appears to be. The artist role, then, draws content from the perception of contemporary work as largely alienating human capacities for expression.[9]

Artists and the Containment of Charisma

Artistic revolt is less a struggle against the social order than it is a selective rejection of the internalization of that order in the form of limits to the aesthetic imagination. The artist figure in a mass society stands for the possibility of charismatic individuality, of iconoclastic self-affirmation in a marketplace deserted of gods. The artistic identity makes available a revolutionary gesture in the perceived absence of any possibility of collective alteration in the political and economic structure. In such an environment, the artist figure represents an exemption from and autonomy within the confines of an all-encompassing social structure; freedom is achieved through critically reworking the received imagery.

The existence of the artist figure in a society in which social change seems to be routinized and its potential for disruption absorbed represents an "inner-worldly" denial of the domination of the mundane world over the individual. The avant-garde artist is able to challenge mass imagery, that objectification of dreams and desires which commerce generates in the form of movies and popular music and which government facilitates so as to absorb and deflect economic and political dissatisfactions, because the artist treats the realm of the aesthetic as a "calling." This calling is a self-imposed obligation to treat aesthetic experience as an ultimate value, a realm whose satisfactions are derived from critical attention. Popular art generated by commerce, in contrast, too often exhausts its potential as the mood-altering music of elevators, supermarkets, and workplaces and the compensatory catharsis of television drama-to-iron-by. Falling beneath the need for a critical response by its accessibility, and failing to sustain an interpretive subculture because of its simplicity and rapid exhaustibility, much of this commercially inspired popular art tends to reduce aesthetic possibilities to an economic and political lubricant. The discipline demanded by the fine-art calling asserts the priority of aesthetic values and presupposes the independence of the artist from nonaesthetic sources of determination.

In premodern societies, art was subordinate to religion, the artistic purpose being undeveloped as a calling in itself, and the artist being one who sought to realize a religious content through sound, images, or movement. Max Weber writes, "The development of intellectualism and the rationalization of life change this situation where art is dominated by religious content. For under these conditions, art becomes a cosmos of more and more consciously grasped independent values which exist in their own right. Art takes over the function of a this-worldly salvation, no matter how this may be interpreted. It provides a *salvation* from the routines of everyday life, and especially from the increasing pressures of theoretical and practical rationalism."[10] In a schematic landscape of bureaucratic grids, the artist figure is the echo of society's desire for an individualism capable of creating new worlds out of the energy and coherence of human personality.

There is a secular mythology in the modern world in which the figure of the artist acts as a foil to bureaucratic man. As such, the artist figure is a phantom presence in the reverie of drowsy commuters; one day they will get out of writing ad copy or importing hardware, and write an acclaimed novel. In the meanwhile, art can infuse their leisure with meaning and humanize the socialization of their children. It might even structure the rebellion of those children so as to reconcile self-affirmation with the limits implicit in the middle-class way of life.

The Artist in the SoHo Community, and the Status Community in Urban Life

As an occupational community of artists granted legal recognition, SoHo is unique. As an example of resident-determined urban planning in the context of far more powerful land use congeries, SoHo is unusual. By what complex process did an occupational community come to have a differentiated existence on the urban map? While SoHo is a community of artists, the literature on community studies does not tell us much.

SoHo is an important focus of urban analysis for several reasons. First, as an urban community, SoHo is an ecologically differentiated area in which occupational necessity and structural obsolescence of

buildings have given rise to a new housing form—the loft as studio and
residence. The residential loft is a rediscovery of a preindustrial urban
concept in which artisans worked at home, while the occupational
quarter is common to both preindustrial and earlier industrial cities, an
urban design disrupted by the development of cheap transportation to
outlying areas.[11] Rather than being a product of real estate trends, however, SoHo's distinctiveness originated as a spontaneous process con-
solidated in a political achievement. It is a product of government zoning
concessions and land-use policies which artists and their allies have lob-
bied to create. SoHo demonstrates that the "administrative" component
of urban communities, the boundary-defining activities of government
described by Joseph Bensman and Arthur Vidich,[12] can be responsive to
spontaneous land-use change backed by the political activism of citizens.

SoHo is important as a focus of analysis for a second reason. It is a
community which has fully emerged from its urban surroundings in response to the needs of its residents. It is unified by an occupational
ideology, by its distinctive institutions and market structure, and by a
common territory. As such, it is exemplary of the status communities
which organize much of urban middle-class life. Status as a basis for
social and, particularly, community organization was given its classic
theoretical expression in Max Weber's "Class, Status, Party."

> In contrast to classes, *status groups* are normally communities.
> They are, however, often of an amorphous kind. In contrast to the
> purely economically determined "class situation" we wish to desig-
> nate as "status situation" every typical component of the life fate of
> men that is determined by a specific, positive or negative, social
> estimation of *honor*. This honor may be connected with any quality
> shared by a plurality, and, of course, it can be knit to a class situation:
> Class distinctions are linked in the most varied ways with status dis-
> tinctions.[13]

Bensman has advanced this discussion with his analysis of musicians
as an occupationally based status group. By his definition, a "status
community is a *consensual* community, in which the individual chooses
to organize his major life interests within a framework of institutions,
culture, practices and social relationships that are consistent with his
adherence to a set of values. Obviously it differs from a territorial community if that territory is not relevant."[14] SoHo is a case where territory
is clearly relevant to a status community. It is the focus of its market in
art and real estate, its land-use privilege, and its arena for social interaction and mobilization.

Art communities, as instances of status communities, consist of individuals who produce, market, witness, purchase, or sponsor works of art. The production of art is central to the norms of the community, and the producers of art are arranged according to these norms into a pyramid of prestige. At the top are the most widely recognized and accomplished performers in a particular medium. Removed one step from these celebrities are the secondary performers. This second rank comprises the bulk of the working artists in SoHo and is a confusion of trajectories, some rising while others are diminishing in promise. Individuals shift among presentational settings and social circles as they try to realize all of the occupational prestige they claim.

The fine artist succeeds or fails according to how well he establishes institutional credentials and cultivates a sustaining social network. This network contains fellow artists and occupational contacts in the market, and includes at its core friends or a spouse whose commitment is personal and made on the basis of emotional attachment rather than as a collegial or market investment in mutual support. The network reflects the structure of the status community in that it is conscious of the prestige of its members and attempts to select them on the basis of a rough equivalence.

Artists who earn their living from routinized careers, individuals such as commercial portrait painters or art teachers, occupy a place still lower in prestige rank. Their aesthetic challenges are presumed to originate outside of their own control.

Beyond the circle of practitioners stands the audience, graded according to the professionalism with which it can appreciate and comment upon the productions of the artists. As an audience member demonstrates increased understanding of an art form, a closer social intimacy with the artist members of the subculture is possible. Museum curators, art journalists, gallery directors, and collectors comprise a professional segment of the art audience. They are linked to the formal associations of the art world which make the artist's sales, grants, and celebrity possible. This professional audience constitutes the art world's "gatekeepers," who not only stratify the producers but also link them with the wider audience. By translating the private artistic venture into terms of objective recognition, they set the price, judge "museum worthiness," and predict the potential for distinction which makes an artistic career "a good investment" for artist and audience alike. Janus-faced, the dealers, journalists, and historians of contemporary art are at once powerful critics and spokespersons, publicists and legitimators, of the artistic enterprise.

SoHo, the national center for the contemporary fine arts, is the focus for many status communities within the arts, each distinguished by its own medium. As the location of New York's largest concentration of painters and sculptors, and of the galleries which display their work,

SoHo is most notably a center for the visual arts. Understanding the SoHo community reveals the status community to be an important communal form in the organization of urban life, and SoHo itself to be central to the dynamics of the contemporary art world.

SoHo is an important focus of social analysis for a third reason. As an artistic community, it is a reflection of and avenue to understanding the American middle class. Caroline Ware, Albert Parry, and Malcolm Cowley, among others, have pointed out that the vocation of the artist and the artist posture emanate from the middle class as a result of a critical impulse felt by a portion of that class to differentiate themselves from the wider society's economic and instrumentalist vision.[15] Yet frequently these rebels reaffirm the values, in substance or in parody, of the class from which they seek distance; they become "commercial" in their vocation as artists or writers, or they pass through a "bohemian" phase of self-definition by negation. A. C. Spectorsky, and J. R. Seeley, R. Sim, and E. W. Loosley have found that in middle-class communities practical success and self-realization exist as dual themes in the socialization of children and in the psychological equilibrium of adults.[16] These two themes, or clusters of values, are in tension with one another. The concern for practical success in a career shapes middle-class conduct, and self-realization acts as a humanist counterpoint channeled into essentially recreational pursuits. Vidich and Bensman have pointed out that the instabilities in middle-class culture affect the youth in particular, motivating them to rebel against the constraints of occupational practicality and political realism as a form of the search for self.[17] Mason Griff has found that young people who define themselves as artists reverse the priorities of middle-class culture, elevating self-realization to the dominant position.[18] SoHo artists desire self-actualization without having to relinquish middle-class notions of practical success, and so involve themselves in a conflict of values which sets the dramatic contours of their occupational and personal lives.

The SoHo community shares an occupational ideology that challenges some of the central trends in modern life, specifically bureaucratization as the mode of occupational coordination, job choice determined by economic rationality, and the breakdown of the work task and its determination according to principles of routinized efficiency. Even the integration of home and occupational life departs from the contemporary organization of labor. But ironically, those who oppose these trends by their calling come, as their careers mature, to accept the consequences of these trends as increasingly necessary conditions of their artistic existence.

In order to secure residential and studio space, artists spontaneously created cooperative housing systems in SoHo; but they found that the real-estate market cannot consistently be transcended or evaded. To sell the work they create, they have had to position themselves dispassionately in an art market and among entrepreneurs who determine which creations will sell. They sought to integrate domestic life and occupation, only to discover that such integration was a burden disproportionately assumed by wives and mothers, and frequently incompatible with the concentration on career required for the husbands' success. They began their residence in SoHo evading housing laws and came to recognize the necessity of protective zoning. They mobilized into a middle-class pressure group so as to defend their community with the tools of the political process. To make the transition from occupational commitment to occupational and residential survival, they drew upon the cultural resources which are theirs by virtue of their educational and economic backgrounds in the middle class. They built upon family experience with real estate, sales economics, the law, government bureaucracy, and the politics of pressure and publicity. Most of all, they drew upon a self-confidence and assurance that, when forced into activism, they could outmaneuver their bureaucratic or commercial opposition. They were able to treat their economic and legal vulnerabilities as problems whose solution required a political campaign, a marshalling of social allies, and the achievement of unprecedented zoning changes. Their tactical confidence and strategic ambition came from their middle-class assurance that, as artists, they were important to society and to the city; and as capable political actors, they could make the city accommodate their presence.

Life in SoHo and participation in its art and real-estate markets, entanglement in its domestic arrangements and in its organizations, has reintroduced the values and conditions which residents, with their career choices, had rejected. SoHo sees itself in opposition to the culture of the middle-class suburb. But while overcoming and so delineating some of the contradictions in that culture and realizing important possibilities for self-renewal that that culture contains, SoHo has come to incorporate much of middle-class culture into its own way of life.

2
The Structure of the SoHo Art Market

New York City is the nation's center for the exchange of art—over one billion dollars worth of all types of art changes hands there annually.[1] Since the early 1960s, when the dominant position of abstract expressionism began to give way to more culturally accessible movements, contemporary American art has broadened its audience and its share of the art market. SoHo is now the principal location for New York's trade in contemporary art, a trade which provides the economic basis of the SoHo community and gives it its cultural orientation.

SoHo developed with the general boom in the art market. Art sales accelerated through the 1960s and peaked in 1968, 1973, and 1979. This expansive atmosphere prompted many uptown gallery staffers to enter the market as entrepreneurs themselves, relying initially upon artists and buyers they could take from their old employers and setting up their new businesses in SoHo where commercial rents were far less than those in the uptown gallery area. At the same time, the established art galleries responded to the art boom by seeking additional space to display and store the larger pieces being produced by contemporary artists. As these galleries expanded their trade, they separated their operations into old master, print, and contemporary divisions, moving the modern works to the cheaper and more available spaces found in SoHo.

The growth of SoHo as an art market has been extraordinary. During most of the 1960s there was no gallery presence at all in SoHo. In 1968 a Park Avenue art dealer, Richard L. Feigen, established the first dealer presence in SoHo when he opened a warehouse to service his uptown showrooms. The same year Paula Cooper, a young woman with experience as a staffer in uptown galleries, saw in SoHo an emerging artist community that could benefit from the local presence of galleries. She established SoHo's first gallery in the fall of 1968 in order to have more ready access to the work of SoHo artists and to take advantage of the large spaces and cheap overhead that her fledgling venture required.

By May of 1975, less than five years after the growing number of residential artists had secured zoning legalization for their combined living and working quarters, eighty-four galleries for painting and sculpture existed in SoHo. In addition, many other galleries and shops had opened to sell photographs, craft articles, and prints. SoHo, by this time known as "downtown" to art buyers, had more galleries handling contemporary art than did the established Madison Avenue district, which had only seventy-four.[2] By 1976 the most influential of the city's art dealers, Leo Castelli, had moved all of his business in contemporary art to his SoHo annex, a business that grossed over $2.5 million a year from the sale of paintings and sculpture.[3] In 1976 New York's first and only auction house devoted exclusively to the work of contemporary American artists, Auction 393, opened on West Broadway, the spine of SoHo's gallery system.

These commercial galleries, managed by professional dealers, constitute the economic foundations of the SoHo community.

SoHo Spaces and the Change in the Presentation of Art

The ambience of SoHo galleries is in striking contrast to that prevailing in the uptown galleries, especially those which sell old masters. In the latter's salesrooms the atmosphere is funereal. The prospective client is ushered across carpeted floors to a viewing room or alcove. This is draped in dark velvet against the distractions of light and noise and features a viewing easel sitting in the isolation of a spotlight. Assistants bring in the "masters," one at a time, and withdraw to leave the client and the empathetic dealer to a moment of communion.

SoHo galleries try to make art viewing an unintimidating secular experience. The dealers, who tend to be younger, have exchanged their three-piece suits for cowboy shirts and casual slacks. The public is encouraged to look around unchallenged and without ostentatious supervision. These dealers try not to crowd their audience, a new clientele for art which includes well-salaried professionals and business people. The dealers try to give the clients time and space to develop their art perception and to establish a comfortable familiarity with new movements without forcing them to articulate their interests to a salesperson prematurely. The appeal of the art itself and the enthusiasm of the other gallery visitors are given time to persuade the potential client. As one leading SoHo dealer explained, "There's a new market down here. There may be a shortage of good artists, but there's no shortage of buyers. Now doctors are buying art. Madison Avenue was a Cardin suit situation, but down here I'm more accessible—just a guy in jeans. I have no back room where assistants bring in a piece and put it on a stand. Here, I leave the client alone to wander around; the client feels freer."[4] While subsequent steps of the selling process are very deliberately directed by the dealer, it is the initial feeling of self-guided and self-determining viewing that softly draws visitors into their first venture in art acquisition. While finding their bearings in the field, these new clients from business and the professions are status sensitive and have not yet developed confidence in their own tastes, so the intelligent dealer does not confront them with anything as disquieting as a purchase decision.

SoHo galleries capitalize on the features of the nineteenth-century manufacturing and commercial buildings in which they have been located to express this new accessibility of art to those without any prior experience as collectors. Space design emphasizes open revelation rather than arcane impenetrability; gallery layouts suggest that there is nothing mysterious or difficult about coming to terms with art. Large plateglass windows invite the passerby into spaces that are up to five thousand square feet in extent and that rise unobstructed to their fourteen-foot ceilings. The bare floors are hardwood and, like all the surfaces, clean and uncluttered. Walls and ceilings are invariably matte white. What examples of mercantile extravagance remain from the nineteenth century—the occasional fluted iron column, for instance— add a historical patina to the setting, as do the often ornate cast-iron facades of many of the buildings in this district. Such ongoing commercial activity as the loading and unloading of trucks and such industrial survivors as fabric-shears makers and hat factories contribute an impression of productive seriousness and an unaffected disregard of surroundings. Here, art has come to terms with the practical world.

Gallery clients feel a step closer to the artists' studios than they did shopping on more elegant Fifty-seventh Street. Sidewalks strewn with packing crates for art, frame and canvas stores here and there, people carrying art portfolios—these impress upon the buyer that in SoHo one has arrived at the source of contemporary art, the creative furnace.

The need for the large spaces that were to be found in SoHo accounts for the locational choices of the early dealers and still draws new galleries willing to pay the now increased rents. Dealers need room to display large indoor sculpture and tapestry-sized paintings. These installations must be easily changed with each new show, and extensive room is required for their crating and storage. The stark gallery interiors provide a flexible and neutral background for the art work, which is set off by the use of variable track spotlights. Designers of home interiors for the new middle class have elevated the gallery-look into a fashionable decor for their cosmopolitan clients who adopt a living style in the spirit of contemporary art.[5]

The crowds which sustain the excitement of Saturday gallery-hopping in SoHo find the area an attractive setting for their dining and entertainment. Restaurants, bars, cabarets, and discotheques have sprung up to meet this demand, spreading from block to block along with the expanding gallery core. SoHo wandering has become an alternative to museum going, an alternative with a social dimension. The urbane audiences who have come to associate themselves with the contemporary in fine art, dance, experimental video, jazz and electronic music, can all satisfy their tastes in SoHo. The art galleries, which often lend their spaces to performing artists, encourage the public to interact with art through exhibits of kinetic "touch" sculpture and holographic light installations. The SoHo marketplace for fine art has evolved into an amusement park and performance area where many degrees of identification with art are possible and where the expression of this identification as a life-style can find support.

The Print Market

Most individuals in the casual Saturday crowds do not buy original oils or sculpture. Many are content to demonstrate their sensitivity to visual imagery by selecting SoHo as their place to drink and dine and by carrying cameras. They do, however, sustain SoHo's emerging restaurant and boutique trades.

The first level of art buyers consists of young, college-educated people starting marriages, households, and professional careers. When they can afford art, they often want what is contemporary. They buy original prints and drawings from several print outlets which flourish in proximity to the galleries which carry paintings and sculpture. Well-known artists occasionally produce work for the print market when their other sales are slow. Some SoHo artists have developed careers as lithographers and serigraphers, typically producing one new work a month in their own recognizable style. The works are usually printed in a limited series of 100 or 150, then hand numbered and signed by the artist. Artists who market this work through a gallery can earn a regular income of up to a thousand dollars per design. Galleries that subcontract the reproduction sell each copy for $50 to $200, raising the price as a design sells enough to become scarce.

Print galleries, especially those which carry less expensive art posters advertising exhibitions, find they are able to make as much profit from the framing—an integral part of the buyer's expression of taste—as from the sale of the art itself, so they have their own frame shops which they refer to as "ateliers."[6] Most print buyers are interested in decorating their apartments with art work. Back in their college days, they were among the half-million students who annually take introductory art history courses, and they probably bought their first cardboard-matted reproductions at the college bookstore.[7] Their college introduction gave them notions of what art is, notions with status connotations opposed to popular taste, ideas which have since deterred them from using furniture-store pseudoart or sentimental kitsch as decorative devices. With signed, gallery-purchased prints or drawings they can make an aesthetic identification with the dynamic trends in society as well as bolster their own claims to individuality. If their careers mature at a faster rate than their expenses, they may celebrate their achievements by graduating into the market of one-of-a-kind originals.

While these modest investors in the decorative arts usually restrict themselves to the poster, print, and drawing market, some of them are introduced in this way to art speculation. Print galleries keep listings of the latest prices at which their stock items have changed hands. The original plates are guaranteed to have been destroyed to insure the rarity of the prints, which differentiates them from a mass culture item and makes speculation in them possible. Print investors can share the excitement of the bigger art speculators, but with less risk. Their conversation in the print galleries often echoes that of stockbrokers at lunch: "I could have bought a Buffet in Paris in 1960 for $100, and now look at the price." Buffet prints and reproductions are now a standard item in the office decor of dentists and certified public accountants in New York.

The print market closely approaches a mass market, reaching out into the suburbs with chain store operations such as the Circle Gallery system. Such systems maintain their flagship galleries in SoHo for prestige and send their salesmen on tours to place art in the furniture stores of elite suburban shopping malls. One SoHo print and poster gallery has a large part of the General Services Administration's business and supplies federal offices with wall decorations. Only the highest government officials have access to the loan services provided by the National Gallery of Art in Washington. Lesser officials make do with prints and reproductions.[8]

The Studio as Salesroom

Artists and collectors have a tradition which legitimates the buyer's going directly into the artist's studio to look over and consider the purchase of works of art. This arrangement enables the collector to buy art at a lower price, because the dealer, who often marks up the price of a work by 100 percent to cover his commission and costs, is eliminated. Lacking the institutional props of the gallery to certify worth, moreover, artists are inclined to accept less for a work sold in the studio. Artists who need sales hope that subsidizing the exposure of their work to a larger audience through a collector will eventually pay off. In the absence of real demand, the artist doesn't know how to price his work and may sell it either too dearly or too cheaply for subjective or ideological reasons. One artist-turned-plumber, whose once promising painting career has faded, explained,

> I used to price paintings at $800. It took me a month to make one, and I needed $800 a month to survive. Now they're $1200, which I need a month. There's no profit in it at all, but I have to ask that much. There's no reason to make a profit if you really like the work [of making art]. Art ought not to get tainted by all that other stuff. You hope someone will care enough to keep the work, so you use canvas and not paper.

Artists who sell very little may allow their isolation from the market to keep their asking prices above the point of sales, but this is the exception. Artists with their market hopes intact willingly subsidize their art by creating bargains for the studio shopper.

Buyers who visit studios are not merely hunting for bargains. They seek to test their perceptions as collectors in the studio, where their taste is unmediated by the commentary of a dealer. In buying art at its source, the collector is claiming to be able to discern the significant work in a crowd of uncertified and unknown pieces. Only the experienced collector has the self-assurance to rummage through studios making judgments. Being among the first to discover, show, and promote a work which later wins significant recognition is the special satisfaction sought by such collectors. Each studio visit, they hope, will unearth an unknown and undervalued masterpiece.

Selling out of the studio is most commonly a tactic of the younger artists who as yet lack outlets in professional galleries. Such artists choose to sacrifice some of the privacy of their working and living arrangements in order to display both their art and themselves to the collector. The collector is allowed "backstage" and extended the privileges of supposed familiarity.[9] Extending Erving Goffman's terminology to cover long-term relations rather than situational interactions, admittance backstage allows the collector to play the role of "teammate" as well as that of "audience." This provides important gratification and legitimation for the collector. Familiarity, however superficial, with the lives of artists can signify the collector's acceptance into the art world as a fellow cognoscente.

Artists with a history of minor critical recognition but without affiliation with a major gallery may cultivate a group of buyers whom they see in their studios on a regular basis. These buyers become friends and promoters of the artist and, while settling on their purchases, extend their visits into afternoons of conversation about the art world. Having been granted social entrée, these buyers have been known to remain patient and loyal for many years while the artist struggles to establish himself.

Even buyers who shop for their art in galleries are not immune to curiosity about the human origins of the art they contemplate. Dealers are quick in making use of this interest. They report that they frequently help sell a client on a program of serious art collecting by introducing the client to one of the gallery's artists during a visit to his SoHo loft. Artists are expected to be on call for such performances. The glimpse of art in-the-making and the acquaintance of a well-known artist often seem to confirm the client's decision to invest in art. The studio visit, managed by an astute dealer, can become a collector's rite of passage into the art world.[10]

Many SoHo artists have participated in a less esoteric tradition of studio selling. In the years before the community was stabilized by zoning amendments and when galleries in the area were few, tour buses brought in groups of corporation managers' wives from suburbs like Mt. Kisco, New York. They became spectators of both avant-garde art and studio living. For a time the SoHo Artists Association, the community organization for the area, helped with these tours by posting notices in its newsletter and signing up artists willing to open up their lofts.

In May of 1970, during the final push for passage of the zoning amendments which would legalize artists' living-working quarters in SoHo, an SAA-sponsored arts festival was held in the area. One hundred artists' lofts were opened for inspection and art sales. Nearly one hundred thousand people, including members of the City Planning Commission, attended the festival activities in lofts and on the streets during the weekend it was held. The members of the City Planning Commission were specifically invited to tour artists' lofts to see for themselves that loft living could be safe, sanitary, and productive. After the artists had made their point to the planning officials, the press, and the public, however, loft tours lost the support of the SAA and of many outspoken residents. The better-known artists complained that too many tourists were coming into SoHo and disrupting the community, robbing them of the solitude they required for concentration.

Artists' Cooperative Retailing Ventures

After 1971 professionally managed galleries opened in large numbers to handle the distribution of SoHo artists' work. But even the present eighty-seven galleries run by dealers in SoHo have not been able to satisfy the demands for exposure by a growing number of artists. In an effort to reach an audience, young SoHo artists have fashioned a number of cooperative and usually nonprofit exhibition arrangements outside the professional gallery system.

Some cooperative ventures take the form of group shows which pool the publicity resources of several artists and are set up in one or several artists' lofts to save expenses. The "Ten Downtown" show, held annually since 1968, is the oldest such area exhibition. Like those in other cooperative ventures, the participants in Ten Downtown are largely unknown artists, but each is selected by one of the previous year's participants. This continues a tradition which encourages "launched" artists to act as mentors and certifiers for unknowns. Mailings and newspaper advertisements for Ten Downtown regularly draw six thousand or more viewers who follow a tour of the participants' lofts in SoHo and other lower Manhattan districts. While on the lookout for inexpensive and adventurous contemporary art, the audience is also drawn by the chance to see artists in their natural habitat, complete with avocado plants.

Artists who can afford a greater and more sustained investment have organized cooperative galleries. Fourteen such galleries exist in SoHo and thirty-six others in various cities on the East Coast. The members share the expenses of rent, sales brochures, and sometimes a paid manager. Members must also rotate as volunteer gallery staff. In return, members are able to show their work every one-and-a-half to two years, depending in part on their own assessment of their readiness. The members choose from among a constantly renewed waiting list for new members to take the places of the one-third who annually give up the struggle or, more rarely, are absorbed into the commercial galleries.

By addressing and mailing their exhibition announcements, by cleaning and running the gallery themselves, and by sharing expenses, the artists subsidize the costs of the distribution of their art, passing the savings along to the client in lower prices. Costs of operating a gallery for a year average $40,000; the annual sales cover only half that amount.[11] Artists hope that the subsidies and the exposure will eventually result in their reputations catching fire. With a demand for their work established, they will then try to move into a dealer-run gallery.

Cooperative galleries operate under some disadvantages. The major buyers and critics tend to give less priority to visiting galleries that are not managed by professional dealers. "My tendency is to go to commercial galleries first," said Grace Glueck, art critic for the *New York Times*.

"Professional dealers have taste, or they wouldn't be in business."[12] The dealers, however, do monitor the cooperative galleries and listen especially to what their own affiliated artists have to say about the work of unknown artists on display. The cooperative gallery functions best as a stepping stone to the more professional market, where the artist can expect his work to be more expensively displayed and more expertly promoted.

Because fine art careers may need to incubate for decades before they take off or are considered hopeless and so abandoned, there is a strong demand among artists for critical notice, however casual, and for sales, however nominal. These can have an importance beyond their function as omens of success. Shows, even those poorly received, mobilize the artist's energies. In a dramaturgical sense, they provide artists with a chance to assume as a public identity what are often amorphous and ill-defined careers. The mechanics of hanging an exhibition and holding an opening celebration with jug wine serves to catalyze the support of, at the very least, personal friends and fellow co-op members.

The elite cooperative galleries are those which are the most selective in admitting new artists. "We try for all top quality artists," said a collagist and co-op member with an impressive résumé of work in major collections. "It's bad when co-op galleries have to advertise for new members." There are said to be benefits in showing at a co-op gallery. One woman painter explained, "My co-op gallery offers certain advantages over a commercial gallery. There's no dealer pressure on one, saying, 'This sells, this doesn't. I can sell more of these.' When they do that, they want you to turn out identical pieces." Like the commercial galleries, elite co-ops try to use the gallery's reputation for discernment to certify the work of their members. Co-op members like to boast that some fellow member has declined an invitation to take a place with a commercial gallery, being so content with their gallery's status and its support for genuine artistic innovation.

Artists looking more frankly at the commercial market see this lack of dealer pressure as the disadvantage of the co-ops. As a sculptor put it, "I'm a realist and not a romantic. If I put art into a gallery, I want it to sell. Once I'm through with a piece, I'm not that interested in it. I'm trying to go beyond it. I like very little of my old work. If it's in a gallery, I want to sell it and make money. It's okay with me if the dealer is a speculator. Art is a business like any other. The dealer and the artist need not be in love. He *should* push the artist."

Cooperative galleries lack the managerial coherence and the capital to "push" the artist by confronting him with the realities of the market. Artists who are independent of dealers describe this pressure as a demand for repetition, a curbing of the artist's innovative spirit, a move toward mass production. "[Commercial] galleries don't like to deal in a single piece,'' said one such artist,''even a great piece. They'd rather see several variations on a theme, and that can be boring for artists. There *is* a pressure to replicate. Well, it really is more profitable to make ten pieces which resemble each other—yet are each individuals, of course. The gallery owner will take the best piece for himself, and steer his buyers to the others. 'You must have this to complete your collection!' I am cynical about dealers.''

The strength of the dealer-run gallery, and its advantage over the cooperative gallery, is not in a crass application of pressure on the artist for replication of what sells, but rather in its ability to commit itself as a gallery to movements in art and thus to help launch buyers, and incidentally artists, in a new direction. Dealers accomplish this by providing buyers with an interpretive context in which a single work is linked to a larger movement. Buyers are thus persuaded that a piece is ''collectible,'' and art writers that the piece will sustain a discursive analysis. Commercial galleries take a risk in throwing their influence with buyers and critics in support of one or another of the trends in art. If the market doesn't sustain them, they lose not only their influence but also the money required to exhibit the new trend. Since dealers use their personal collections and those of their galleries to create momentum for a new trend, these investments can also be lost on a mistaken judgment.

The cooperative gallery lacks the entrepreneurial ability of the well-connected dealer seeking to lead the market in a new artistic direction. The co-ops do not even try this sort of maneuver. Instead, they have attempted to make more democratic gains for artists in SoHo. The fourteen co-op galleries in SoHo, along with fifty-one others nationwide, have formed an association to further the interests of unknown artists seeking exposure. Since 1976 they have sponsored a street fair, Artists' Day, held in SoHo each May. Along with trying to draw a larger public into the cooperative galleries and attracting the critics, the co-ops are seeking to publicize the plight of the many unemployed artists. This effort has succeeded to the extent that in 1977 a representative of the mayor of New York attended Artists' Day and promised the crowd that 300 of the jobs made available through federal funding for the long-term unemployed would go to artists. By 1978, 500 such jobs had been offered to artists.

While not against government jobs for artists, the commercial galleries are sensitive to what they see as a possible degeneration of SoHo into a semipermanent street fair. They fear that SoHo will become choked with hawkers of leather crafts, performing dog acts, and tightrope walkers. Many close their galleries ostentatiously for Artists' Day, putting signs in their windows explaining that they are ''Open by Invitation Only.'' The professional dealers have a more genteel market to protect. They have thus far fended off any incursions of street art peddling from the annual Washington Square outdoor sale, held directly to the north. However, Artists' Day and street fund-raisers held opportunistically in SoHo to benefit midtown art schools, have brought regular, if disdained, sidewalk art sales to the district.

The commercial dealers look upon the cooperative galleries as a feeder system, which in fact they are, for artists who can attract attention to their work are usually promoted to the professional galleries. The dealers can comfortably coexist with alternative forms of merchandising art, at least so long as it is not on the street, because they believe that the best artists will come to them, recognizing that they offer the best services. One prominent commercial dealer explained benignly,

> A number of artists today manage their careers very nicely from their studios. It's not because they are such private persons and they have refused to become involved with gallery and commercial activity. It's that the artist usually hasn't achieved any exhibition opportunities and says, "My work is awfully good," and he gets together with other artists who haven't had the opportunities either and says, "We're going to try to do something." And this usually has caused cooperatives to form. There a number of cooperatives in the neighborhood; some of them are rather good.
>
> Artists like to be managed, however. They like to have a strong guiding hand. They like the idea of a commercial premises where they're going to be sold. There's no reason why work can't be sold in a cooperative gallery, and it is. They just like the idea of what they consider the professionalism that goes with commercial galleries.

The New Art Buyers

The majority of the new art buyers who support the proliferation of SoHo galleries for contemporary painting and sculpture are people with earned wealth who are new to the pleasures of living with art. They are surgeons, corporate lawyers, and upper-management personnel— individuals who have succeeded within meritocratic institutions. They use contemporary art to express their own achievement of status. In collecting avant-garde art, they find their new sense of social position reflected in works which stress innovation rather than tradition and a radically individual, rather than a collective, social vision. The new middle-class buyers approach art from what they feel is a plateau in their prosperous careers. Art collecting poses a new adventure in self-expression for them, one legitimized by the recent trend toward corporate sponsorship of new art.

Art, commissioned or chosen from the storage racks of artists in SoHo and elsewhere, has become integral to the environment of corporate

offices as well as government buildings. Such art is being used to differentiate the white-collar worker from lower prestige strata, and to
humanize the image of bankers and executives. This trend has its origins
in the decision of the Chase Manhattan Bank to build a new office tower
in lower Manhattan in the late 1950s. The bank's chairman, David
Rockefeller, said of this move, "We wanted to get away from the marble
columns outside banks and from the image that bankers are glassy-eyed,
hard hearted people. So we first determined that we would have a contemporary type of architecture." The severity of the building "called for
paintings and sculpture that could be thought of as built-in, decorative
features."[13]

Chase embarked on a program of art purchasing, largely of contemporary pieces, not only for the new Chase Manhattan Plaza but for its
eighty overseas offices. More than 4,700 works of art by 1,550 artists
have been purchased in this one corporate program alone. Said Rockefeller, "The collection [was intended to] provide enjoyment and education for members of our staff and visitors and serve as a means to give
encouragement to contemporary artists."[14] Other corporations have
developed similar programs, especially for their headquarters.

For those who are conscious of rank, it is gratifying to work with an
original painting on the wall, quite apart from the artistic experience
itself (which, presumably, is not considered overly distracting). The
gradations of artistic "value," from less expensive prints to more expensive paintings, from smaller to larger, are easily reconcilable with the
other symbols of achievement and position which orient the inhabitants
of the office world. However, art in the office is not merely a parallel
symbol system communicating degrees of power; art adds a dimension
to the humanity of the office occupant. It says, "Here is a person aware
of values greater than, or at least in addition to, mere money." It is for
this reason that, while their art collections are often among corporations'
better investments (Chase's collection has doubled in value), corporate
spokespersons are at great pains not to discuss their collections in
profit-making terms.[15] In the bureaucracy, art has come to represent a
system of humanistic prestige parallel to more obvious gradations in
rank and income.

The new art buyers are not moved by the ownership history of a piece,
a consideration which enthralls collectors of old masters. The latter
authenticate their purchases and add relish to their ownership with research into the twists of a marketing pedigree. Dealers report that new
buyers seek to develop an interest and knowledge in a still developing
line of art. Some go to great lengths to anticipate new trends. Hanns
Sohm, a middle-aged German dentist, for example, collects the eviden-
tiary material documenting "happenings," performance art, and other

creative events—scripts, posters, programs, photos, and newspaper reviews.[16] He has succeeded in making collectible items from such in-
tentionally uncollectible and untradeable occurences as Charlotte Moorman's avant-garde festivals and the events of Red Grooms.

Recently, new collectors have been buying the highly technological
art of the new realists, which includes deliberately ordinary urban scene
painting, popular-culture iconography, and large, Byzantine-sized portraits of anonymous individuals. This work is accessible and appealing to
those whose success allows them to objectify the familiar objects of
contemporary culture, but whose lack of alternative historical awareness blunts the critical edge of their response.

The buyer of contemporary avant-garde art acquires assurance more
quickly and moves in a more volatile and more exciting market than does
the collector of old masters. In the contemporary-art market, prices and
reputations can change quickly. It takes time for artists to achieve recognition as "twentieth-century masters," and that recognition seldom
comes during the artist's lifetime. Critics and art historians are more
concerned with the formation of a consensus about the prestige of art
accumulated from the past. They resist certifying the most recent work.
The largest-selling college art-history textbook devotes a mere 26 illus-
trations out of 1,268 to post–World War II art.[17] With less critical opinion
to guide the buyer and, in the case of a still productive artist, with the
number of works in the market still uncertain, it is difficult for a consensus to emerge about the merit or fair price of an avant-garde piece. A
buyer with strong enough convictions to take risks can more easily become influential as a collector of contemporary, rather than of
older, art.

The buyer of contemporary art finds much cheaper prices than would
a collector of old masters. Realizing that the experience of acquisition
excites the buyer as much as looking at his purchases, SoHo dealers try
to keep the young collector in the lower price brackets so that, within a
given budget, the buyer can multiply his purchase anticipations and
completions. The newer the artist, the cheaper the prices, so new collectors are steered toward less established artists. Explained one dealer,

> In one case a twenty-six year old real estate investor came to me
> wanting a program of collecting. He told me he had $10,000 to spend.
> I told him to buy five pieces, one each at two month intervals. This
> sustains the excitement of constantly buying. He took six weeks to
> buy his first work, at $1,500. He waited two months more, and de-
> cided he really wanted a piece that cost $8,000. I tried to dissuade
> him, and told him to think about it. Then I let him go ahead. It was
> such a good piece that I knew I could sell it and get his money back if
> he got into trouble.

Knowledge of the contemporary art market is acquired by a collector in the pleasant context of studio and gallery visits, viewing, discussing, and gossiping with artists and dealers. For the executive or the psychoanalyst, acquiring this knowledge can be a relaxing break from work. Moreover, there is always the chance that a piece will undergo a spectacular appreciation in value. Jackson Pollock's painting *Lavender Mist,* for example, set the record for rapid appreciation when the National Gallery of Art paid over $2 million for it in 1976. Pollack had died in 1956, and the following year his widow sold the painting, on the installment plan, to a collector for a mere $1,500; it was this same collector who made the sale to the National Gallery.[18]

The contemporary-art market is the most volatile of art markets because public institutions and major private buyers invest far less in it than they do in the old masters. The highest prices for paintings are paid by public institutions which are, for the most part, inhibited from acquiring avant-garde or disturbingly modern pieces.[19] The highest price paid to date for a work of art was "about $8 million." It was paid in 1974 by the National Gallery of Art in Washington for a painting by seventeenth-century French artist Georges de La Tour. Second- and third-highest prices also went for old masters, $5 to 6 million paid by the same museum for a Leonardo da Vinci in 1967 and $5.5 million paid by the Metropolitan Museum of Art for a Velazquez in 1970.[20]

Wealthy entrepreneurs in industry and finance constitute the most prestigious collectors in the private realm. They collect for reasons of largess, tax advantage, and personal expansiveness, usually lending their acquisitions for public display and eventually donating them to museums. Dr. Armand Hammer, chairman of Occidental Petroleum Company, for example, recently established a record price for a Rembrandt painting, paying $3.28 million against the bidding competition of J. Paul Getty. Hammer donated this piece to the Los Angeles County Museum, which he supports in a rivalry with the Norton Simon Museum of Art in Pasadena.[21]

These wealthiest collectors avoid the contemporary market entirely, thus leaving it unstabilized by the commitment of the largest private collections. They consider it to be too speculative and lacking in critical certification. Norton Simon, owner of the world's largest private art collection, spends up to $20 million each year acquiring art for holdings worth "several hundred million dollars."[22] But Simon will not buy in the avant-garde market. Neither would Getty, a collector who was willing to pay $1 million for a Rubens painting.[23] The principal motivation for investing in the prestigious old master market is not a desire to profit through speculation but the wish to demonstrate that one has financially and, one hopes, culturally arrived. These investors certainly have no

inclination to express symbolic attachment to a disruptive and historically scornful avant-garde.

There is, along with the main body of middle-class buyers of contemporary art, a handful of prestigious buyers who contribute some
buoyancy and glamour to that market. SoHo's largest dealer reports that
less than ten of his buyers are in that class.[24] Collectors like taxi-fleet
owner Robert Scull would be included in that category. For the most
part, however, American collectors remain reluctant to commit large
amounts of money to the work of living American artists. Many of the
largest buyers are European industrialists secure enough in their aristocratic credentials to be able to indulge a taste for the American avant-
garde. Of these, Dr. Giuseppe Panza DiBiumo may invest the most. He
is a Milanese industrialist living in a 225-year-old ancestral home of fifty
rooms. One entire room is devoted to the display of the work of a SoHo
minimal sculptor, another to a constructionist. DiBiumo and the German
industrialist Professor Peter Ludwig "have the most outstanding collections in the world today of American art," according to SoHo dealer Leo
Castelli.[25] With its many European clients and branches of European
galleries, SoHo has become an international art market.

The inadequate backing by art historians and the major collectors and
museums, subjects contemporary art to the ups and downs of the general
economy. After a boom in both stock market prices and art prices
through 1973, both markets began to slip, and by the spring of 1975,
dealers faced hard times. Popularly styled, if not priced, galleries were
openly discounting their art up to 60 percent in department-store-like
sales. Dealers generally believe that the art market follows a curve that
is parallel to the stock market. When the nervous small collector runs
short of cash and tries to unload his art, the market is further depressed
and the efforts of the dealers to hold the posted prices fail. In the spring
of 1976, one year after the slump, a general economic recovery had
carried the art market with it, and Parke-Bernet reported sales up 40
percent over the previous year.[26] Record-high interest rates and inflation
in 1979 sent speculators into art in such numbers that the auction houses
were setting record prices for major works in all categories.

Conclusion

Artists and buyers meet in a stratified SoHo art market, where the
ideology of unrestricted creativity must come to terms with the aesthetic
outlook of a new art buyer—the successful manager, business person,
and professional—the upper tier of the middle class. This buyer is unlike
the economic aristocrats who use art to link themselves with older aris-

tocracies of birth through the display and public donation of certified masterworks.

The new art buyer seeks an aesthetic experience and market product which meets five requirements. (1) It must affirm that the investor's awareness is superior to that of those individuals presumed to be immersed in mass culture. It should obviously depart from older art traditions and folk or ethnic themes, none of which have much meaning to the arriviste perspective. (2) It must be avant-garde in style, and so be expressive of the optimism and orientation toward the future that accompanies occupational achievement. (3) The art should be a contemporary product, so that its acquisition may offer the buyer a socially involving adventure in the art world, an adventure which provides a break from the routinized aspects of a successful career. (4) The art should be conceptually accessible in nonart terms, as having a pleasing design, as enhancing domestic or office decor, or as having familiarity of imagery. The conception must not, of course, be embarrassingly obscure so as to leave its owner with little to say about it. It may be bold in form, even graphic, but in a way that is so clearly artistic that it is secure against the label of ''bad taste.'' (5) The art should be presented by its seller in an interpretive context that convincingly depicts its aesthetic and economic advantages.

Because the contemporary art market is comparatively deficient in the reputational investment of art historians, in the showcasing activity and prestige lending of major museums, and in the acquisitional interests of the largest collectors, the tastes of the new art buyers have a dominant influence on SoHo art.

3 The Dealer
Gatekeeper to the Art World

A contract with a SoHo commercial gallery and its dealer-operator is the goal of the swarm of artists who come into New York each season in search of an exhibition showcase and professional management of their careers. More than 4,500 artists receive bachelor's or master's degrees in fine arts each year, and an acute job shortage has developed, especially in such institutionalized positions as art teachers. There are said to be 150 candidates for every available position in the art field.[1] Graduates with art degrees coming to SoHo and hoping to make a name for themselves must adjust to the competitive reality. In recent years, many have prepared themselves with college courses in studio economics. They understand the techniques of career advancement and realize that they must locate themselves along the moving line of artistic innovation and fashion if they are to gain the attention of the buyers and critics. The painter who repeats art history is ignored. As more innovators struggle for attention, however, the pace of art development accelerates, tending to leave the critics and the schools behind. The new buyers seem more willing than the critics and the schools to keep pace with the new developments. The dealer who coordinates the career of the aspiring artist with the hopeful collector has assumed the central position in the market. The commercial gallery has supplanted the museum, the critic, and the school as the arbiter of success.

Designating the New Art

The SoHo dealers have the problem of sifting through these aspirants—"unknowns," for the most part, without previous recognition by critics or buyers. The dealers must decide which of them are producing work that might be marketable as well as aesthetically significant. Dealers deny that they can or do force the market to accept an artist, just as they deny that they persuade the artist to accept or adopt the market's standards. Dealers describe their function in more positive terms: they propose and the market disposes. As one of SoHo's most prominent dealers explained it,

> We try to identify work that seems important to us and to the development of American visual experience. And if we think that a thing is significant enough, then we will exhibit it. And then we hope for the best. But then, it is usually only one-third of the exhibiting artists who have what you might call commercial fame. They may get a certain amount of attention from the critics and magazines, but it doesn't always result in the artist gaining material goods. It is very infrequent that an artist is able to support himself on the sale of his work. We show very off-beat stuff here, you know, and we just hope for the best.

The dealers try to winnow the field of aspirants down to a commercially manageable group that still includes all of the authentic talent presenting itself at any one time. The dealer's strategy is to remain accessible to all artists with work to show yet to be very selective about which works will be sponsored for exhibition. Great art works remain scarce, according to the dealers, despite the increase in the absolute number of fine artists. However, the dealers are convinced that their direct and extensive familiarity with the art being produced, and their educated perception, enable them to locate all of the real talent. As one put it,

> If an artist of major consequence comes along at this time, it's not likely that he would go undiscovered, even if we didn't discover him here [in this gallery]. In other words, there's so much interest and perception about modern art that it's not likely that an artist is going to be left forgotten, at this point. I mean, an artist may be neglected for a while, an artist of consequence may be left in the shadows longer than he should be, but it's not likely that he'll be totally forgotten. It's not like it was in the eighteenth and nineteenth centuries, when maybe a great artist, a man like van Gogh, for instance, who never developed any audience at all for his work, could occur. If a painter or

sculptor of any consequence came up in this period of time, the work would be identified. We like to think [this gallery is] there at the beginning to identify it.

The well-known artists agree with the dealers that little genuine talent is overlooked, nor is substantial success possible as a result of favoritism or publicity flukes. Said one eminent artist, convinced that the market recognizes talent, ''I don't agree with these charges of art-world corruption, the attribution of success to who you know, who you sleep with, whether or not you're homosexual, and what not. That kind of charge is all overrated.''

SoHo dealers explain that they use the most demanding criteria in selecting their artists. According to the head of one of SoHo's leading avant-garde galleries, the dealer seeks to identify work that is the germ of a new movement: ''We do have a philosophical outlook. There are certain kinds of work we prefer. We like really adventurous work, that is, the work has to be innovative, and it has to break away from established traditions as much as possible and begin new traditions.'' Dealers describe their function in the market as recognizing, ahead of other art-world institutions, such as the museums, the exceptional work of art. They distinguish it from the far more numerous pieces of inferior and repetitive work and display it prominently. The dealer sees himself as the art world's gatekeeper, or as an explorer picking through uncharted territory in advance of the critic and curator. According to the dealers, no other institution accomplishes this public service. One dealer explained,

> I think the art gallery has become the pioneer, the trying-out-ground for artists. The museum doesn't do the kind of creative work now that galleries can and do engage in. The gallery generally does locate the most important work of its time. The museums just do not have the facilities or the ability to do that, or the willingness to do it.
>
> Institutions like the Whitney have tremendous pressure on them to acquire all kinds of art and are subject to all kinds of internal strife. The Museum of Modern Art is too limited in its funds and is trying to be an educational institution, so it can't do the kind of avant-garde work that they used to do. The Guggenheim, it seems to me, is an historical museum. It's rather sleepy in its attempts to unfold new currents of art. . . . So it's really the art galleries of the major centers of America that can do all this necessary pioneering work in getting the best artists shown.

Critics such as Hilton Kramer of the *New York Times* admit that it was once true that the entrepreneurial dealer was the primary midwife of new art movements. But this is no longer the case, Kramer maintains, because "both the media and the museums maintain a steady and unremitting surveillance of everything new, and middle-class collectors vie with each other to embrace it."[2] Judging from the role of SoHo dealers in introducing collectors, curators, and critics to new art and in providing a context of developmental interpretation for it, Kramer would appear to be displacing the dealers from their front-line position without warrant.

Sorting the "Unknowns" and Distributing Aesthetic Territory

SoHo dealers continually look at the latest works of young and older unknown artists so as to be ready to reposition themselves in the art field. The most influential of the SoHo galleries are exemplary in their accessibility to new artists who come in every day seeking an audience and an encouraging milieu. The director of one such gallery declared, "We look at more new talent than almost any gallery in the United States, in the whole world, I think." Artists bring in photographs, slides, and sometimes the works themselves for a viewing. Some truck in their work from out-of-state locations and set it up in the SoHo loft of an artist friend or in the gallery itself when it is empty for a day or two between scheduled shows. Since some works do not photograph well, there is an advantage to bringing in the works themselves. Often a dealer will allow the artist to invite other dealers to look at work that has been temporarily installed in his gallery. Sponsoring experimental work, however tentative that sponsorship is, enables the gallery to assume a prominent position in the forefront of emerging styles. It is good public relations and channels more of the stream of promising artists through the gallery.

If an artist is merely interesting he may not be invited for even a try-out show with a SoHo commercial gallery, so extensive is the available pool of talent. One dealer explained,

We see upwards of fifty artists a week, and we do it with tremendous democratic generosity. We don't make any appointments, or anything like that. All artists are invited to come in and make a submittal of some kind, usually evidence of their work, or they can bring in the work itself. We're open at all times to looking at people's work. We can only show so much, however. During the course of a season, we have here, considering that we have a very good space, we have thirty-three shows a season, and that's more than any other gallery in the country. And we're still limited to the number of exhibitions we can have.

The artist who walks in with slides or a portfolio helps to keep the dealer informed of art developments. Several SoHo dealers, such as Ivan Karp of O. K. Harris Gallery, lecture extensively on contemporary art on the college circuit, absorbing new developments as they travel. When a dealer judges that a work is part of a new direction in art, one to which respected artists are themselves seriously committed, then he is likely to show this work even against the contradictory opinion of art critics. Whereas the dealer must be willing to act quickly to establish a lead in a new turn in art, the critic tends to be suspicious and is hesitant to identify a trend that might prove to be only an insignificant wrinkle in the history of art. Being closer to the artists, upon whom most of them rely for advice about which new artists to treat seriously, the dealers can more easily synthesize the judgment of the artist community than can the critics. This has been the gallery owners' advantage since the great Paris dealers of the late nineteenth and early twentieth centuries.[3] A SoHo dealer described his gallery's position in the following way:

> We've exhibited here a number of so-called photo-realist or new-realist paintings. We take a lot of punishment for that. In some cases it's considered pretty reactionary, and so forth. But we think it's the best work being done now. And we think there is a freshness of vision, and if a number of very intelligent artists decide to embark on investigating pictorial ideas like this, then there must be something going on. And we feel very genuine enthusiasm about it. We're wise and mature perceptors. I think we've identified some very, very important artists. It's a significant movement.

When an artist who walks in off the street, or far more frequently, who is mentioned to the dealer by one of his affiliated artists, proves to be more than merely interesting, "if he really rouses us up," as one dealer said, then the investigation of the artist will be taken a step further.

> Out of fifty artists that we see during the week, we'll go to see three or four studios at the end of the week. We'll say, this guy looks awfully good, let's go to his studio. And I'll go or [my assistant] will go and visit the artist in his studio. Often, it doesn't look as good as it did in the photographs, but if it holds up, we'll proceed to the next stage. If we can, we'll try to schedule the artist [for an invitational show].

The SoHo dealer usually has his exhibition schedule worked out a full year in advance, sometimes two years. The larger commercial galleries have eighteen to twenty-five affiliated artists who expect, and whom the dealer expects, to show at about eighteen month intervals. Special exhibitions and invitational group shows of unaffiliated artists fill up gaps in the gallery calendar. Dealers will try to schedule an exciting unknown artist into one of their invitational group shows, which are usually held at the end of the season, the slack period which coincides with the summer vacations of the buyers. These invitational shows allow the dealer to gauge the public reaction to the artist's work without having to commit the gallery to an extended affiliation with the artist.

It may sometimes happen that a delay of six months or a year in showing an artist will allow other artists to establish themselves in the same style and become the focus of attention. Artists working within the competitive and fast-paced New York market may discover that they are innovating along parallel lines. Where the parallelism is close, the artist who is the last to exhibit may have difficulty establishing a place within the style. Dealers sensitive to this problem may help an artist stake out his territory by mounting a show of the artist's work earlier than would ordinarily be the case. "Now, if an artist looks incredibly good," one such dealer said, "and it seems important that the work be seen right away for his own sake, in other words, that his vision not be preempted, then we'll try to get it shown as fast as we can."

Of course, the field covered by the artists in any one gallery is itself a territory, and the dealer may be accused of allotting areas to his artists based upon the interest of the gallery alone. In the spirit of rationalizing labor, one dealer told an abstract artist to stay with it. The gallery had enough realists, he explained, and "You're my abstract person."

The Packaging of Styles

The SoHo galleries that have been most successful in finding new markets for American painters have done so by aggressively promoting trends in art. If a trend and its leaders are recognized and raised to public prominence under the sponsorship of one gallery, other galleries will follow by promoting the new style with lesser exemplars of their own, and critics will be obliged to review the work of significant artists of that school. As one long-time SoHo artist describes this tactic, "The galleries who control the scene down here do it by getting the other galleries to promote their trend. They set up the initial shows. Then, everything is more coherent. There's less risk for buyers, and it's easier for critics to see what they should review. They are ignorant and conservative anyway, and take to consensus opinions." Dealers hope, moreover, that by establishing the trend as a discernible parameter for the guidance of collectors they will also be in a position to identify its true exponents and persuade them to form an affiliation with their galleries.

Dealers occasionally manage to transform a tendency among some artists into a named and defined trend or movement. For example, Louis

Meisel, a young dealer from Madison Avenue who moved to a SoHo gallery in 1973, opened with a collection of works consisting exclusively of photo realism. Meisel was clarifying the outlines of a movement exhibited earlier at other SoHo galleries, but doing so in a big way. He was hoping to capture a leading place as its sales representative. Meisel discussed the organization of his opening exhibition in its handsomely printed catalog.

> In the fall of 1972 Stuart Speiser informed me that he was interested in assisting the arts both through legal innovation, in his capacity as an attorney, and also through direct involvement as a collector and patron. His special interest was realism, as was mine. I made the following proposal:
>
> I asked him to commission me to assemble a collection of the best Photo-Realists. The method was to be unrestricted commissions for the artists, and the result was to be a semi-public collection which would be made available to museums throughout the world. The idea of a theme had occurred to me several times in the past few years for a number of reasons. The idea of aviation as a theme came about as a result of Mr. Speiser's interest in aviation. He is one of the country's foremost aviation and aero-space attorneys, as well as having flown numerous airplanes, and is also a collector of aviation art and memorabilia. I felt that the airplane was not unrelated to the imagery which interested many of the Photo-Realists, and after discussing the idea with about ten of the artists, and finding no resistance, but only an interest in the added problems, I adopted the theme concept.
>
> It was emphasized to the artists that we wanted a major work which would be consistent with their work in 1973. The theme was of secondary interest. Each one does include something to do with aviation, but upon seeing each one separately, the viewer would not realize that there was a commissioned theme.[4]

None of the works in Meisel's exhibition were for sale. He gambled that if he could appropriate a trend for his gallery and publicize it in such a way that critics and ultimately buyers couldn't ignore it, buyers would come to the gallery on a steady, long-term basis. Publicity was to be achieved not only by ads in art magazines and full-color brochures, but by scheduling the show for a subsequent tour. Galleries and museum curators in the smaller cities and universities frequently call on SoHo dealers to provide them with work for exhibitions. In this case, Meisel had packaged for distribution a large exhibit of twenty-two major works, complete with interpretative literature.

This type of cultural dissemination insures that an art development that originates in New York, or whose practitioners migrate there, spreads rapidly across the country through networks of galleries affiliated with SoHo dealers and through the more adventurous small museums. This may occur before the major museums have gotten around to including the new style in their periodic shows of new material, but they cannot thereafter forever ignore the well-disseminated trend.

Dealing and Collecting

SoHo dealers, then, accelerate the developments they observe in the artist community and persuade critics, patrons, and museums to reinforce these developments by adding their institutional certification. This publicity and the widening basis of support it mobilizes becomes the leverage with which the dealer creates a place in the art market for the new trend, and with it, for his artists.

Those who get in on the ground floor—the patrons who subsidize a new movement, the artists who become historically linked to its inception, and the galleries which sponsor and affiliate with those artists—all benefit if the publicity strikes a responsive cord, and the trend, one of the many that are emerging or dissipating among artists at any one time, coalesces as a fixture on the art-world landscape.[5]

The major SoHo galleries are those which have succeeded in identifying themselves with a new turn in art and in raising it to prominence. As they affiliate themselves with its major artistic figures, they simultaneously help to determine who these figures are to be. In this process museums and the critics are maneuvered into providing broader institutional exposure and support. The major collectors linked to the gallery are the first to be given a chance to buy and so to subscribe to the new art. Depending as much on their evaluation of the dealer's perspicacity as on their evaluation of the art itself, they make their decisions on early purchase. The dealer himself almost certainly is among these early buyers. Dealers rely upon their inside track for purchasing the best pieces by the pacesetters of a movement in order to make their personal fortunes. Lesser galleries and lesser buyers can be trusted to follow an established trend, usually creating support for the works of artists more peripheral to the now-delineated movement.

Leo Castelli, often considered the shrewdest among SoHo's leading dealers, acquired his top stable of artists in his pre-SoHo days. These include Jasper Johns, Robert Rauschenberg, Roy Lichtenstein, Andy Warhol, and Claes Oldenburg. Castelli accomplished this by making the decision in 1957 to support the then emerging pop art, while the rest of the market remained loyal to abstract expressionism. Castelli says his wealth is based on the fact that dealing has allowed him to collect art, though he modestly declares he bought works that were left over from shows and which no one else wanted. At the first Johns exhibition in 1958, which Castelli helped arrange at the Museum of Modern Art, everything was sold to the museum benefactors, who were offered the first crack at them, except one, a blue and yellow target with a row of dismembered body parts set in boxes. The piece was considered too sexually frank for the museum to acquire for itself, and Castelli finally bought it from the artist for $1200; he recently turned down an offer to purchase it for $400,000.[6]

The collections which dealers accumulate are often used to generate publicity for a new art movement. They are "reinvested" by being lent free for other exhibitions. As both collectors and traders, dealers focus the attention of the market and its other participants—magazine critics, museum curators, buyers, and even the artists—on a limited number of art developments. Dealers prune the chaotic possibilities inherent in the artist community to strengthen a limited number of developments. These then can be analysed in the art press, honored by museums, and coveted by collectors. In a market whose only philosophical consensus is a commitment to modernism—that is, to the value of transcending conventions—there is no other market element that can perform the function of establishing coherence but those dealers close enough to the artists and the point of artistic production. One SoHo dealer summarized the process.

> Publicity is the key. I advertise and spend a lot of money on it. [Not every dealer] does this. For example, I get a page in *Art in America* and pay $1000 an issue. I lend to museums. I have 300 pieces on loan now. This is a big headache. There's a lot of work—making sure insurance is okay, that things are kept track of. I use one artist to get another [into a museum exhibition]. I'm doing them a favor, I tell them. If a curator wants a big name, I ask them to take a look at a lesser artist as well. I don't twist their arms. I say, "Please, if you like the work take it too." They usually do. This builds up the résumés of the artists with lots of museum shows.

If the museums are kept supplied with front-line information on art developments by the dealers, so are the art magazines. The dealer quoted above continued,

> The magazine people come around, with no idea of what to do three issues down the line. Many dealers hide. They see only an ad salesman. But I talk to them. I give them ideas, and presto, I've got a cover story and 26 pages in *Art in America*. In eight years and 100 shows, I have never had a word in the *New York Times*. I always thought that they couldn't be bought. But for this show [the artist] insisted on an

ad there, and I said, if you want one, you pay for it. And she did.
Now we'll see. I don't like the idea of buying coverage, but if you
have to do it, I would to promote my artists.

One problem with promotionally accelerated art movements is the
rapidity with which they may succeed one another, leaving the market
closed and cold to all but the established leadership. Dealers don't promote out of thin air, of course. They follow the existing contours of
developments they observe among artists they know and respect. And
they try to prevent confusion and charges of "ahistoricism" from the
critics and curators by elaborating links between the new movement
they invest in and the fine art of the past. Each new trend is construed as
following a developmental logic. Art commentators and custodians,
concerned with a coherent art history, are offered the new movement
within a context of analysis by the dealers. Explained one SoHo dealer,

> I'm promoting abstract illusionism. The Taft Museum was setting
> up a show—strictly nineteenth-century illusionism—and I suggested
> to them that they tie it in with contemporary pieces. I showed them the
> logical steps of the development—nineteenth-century realism, trompe
> l'oeil—the historical flow. This gave them the idea for an exciting
> show.
>   Not everyone will see [this show], but it builds [abstract illusionism].
> I lose money on things like this. I often have to pay the shipping. But
> my artists are in, and in five years it will help. They can look back and
> say, that was the show that started it all. And [my artists] were in it.
> These shows at museums are a useful tool.

An activist role in the market does not guarantee that a dealer per-
ceives which developments are rooted in the enduring commitments of
truly talented artists, and which are merely fads. Neither can the use of
publicity replace the ballet-like timing that a dealer may need in order to
anticipate the tastes of the market. Dealers do go broke, are forced to
sell off their collections, and are reduced to selling antique furniture in
their galleries.

But it remains true that major dealers rely on the same strategic ma-
neuvers: (1) They co-opt and concretize an art development of genuine
concern to producing artists; they try to sign up its leading practitioners
and may name the movement so as to lay better claim to it. (2) They
accelerate the rate at which other art organizations, chiefly museums
and art magazines, become aware of the new movement, and they use
the attention of these institutions as evidence of broad support for the
movement. In lectures and in their publicity, dealers help fashion the
intellectual defense of the movement. (3) Dealers take the recognition
given the movement they underwrite as certification of its importance,

and present the buyers with this certification. Using their own purchasing initiative and that of preferred customers who have their confidence, the dealers prime and cultivate market demand for the new work.

Selling to Clients

The customers who spend substantial amounts for contemporary art are but a handful of the total buyers, and consequently SoHo dealers must encourage many new middle-class buyers. Dealers hope to convert the occasional customer into at least a modest collector, one who will have a long-term commitment to the dealer's artists and thus his gallery. Dealers prefer to work with collectors, not only because they buy more and their purchasing can be channeled into support of the style which the gallery sponsors, but also because the collector is a secondary sales agent. Collectors socialize with one another, compete at auctions, and influence each other's buying determinations. Hoping to place their acquisitions within the center of the market, collectors have an interest in reaching a consensus among themselves.

Dealers assess their clients in terms of the prominence and influence of their collections and offer those who assemble the more important collections cheaper prices and longer payment terms. Castelli suggests that his prices vary for a particular work, depending on his friendship with the purchaser, the distinction of the purchaser and his collection, and the frequency of his purchases.[7] According to Larry Fleishman, a partner in Kennedy Galleries, "Big museums will pay 20 percent below the market, but my best collectors are like museums to me. I try to keep them happy."[8]

Dealers also favor their best customers by making available to them the gallery's most important art pieces. "Placement" of such pieces in prominent showcases is the most prudent tactic the dealer has for maximizing the impact of a piece, to the career advantage of the artist and of his sales agent. Explained one SoHo dealer,

> Buyers have to buy a lot, they have to be serious about building a collection, or I won't place important works with them. Placing is important for the career development of artists. If someone came in and wanted to buy an important picture off the wall, I'd first ask, "Who are you? Do you understand the responsibility of ownership?" They'd have to be willing to lend to museums. They'd have to be the kind of people who talk with other collectors so that each will buy each other's things. I don't want a piece to simply disappear.

SoHo dealers compete in making themselves available and gracious to new gallery visitors who are contemplating a first purchase. Like many of the artists they see, buyers are often unknowns. First encounters, handled correctly, can pay off in the emergence of a new collector who adopts the gallery's aesthetic coordinates. Giving the brush-off to someone taken for a small-fry buyer can be a mistake. A SoHo dealer tells the following cautionary tale:

> An anesthesiologist, five years out of Czechoslovakia, accompanied by his wife, an art historian or would like to be, went to [one of the top SoHo galleries]. They had $20,000 and were doing well, and told the receptionist they wanted to see [the gallery director]. The girl at the desk said she'd take care of them, but they insisted on seeing [the director] and said they wanted to buy a [prominent artist in the pop art movement]. Finally, [the director] came out and right off the bat asked, "How much can you spend?" They said "$20,000," and he said, "You know, you can only get a water color or a drawing for that," and he went over to the girl, whispered in her ear, and went off to his back room. Without even a "Goodbye" or a "Thank you." She came over and said, "[The director] asked me to show you some water colors and drawings."
>
> They told me all this after they had been buying here for a while. Here it was a different story. They had a drink upstairs, asked to see a studio, and I called up [a top painter with the gallery]. She obliged. Months later, they bought. They've spent $180,000 in two years. I've sent them to [a different SoHo dealer] for some things they needed for a valid collection.

Dealers socialize with their clients at the point of sale and in the more diffuse surroundings of charity affairs. The latter, held for such causes as "saving Venice from sinking," are sponsored by dealers to generate good will. "The art world is all my time, really," said one dealer, "social, business, and spare time. But I do race hydroplanes. That's the only time I get away from the art world and into middle America. But I got into it through [the painter son of a painter father]. Otherwise, my social life and my conversation are all the art world."

Because socializing and sales are so closely linked, several dealers have renovated large lofts next to their SoHo galleries in which they can hold charity parties and entertain individual customers. At the home of a representative SoHo dealer, a client will be dined, asked to play pool with the host, and ultimately seated on a semicircular banquette facing a wall thirty feet away on which is hung the particular painting the dealer intends to sell that evening. It is usually the client himself who brings the conversation around to the work in question.

Major dealers are always collectors, and their homes reflect this. Ivan Karp and his wife display a collection in their SoHo loft which includes

American salt-glazed crocks, nineteenth-century landscape and portrait paintings, twentieth-century painting and sculpture, art nouveau and art deco sculpture, antique kitchen and carpentry tools, turn-of-the-century tableware, commemorative spoons, Coca-Cola trays, and more.[9] Another SoHo dealer has displayed in his loft, besides a portion of his 800 personally owned paintings, Victorian glass and silver objects, the world's largest collection of "Fiestaware" table china, traveling cosmetic cases from several centuries, and antique desks.

Dealers seem to be addicted to collecting. It is not merely the desire to own and display objects that moves them to collect. They like to play the market in anything "collectible." One dealer offered a free hint on the next collectibles boom, old group photographs, and invited his listeners to get in early.

> They have to be, like with any of these boomlets, of some aesthetic interest, placeable by period, and perhaps historically important. They can then derive a nostalgic or an historical value. You have to buy them cheap—after the word gets out, prices will go up and you stop buying. I told [another SoHo dealer] about this and [he] bought 300 of these historical group photos. I don't know where he could have gotten them.

This dabbling in collectibles is, of course, a busman's holiday. The dealers are playing, half seriously, with the skills they use in their fine-art dealing. They pioneer the delineation of a field for collecting, buying up the bargains. Then they spread the word to others to accelerate the demand. When the market peaks, they sell. They appear to be as enamored with the game itself as with the possibilities of gain.

Dealers generate a contagious atmosphere by their constant and, as they report, profitable trading ventures. In the dealer's gallery, and even more so in his home, the client is exposed to a persuasive example of the advantages of buying art. Ensconced in art-ladened surroundings and told exemplary tales of the profits and excitement opon to those who buy art, the client is tempted to identify with the evident success and pleasure of the dealer. If he will seize the bargain presented to him, he may, with the dealer, share in the next art boom.

Fine art, often beautiful and always displayable as decoration, is also interpreted to the client as a socially important legacy of which the buyer becomes custodian. The buyer is offered, then, a variety of gratifications that differs significantly from the unleavened appeal to greed which attracts, for example, commodity traders of futures in frozen pork bellies. Along with feeling perceptive and shrewd, the art purchaser can also feel socially responsible.

This layering of motives—profit, status, beauty, and altruism—is sometimes exploited by the dealer. One dealer, who in the last year reported that he had placed eighty paintings in museums—more than he had sold to private collectors—explained the multilayer approach to art clients. He uses the gift-donation system. As a dealer, he lines up a benefactor who wants a particular painting. The benefactor is induced to make an offer of an equivalent work by the same artist to a museum, a gift which is tax-deductible. The price for the latter work is doubled. The benefactor pays the artist, donates the work to a museum, and collects his tax deduction on 100 percent of the doubled price. Then the artist, having been paid twice his usual and established fee, "gives" the originally desired piece to the benefactor without charge. The museum, usually chronically short in its acquisitions budget, gets a significant piece of art. The artist gets additional exposure and may be able to raise his previously established prices. The donor gets his art and his tax break, while the dealer collects his commission. Everything is legal, and sweetened with altruism.

On Managing Artists

Dealers try to maintain as much flexibility as possible in their commitments to particular avant-garde styles and artists. The pace of artistic innovation is rapid, and the danger of stylistic obsolescence is always real. To cope with the rapid changes in the field of contemporary art, the dealer is ready to emphasize, when appropriate, that his professional commitment is to the art and not the artist. Explained one dealer,

> We're loyal more to the artist's work than to the artist. In other words, we don't commit ourselves to a personality so much as to his performance. We try to keep neutral that way. And as long as the artist's work is interesting, we continue to exhibit it.
> We'll show an artist's work as long as we like it. And we don't say, "You're fired!" at a certain point if the work is not good. We'll say, "We can't show the work right now, it doesn't look just right to us. You can show it later if it's good." Of course, that sometimes disgruntles an artist. An artist who has had two or three one-man shows expects to show regularly. But we just don't do that. We show only the work that consistently looks interesting and engaging or provocative, or, you know, of interest. For us, the artist's performance is very important from event to event. We won't show an artist just because he's a sentimental favorite. We really have to like the work.

The notion that the dealer's commitment is to the work and not the artist finds its most useful moment when an affiliated artist declares to his dealer that he's ready to show, and the dealer tells him he's not. The dealer must communicate the nonarbitrary basis of his decision so as not to drive the artist out of the gallery permanently. The dealer stands for higher standards in art, he must assure himself, than the artist might follow on his own. One dealer illustrated this function of maintaining standards and the problems it raises with dealers whose self-evaluation differs from that of the dealer.

> We have a very loyal group here, and we treat them with great courtesy. But we have turmoil, too. We had an artist this week who announced to me that he was prepared to leave the gallery, and I asked him why he wanted to leave. He said, "Well, you didn't like my work this year." "But," I said, "I've given you three one-man shows and you've done quite nicely here, and here I've rejected your work for this season—maybe I'll like it next season. Why do you want to leave?" Well, his feelings were hurt and he felt terrible. He'd never been rejected before. He was singularly hurt, and it was basically an act of self-spite that he decided to withdraw from the gallery.
>
> And I convinced him not to withdraw. I said, "Let's keep looking and see how it goes, you know. Maybe next year everything will blaze with glory for us." He said, "Well, you're misconceiving these works; you're not reading them." And I said, "Well, we have to show what we're really committed to, what we really like, and it's senseless for us to put on exhibitions just because we think you're a fine fellow. We really have to like the work, and we have to relate to the art, rather than to the person." Well, he seemed to understand that, to a certain extent, and we came to a sort of mellow understanding that he wouldn't retire from the gallery and that we'd keep looking at his work and hope that we'd both come to a happy moment again.

The dealer's confidence in his definitive role as a judge of aesthetic value is necessary if he is to sort out the market. In resisting the pressure of artists for self-inclusive definitions of what is significant in art, the dealer must be willing to make categorical decisions. Prior to the critics, the collectors, and the museums, it is the dealer who decides whether a work is interesting enough to merit exhibition, or if it is to be ignored by the whole institutionalized art world.

Dealers describe their role in the art market to new artists in passive terms. They say that they are there to recognize the few distinguished and important works which occur among the many that are neither. They can only hope, they explain, that the wider art public will confirm their evaluation of a new talent by praising the buying those of his works which they exhibit. But dealers emphasize that they are in a risky business and that very often an artist's early promise and his dealer's enthusiasm find no sympathetic echo in the market. Such a fatalistic view of his position in the market is useful to the dealer who must reconcile an unknown artist to modest prices for his work and to the typical 50 percent commission charged when the work is sold.

The more established artists expect the dealer to be more active in the market, and dealers will accordingly offer their services to those artists who are proven sellers with a different argument. To these artists, the dealer represents himself as a successful promoter. As one dealer said,

> I don't just hang them on the wall. I promote their careers. With [one of my best selling painters], when she started with me she got $3000 [per picture] and was not really known. Now, she's in 112 museums and she gets $30,000. I emphasize public relations. I get my artists into museums within one year and get them an article, if not a cover, in an [art] magazine. I work for this.

With the successful artist, the dealer has more room to be an active agent, concerned not so much with simply selling his work as with placing it in those public or private collections where it will have the highest visibility and the most status enhancement. The successful artist has, of course, a different market position than the unknown. Other dealers are anxious to accept such an artist into their own galleries and may already be ingratiating themselves with the artist so as to lay the groundwork for a "raid."

Many of the material and psychological services which dealers offer to their established artists are designed to strengthen their loyalty to the gallery and to the dealer. Many of these dealer services are financial and professional. "I'm trying to work out a complete plan for my artists to get Blue Cross and accounting services," said one dealer, "and, if they have money, investment counseling." Others reveal a strategy of encouraging the personal dependency of the artist upon the dealer, the very dependency and personalism which the dealer repudiates as unprofessional in his relationships with lesser known artists.

> At 3 A.M. I will get a call from [one of the highest priced artists in my gallery]—he can't work, he's upset. I reassure him. Though he's the most successful of the realists, he's the least secure personally. This is a big drain on me, but I'm glad to do this. For another artist, I had him live with me for a month, I got him off the bottle and settled down and working.

A dealer would have to be exceptionally insistent on drawing the line if he wanted to resist the role of therapist and confidant which some artists thrust on their dealers. Few dealers can resist its advantages.

> You can find yourself developing relationships with artists which are based on sentimental affection. There are many pitfalls in this. I should not come to that, but you know, it's a family scene, and you may automatically find yourself in the relation of a maternal or pater-

nal guide. Now some dealers aren't really mentally or psychologically equipped for that, but you find yourself obliged to take that role. And some of us are reasonably equipped to play a strong leadership kind of a thing. It works out okay.

The list of services performed by dealers for their successful artists is extensive, and its emphasis on personality-propping suggests that artists are not reluctant to exploit the role of the gifted but demanding child.

> For one artist, I reorganized a land deal he had made. He had bought an old lumber mill to live and work in, with his family, but there was no one else around. There was no one for his kids to play with or for his wife to talk to. So I restructured it as a co-op for five artists and their families. This solved the isolation. He didn't seem to know how to go about doing it, even if he could have conceived of the idea.

Dealers simplify daily life for those of their artists who demand these services, thus allowing them to act as if their creativity were a license exempting them from sordid, commercial details. "I handle car payments, rents, advances, divorces," said a dealer, "so that if an artist wants, he need only pick up a paint brush and not balance his own check book at all. This does take a great deal of trust. It is for these reasons that many dealers do not want to handle living artists and contemporary art."

The dealer wants to be friendly and fair with his or her artists, and sympathetic and emotionally supportive. The dealer must sustain their belief in both the objectivity of his judgment and his personal interest in them. The typical tie between the artist and a gallery of affiliation is not a long-term exclusive contract but a diffuse conviction that, for personal and economic reasons, the dealer is indeed working on the artist's behalf. Belief in the dealer's obligation to him bonds the artist to the dealer. The perception of a personal loyalty, of course, operates within a wider market context of external pressure from the many artists seeking dealer affiliation and the artist's expectation that the dealer will boost his career. Given these considerations, a mutual if qualified trust usually develops between artist and dealer.

> If the artist likes the way we exhibit his work and the way we describe it and everything else, then maybe he'll stay with us. If he feels that we haven't been serving him, he or she might leave. There's no rigid arrangement that way. We don't have any contractual arrangements with artists where we say "You're our man and you can't go anywhere else." It's based on what you call mutual faith.

These relationships may, of course, be strained from time to time, as when an unknown artist is accepted into the gallery for further trial and is scheduled to be a part of a group show with the gallery's established artists. Successful artists may feel that a grouping with an unknown or a lesser known artist is a challenge to their achieved status within the gallery and the art world. So peer conscious are established artists that some have left galleries and taken their future work to new dealers in order to protect their reputations from this status contamination. Dealers, however, guard their right to offer new talent its chance. Explained one dealer,

> They can't hold leaving over my head to get some concession or other. "I don't want my things shown with this somebody else," they say to me. This somebody else may be an unknown. I tell them, "You were young, give him a chance." I have a tryout policy, you see. One thousand artists come by in a year to show me slides. I look at their work in their studios maybe in fifty cases each year. Five will measure up. This five I will bring into the gallery [in separate group shows], and eventually four will have to go. One will hold up. It is this one that a top artist may resent being shown with. That's too bad. That's my end of the business.

Innovation, Inflation, and the Gallery System

The prerogative of the dealer to introduce unknown artists to the market represents the heart of the gallery system. The search for new talent and its ultimate incorporation into the gallery keeps the gallery alive. When the gallery exhibits unknown artists whom the dealer has certified as having major promise, buyers of art are persuaded to invest in the rising value of the artist's reputation, in anticipation of a substantial appreciation in the value of what they buy. As art lovers, such buyers also have the opportunity of sharing in the discovery of a major talent and so demonstrating the sharpness of their aesthetic perceptions. It is this raising of unknowns into wide acceptance and the accompanying rapid increase in the prices of their work that constitute the gallery system. Dealers have to be accessible to new talent in order to keep the cycle of renewal alive, despite the understandable wishes of some established artists to freeze the process at a point advantageous to themselves.

Bringing new artists into the gallery at regular intervals not only lets the dealer offer his clients bargain pieces prior to their price appreciation, but it also allows the dealer to speculate in inexpensive acquisitions for the gallery. The dealer's own collection, so useful in publicizing art trends when lent out and in priming the market, also has uses in regulating the exchange between dealer and artist and in capitalizing the gallery. Pieces in the dealer's collection constitute a kind of currency which augments the often scanty cash reserves of the gallery.

The purchase of work from affiliated artists also solves the often difficult problem of stipends. During periods when the sales of an artist's
work don't meet his expenses, the dealer's offer to purchase is appreciated. Many dealers and artists prefer such purchases to stipends or
advances of money charged against future sales because the purchase is
less entangling. The dealer will pay the same price as the artist has
established by his most recent sales, or perhaps a lower one, and if the
work appreciates suddenly, a large profit is possible for the dealer.

The Barter Trade

Recently, dealers have begun to trade paintings directly for merchandise, dental care, psychiatric counseling, and tax advice—as, indeed,
have artists themselves. When one dealer, who had opened his first
gallery in 1967 in the uptown art district, moved to SoHo after five
successful years, he had accumulated from one to five works of each
artist he had represented, a total of well over 500 pieces. "This ex-
presses my confidence in them," he explained, pointing out that some
other dealers do not take such risks. In SoHo he renovated an obsolete
industrial space to create his gallery and living space, using only $15,000
in cash, which was all he had. For most of his purchases and expenses,
he traded paintings. All his furniture, including an Eames chair, a deli-
catessen refrigerator with glass sliding doors, and a marble bathroom,
are the fruit of such bartering. There are art collectors among the pur-
veyors of furniture and appliances who find trading for art more profitable than buying it. The largest of these issue virtual "Sears catalogs" of
merchandise from which those owning art can choose. "If you want a
thousand dollars in appliances," explained the art dealer, "you make a
selection, deduct the 20 percent discount which is a wholesale courtesy,
and trade him $800 in paintings." The artist or dealer who trades his art
avoids sales taxes, and is able to distribute pieces that might not otherwise be readily sold. The dentist, paint store owner, or large collector
who barters is able to enjoy the satisfactions of the patron's role and to
absorb the cost into business overhead.

Conclusion

The study of SoHo's art market supports the contention that the locus
of creativity includes the entrepreneurial initiatives of the art dealer. The
development of the SoHo community and its galleries has coincided with
specific changes in the art world—the growth and openness of the market since abstract expressionism, the introduction of a new contemporary art buyer who seeks artistic coordinates from the market itself, and

the absence of any single critical definition of what is important avant-garde art or theory—and the result of these changes has been to elevate the dealer to the central position as arbitor of taste in fine art.

The elevation of the dealer role is possible because the critical function in the art world has devolved. What is common to all the newer styles and movements—earthworks, minimal art, conceptual art, the random scattering of found objects, and the appropriation of nonartistic "reality" into art in the form of commercial iconography and the photograph-like representation of the everyday—is an emancipation of the work of art from control by the professional critic. Either the work can be immediately apprehended in nonaesthetic terms, or else the artist or the dealer has taken on the function of generating the conceptual wrapping which makes the hole in a Nevada desert, the plywood box, the stacked railroad ties, or the pile of felt waste "art." In either case, the critic as a powerful and autonomous participant in the dialogue about art has taken a beating. The new art found in SoHo is frequently either material speaking for itself or concepts defined at some length by the artist and illustrated by intrinsically uninteresting material. The gallery installations present the art objects in their untainted accessibility as "reality" or propped by explanations which are themselves "meta-art."

Critics believe that this claim of art to be its own critic or to be beyond criticism stems from an aggrandizement of the artist figure into what I call the "celebrity artist." Celebrity artists presume to operate in the spirit of Andy Warhol's reply to the question "Why is *The Chelsea Girls* art?" Said Warhol, "Well, first of all, it was made by an artist, and, second, that would come out as art."[10] Writes critic Harold Rosenberg, "Actually, the artist who has left art behind or—what amounts to the same thing—who regards anything he makes or does as art, is an expression of the profound crisis that has overtaken arts in our epoch. Painting, sculpture, drama, music, have been undergoing a process of de-definition. The nature of art has become uncertain. At least, it is ambiguous. No one can say with assurance what a work of art is—or, more important, what is not a work of art. Where an art object is still present, as in painting, it is what I have called an anxious object: it does not know whether it is a masterpiece or junk."[11]

The SoHo data indicates that what has actually taken place is that art has become unabashedly an entrepreneurial field. Some artists, celebrity artists, have become entrepreneurs as well as artists, either through showmanship or by articulating their own theories about art, their own context of interpretation. The celebrity artist may use a dealer, but only as a representative, and will conduct his or her own salesmanship and conceptual defense.

For most artists fortunate enough to be shown in a SoHo gallery, the dealer functions as their impresario. It is the dealer who spins out a mantle of legitimating commentary on the lecture circuit and in gallery publications. It is the dealer acting as market entrepreneur who collects investors, solicits external critical commentary and press coverage, and orchestrates the fact and the appearance of a concerted art-world movement, as distinguished from an artists' movement. Where the critical function is not usurped by the dealer or the celebrity artist, it must compete with a new kind of commentary that is essentially descriptive journalism, in which the review of a gallery show approximates the movie review in being a guide to the enjoyable consumption of an experience rather than a theoretical critique. Press attention, then, becomes something distinguishable from critical attention; the first can be sufficient to enable the art work to survive the second.

Dealers, consequently, are the gatekeeper figures in the SoHo market for all but those artists who act as dealers on their own behalf, and only the celebrity artists can succeed at this game. For the unknown artist seeking sales and exposure, there is no realistic alternative to a professional dealer. For the artist wishing career management, the dealer is the most widely used and effective agent. In the creation of artistic culture, dealers are coparticipants rather than mere administrators of the market. As Richard Peterson has pointed out, the infrastructure between cultural producers and consumers is not a neutral mechanism in a market society.[12] Dealers make their selections prior to the review of art collectors, public and private, and it is their gallery exhibitions that become the interface between the artist and the critic. Other institutions of the art world, organized to consolidate rather than to challenge new artistic directions, are used to amplify the consequences of the dealer's selection of art and art movements, to reaffirm the dealer's own judgment as the most definitive statement about what is important in contemporary art.

4 The Unsuccessful SoHo Artist

The Social Psychology of an Occupation

Sources of the Artistic Commitment and the
Differentiation of Self as Artist

Looking back, SoHo artists locate the source of their career decision in their childhood experiences with art. They were talented children. Many report that in grammar school they had the ability to "copy anything." While their parents and teachers occasionally applauded this interest in art, the children felt insufficiently supported. Art provided the vehicle for both their rebellion and their legitimate achievement, and it took the place of intense peer-group socialization. The developing sense of self became identified with art. "From as far back as I can remember," said one painter, characteristically, "I always felt I was an artist."

As children, these artists shied away from the majority of their school companions, who did not understand their interests, and they often reported keeping the seriousness of their interest in art to themselves. "I never felt a part of the student crowd in high school," a collagist explained. "I was too out of it to work on school art projects like the yearbook. When I got praise sometimes for work I did for art teachers, they would say, 'You could be a fine illustrator.' But I thought of myself as an artist. That is a prime example of how school tries to lower your expectations of yourself."

An early sense of vocation combined with a lack of empathy from those around them caused the young artists to be acutely self-conscious. "I used to wear a long raincoat everywhere," said a photographer whose childhood talent had not been encouraged. "I felt I was hiding." A further retreat into art soothed this consciousness of being different. A painter recalled, "Art was an escape from teenage things—dances, dates, the changes in my body. I was convinced that I and my twin sister were ugly. We had acne. Thinking back, I guess everybody did. But I would draw with my sister for hours in the basement of our house."

Once an artistic self-concept was made available to these children by parents or school, and it meshed with evident talent, the social anxieties that accompany childhood were turned into support for the artist identity. "I had the romantic idea," said one painter, "that the artist was also a misfit, and it was easy to identify with them."

Parental Pressure

For most SoHo artists, the usual stresses of childhood were complicated not only by an ability and interest in art but also by parental opposition to that interest. Typically, their parents came from the more modest managerial, business, and professional segments of the middle class.[1] They sought to steer their children, sons and daughters alike, into economically sound professional or business careers. Fine arts was not perceived to be an acceptable alternative. In seeking to become artists, the children had to break away from the influence of their parents, who considered the arts an economically irresponsible choice.[2] Many of the artists recall with bitterness that their parents, especially their fathers, used the strongest psychological and financial leverage to get them out of fine arts and into more practical occupations. Some fathers stopped speaking to sons for years after they chose art over a place in the family business. Parents cut off tuition payments in the middle of the academic year for children who had switched to art programs, thus forcing them out of school. Resisting such pressure required, and perhaps fostered, substantial strength of will.

Although they were aware of their talents early in life, SoHo artists backed into their vocational commitments gradually, first denying the seriousness of their interest to their parents, then defiantly defending their identities when pressured, and finally sabotaging other career possibilities. They might, for example, flunk out of business courses or teacher-training programs in college and then go on to win full scholarships as art majors. The process of freeing themselves from their parents' expectations sometimes occurred earlier than college. One SoHo painter said of his youth,

In [grammar] school I was lauded for my ability to copy pictures. I was very good at it. They sent me to a separate room sometimes to copy magazine pictures. They really didn't know what else to do with me. You see, I was a bad scholar. I was always forgetting my books. Once I did this every day for two months in spite of writing notes to myself and putting my books inside my coat at night. And I was late all the time. I was good in art so I guess I felt I could be bad in other ways.

The artists traced their parents' restrictive definitions of permissible career possibilities to a materialism they had assumed in response to business setbacks or difficulties in upward mobility. These parents were harsh critics of their own financial performance, judging it against that of more successful relatives or in the light of their own earlier ambitions. Haunted by this standard, these financially comfortable families were tense with status strain.

To cope with a business decline or a difficult career climb, the parents of these artists had turned to hard work, self-discipline, and self-denial to attain what they considered to be economic respectability. They considered their art-prone children to be not merely foolish but also indifferent to the meaning of parental sacrifice. Relations between the young artists and their parents, particularly, as has been said, their fathers, were therefore often bitter. The following are fairly typical recollections by artists of parental opposition and the conflict that resulted:

My father was wealthy until I was ten. I started out in private schools and summer camps. Then the money was lost. This was hidden from me to some extent, but I knew, of course. My mother had to go to work. We moved several times to cheaper neighborhoods. Later, my father got his business back on its feet. He never thought I'd follow through in art. He thought I'd become a businessman. When he finally realized I intended to be a sculptor, he stopped speaking to me. Even now, we usually communicate through my mother.

My mother had been on the stage before she got married, but my father was a fireman. He saved his money and finally bought a home-furnishings store with a partner, but I don't think he ever felt he was successful. And I've never felt close to him. My being an artist hasn't helped.

I grew up in a town of five thousand in rural Ohio. It was without any cultural facilities at all. My mother was a hobby sketcher. She always gave me the feeling that she felt she was wasting her life there. She taught kindergarten and would talk a lot about the talent of her kids, talent that was going to be socialized out of them. My father taught, too. He had been in a few bad business deals and had become too much of a miser to spend any money on art lessons for me, or that kind of thing. Miser was his middle name.

My father was a frustrated pianist. He never touched the piano while I was growing up, though. He tried to steer me away from art. . . . He ran a textile business, but I was always aware of his frustrated music interest from the stories I'd hear. Maybe that's the aspect of him that I wanted to latch onto. But there was no support for art at home. I was seen by my father as no way to make a living. . . . After my first year in art school, he and my stepmother withdrew the support they had promised me.

But some young artists did not make their way completely without solace. The mothers in a few of these homes were remembered as having provided some covert support for an interest in art. It was often the mother who gave a son his first box of paints or who encouraged a daughter to try to market a photograph. Those artists who in later years held successful shows and discovered that as known painters they could cash checks at art supply houses shared their success with their families by first informing their mothers.

In general, however, the childhood homes of these artists reflected little awareness of art, though they often contained antique furniture or ethnic mementos prized as embodying heritage rather than aesthetic value. Only one artist recalled that his parents ever entertained a fine artist at home, but there were relatives in the families of each of the artists who represented a genteel tradition of interest in the arts, usually in the form of hobby painting, the restoring of antiques, or career plans in music or the theater that were ended prematurely by marriage or financial necessity. It was highly memorable to one artist, for example, that stories were circulated in the family about her father's having had to abandon an early career with a dance band and turn to public school teaching in order to support his family. Another artist recalled that his aunts described his father, a clothing manufacturer, as a once promising pianist. The parents themselves usually did not volunteer this information to their children.

Artists seeking to evade parental pressure had the need to exaggerate these characteristics of unfulfilled parental promise. In one instance, an artist saw in her deceased mother, whom she had never known, a substantial lost drawing talent. Artists typically traced the present unhappiness which they saw in their parents—together with the ulcers, cramped emotional expression or stinginess—to a turn in the lives of their parents toward the single-minded pursuit of financial security. A mother's interest in sketching or a father's in music were thought of as recessive characteristics, overwhelmed by economic considerations.

Art as an Affirmation of Middle-Class Culture

SoHo artists did not rebel against their parents with clear consciences. They acted with the strength and limited objectives of survivors. They conformed to parental values in that they viewed their work in terms of a chosen career, and they protected their identities by attaching themselves to those aspects of family background that could be construed as supporting the quest of the artist. They were not bohemians, but rather hoped for economic respectability as a component of their artistic ambition. By holding that a person's identity resided in a vocation, a cumulative career achievement, they also agreed with the class perspective of their entrepreneurial or professional parents. But when art did not yield financial success, these artists interpreted vocation in expressive terms as a journey whose meaning lies in the progressive realization of the self. In their middle-class backgrounds, unsuccessful artists found the ideological material to transform a failed career into a successful "calling." As artists they were salvaging both their identities and their society from a reduction to the commercial values that seemed to have impoverished their parents' lives. Like their parents, who maintained the outlook and economies of the marginal professions and of small business in an era of corporate bureaucracies, the children chose in art one of the least bureaucratized, least rationalized, and most individualistic of occupations.

Failure in the Fine Arts

Erving Goffman points out that even ascriptive identities are qualified by some degree of failure or ambiguity and so can be managed in a way which minimizes the repercussions of that failure.[3] Occupational identities, the result of achievement, exhibit the same characteristics of ambiguity and potential failure, and that of the artist more than most. In SoHo, where exhibition openings are highly visible, art prices are the stock of street gossip, and notices of foundation grants to artists appear in the local press, failure is all the more bitter by its ready contrast with success.

Success means two things to the young SoHo artist: critical recognition of an enduring nature and sufficient sales to allow the artist to work undisturbed by the need for a different job to maintain the middle-class standards of his family. The artist does not want his children to visit their grandparents and be taken immediately on shopping trips for "decent clothes," an occurrence which is commonly remarked upon. Success in both income and recognition, however, appears to be so rare for the young artist that failure is converted into an occupational norm, and each artist must to struggle to maintain the belief that he or she is destined to be an exception.

Working to Support an Art Career

Artists commonly believe that only 1 percent of serious aspirants will succeed. There are no reliable figures available because those who abandon their careers usually adopt another occupation and shed the "failed artist" identity. The census lists 15,374 painters and sculptors in the New York Standard Metropolitan Statistical Area (SMSA) in 1970.[4] Since the census excludes nonselling artists with independent financing and the many whose sideline jobs provide their incomes and census identities, this is a very conservative figure. It is estimated that each of the 160 galleries representing contemporary American artists in the New York market handles, on average, 18 artists at any one time.[5] There are thus 2,880 slots for galleried artists in the New York market. Since this is the central market for the country as a whole, some of these slots are filled by artists from outside the New York SMSA, and thus only about 18 percent of aspirants find places in galleries. Artists sell to friends, family, and old clients out of their studios, but it is considered impossible to make a living without representation through a dealer. The obverse, however, is not true. Dealers carry slow sellers and try out lesser knowns, with the result that only one in four galleried artists is a significant seller; 94 percent of all the artists in New York are not, then, significant sellers. Five percent of arrivals to the New York art market may succeed—a small number, but one which exceeds the pessimism of many artists.

The career choice of fine arts is difficult to defend on economic grounds. Artists typically earn low incomes and experience the stress of having to earn most of this income from either low-paying, casual work or from quasicareers which continually threaten to take over their fine art identity.[6] Artists find themselves backing into other jobs to supply necessary income and acquiring such secondary identities as art teachers, cab drivers, or script coordinators in the production of television advertisements. While these jobs pay the rent, the more substantial they become the more likely it is that they will swallow up the fine arts identity. The more menial jobs leave little time for painting. The artist resists the erosion of his identity by alternately cultivating the secondary career and then dropping it. Those who become dependent on a higher standard of living than art can provide, who see a two-day-a-week adjunct teaching schedule grow into full time, or who find they can earn $400 or more a week doing advertising layout, let their primary identity slip away.

As the artist ages, it becomes more difficult to develop a sideline career. Some artists are exceptionally fearful of contaminating their imagination and sensitivity with advertising layout work and book jacket design and so avoid developing these related skills as lucrative sidelines. The high salaries paid for some commercial art work and the ready availability of such work in New York on a freelance basis are viewed as threatening by those artists who feel their vision depends upon their sustaining some occupational marginality. These artists restrict their commitment to fine arts and discover, at the age of fifty, that in order to live they are "pushing" a taxi forty-eight hours a week and painting only on Sundays, and that they have no prospects at all.

Older painters and sculptors who endure in the face of economic discouragement have already received some form of recognition. But because recognition dispensed by the art world is often momentary, casual, and uncoordinated, it does not always bring lasting fame or market demand. But it does nourish hope. Living on unemployment compensation or part-time teaching, supplemented by support from a working spouse, the older artist persists. He works for the day when the critical success of a show five or fifteen years ago may be repeated or surpassed.

Older Artists and Career Stress

The situations of three artists in mid-to-late career who lack full success may illustrate the tenacity of the artistic identity as well as its vulnerability.

John is in his mid-thirties and has a B.F.A. and an M.F.A. from a large state university. He came to SoHo from California and paints in a loft on an anonymous commercial backstreet, ignoring the art-world social "scene." He and his wife, a public school teacher, share a spacious loft more than half of which is devoted to his work space and the storage of his finished pieces, raw canvas, and supplies. He teaches three mornings a week at one of the most serious of the city's art schools, one preferred by teachers who desire a minimum of administrative supervision and an adult relationship with their students. During the rest of the week he produces abstract oils and prints. He is a lesser-known painter affiliated with one of the top galleries, "low man on the totem pole," he says, among twenty-five artists. He is friendly with some of the gallery's better selling new realist and minimalist artists, but he is worried about his place in the art world. While he goes to the mountains on his holidays, he spends the time painting in a closed room.

John and his wife have been living on their teaching pay and on a stipend John has been receiving from his dealer. John has not had a show for three years, and it has been a year since his dealer last sent a client around to his studio. That client was a psychoanalyst who visits New York regularly in an effort to become a serious collector and to mix socially with artists. John thinks the man is bored with his work and buys art as a diversion.

Recently John has had a show scheduled. Both he and his dealer feel that he is ready, and he hopes that with a show impending, the dealer will begin to push the sale of his work. He is at a critical point in his career: if this show is not successful, his dealer will cut his losses and end their relationship. John knows that the gallery is carried by a few internationally known artists and that the system requires him to move up in prominence, or to get out. If he leaves, he will have less time for art as he searches for other income, and he will lose the opportunity to show and sell what he can complete.

He enjoys the stimulation of teaching and the chance to talk with students about issues like the relevance of art to life. He feels making art is worthwhile, particularly when compared to vocations such as that of his father, a salesman, or that of his mother, an accountant. Art, even teaching art, lifts you out of the ordinary day-to-day routine, he explains. But his discussion of the pleasures of working with students suggests an anticipatory resignation to a teaching career.

As happens with many artists who have had only moderate success, John is now at a crossroads. He cannot continue as a full-time painter if he loses his gallery stipend, which provides half his income. Whether he sells or not depends upon the subjective and unpredictable decisions of art buyers. In teaching, on the other hand, he can find the immediate satisfaction of an appreciative student audience and earn a steady and reliable income, but he will have lost the status and potential of an affiliation with a prestigious gallery where he could hope to go to the top.

Jane paints in a large loft studio in a SoHo artists' cooperative building. She bought the studio with her savings and with help from friends, and she has divided it in half, renting space to another artist to help defray her expenses. Jane has an impressive résumé. Several of her large abstracts are in the collections of prominent buyers such as the Rockefeller brothers. Her work hangs on the walls of Chase Manhattan Bank's headquarters and at the Whitney Museum of American Art. An important art magazine featured her work, paintings subtly textured with stone-color shadings, four years ago. She keeps the article on a shelf next to her kitchen table.

Notwithstanding her past critical success, Jane has never made much money from her art; last year she made "less than a thousand dollars." She subsidizes her annual show at an elite cooperative gallery where sales do not often meet the expenses of the printed brochures. She has to address and mail the brochures herself, but she feels that the cooperative gallery has advantages. "There is no dealer pressure, no one saying, 'This sells, that doesn't; I can use more of these.'" Her income now is from unemployment compensation derived from a clerical job she once held.

Her work is on a large scale, and the walls and floor of her loft are lined with finished and unfinished pieces. There is no room for anyone else to work in the space, nor would she want to have the distraction of other people about. Her one complaint with SoHo is that there is not sufficient anonymity. "I have to say hello to twenty people in the morning when I go for cigarettes." She does not want to meet an audience until she is ready.

Jane fled a Nebraska town of 600 people with "wheat fields that came up to the door." "My father was a mortician, and I used to help him make up the corpses," she said. She studied art in college, moved to New York, and worked as an actor and model. She had rented several other lofts for painting before coming to SoHo. Her social identity is urban, and she could not go back to small-town life. Although she is in her forties, her solid accomplishments still lack the configuration of real career momentum. But the recognition that she has received makes her feel that she can still "make it." She is not ready to quit.

Jane's situation is typical of many artists who discover that they may be in the denouement of a career that has peaked without their having realized it. The hope which drives them struggles against the gravity of age and discouragement. The artist in mid-career must continue to generate excitement among critics and on the market if interest in his or her work is not to go flat. Though such artists commonly complain that dealers curb the artistic freedom of the artist by asking them to repeat marketable work, it is never their own dealers whom they accuse of this pressure. They know that other market arrangements are an inadequate substitute for the dealer, being unlikely to generate the momentum which a career requires in order to "take off."

It is not merely the hope of success and a passion for the artistic experience that lock the older artist into a declining career. The pattern of an established life-style, the mature sense of identity, and the difficulties of starting over also inhibit the marginally successful artist from beginning a new career.

Carlo is a painter-sculptor in his late fifties. In his youth, he was the top student of an eminent Argentine artist and has received important commissions for murals, mosaics, and sculpture in South America. He came to New York City fifteen years ago seeking a wider market and a less parochial recognition. But he found that his organic, humanistic pieces, which incorporate folklore and biblical imagery, did not find a ready market in the technological and secular culture of the New York art world. He has not sold well here and is presently without an American dealer.

For a time Carlo was given a stipend and rent subsidy by one of New York's most active patrons, an industrialist with an interest in the arts and in artists. But when Carlo's promise of an American career began to fade, the patron suggested that he develop his work in other aesthetic directions. That suggestion ended the relationship in an atmosphere of offended pride and charges of ungratefulness.

Carlo shows and sells through outlets in several South American cities and at international exhibits, but this brings him only a few thousand dollars annually during most years. To meet his expenses, he has to make store display cases and to take on students. If living costs continue to rise and he does not experience a break in his career, he will have to move out of SoHo, perhaps out of New York, to cheaper work space. He has thought of returning to Argentina, where he recently had a show. His sales at the show were few, and he was paid in Argentina's inflated currency, but his return home was an event noted in the daily press there. He could live more cheaply in Argentina and expect some government aid, but he fears the government and disapproves of its repressive treatment of dissidents. Soon, however, he will have to make a decision, and he is an artist, not a politician. In the meantime, he hopes the American market will change in his favor. Despite his age he rejects any suggestion that retirement is a legitimate choice for an artist. He spends his days in his studio and his evenings with old buyers who have become friends, with other South American artists with whom he exchanges help and sympathy, and with his wife whose understanding supports him. "Of course artists do not retire," he says flatly. Nor do they easily abandon art.

These three cases do not, of course, exhaust the possibilities of career dilemmas faced by serious artists whose talents provoke more critical recognition than market support. In an effort to hang onto their beleaguered occupational identity, less successful artists are tempted to transform it into a master identity affecting all their social roles. The nonartist roles are thus inhibited from functioning as points of independent leverage from which the artistic commitment could be criticized and perhaps dislodged.

Artist as Master Identity

Artists who sell little and must therefore subsidize their true vocation with other work usually continue to interpret their occupational choice as a response to a calling. Maintaining the conviction that one is "an artist" as a matter of personal identity is necessary to sustain the producer of art through the prolonged incubation of his career and the erratic nature of the market.[7] In contrast to other occupations, that of the artist does not follow a daily routine interwoven with work routines of others. It lacks explicit directives and rules and regular pay. The role of the fine artist, as opposed to the teaching artist or the commercial artist, lacks institutional underpinning. The struggling artist's personal resolve gains support only from a small informal network of fellow artists, from a friendly collector, perhaps from former teachers or students, and usually from a sympathetic and employed spouse. The production of art is a solitary and self-directed activity, which is why dealers search for artists with personalities strong enough to continue with their work while enduring the neglect of the critics and of the market; talent alone is insufficient for the artistic career.

While successful artists are more secular in their outlook, the yet to be successful tend to mythologize the occupation which gives them an identity but not a living. In order to nourish a commitment to art while working at something else, the artist sees his occupational identity as a mode of consciousness, a way of being in the world, not simply as a type of work. As a cab driver or newspaper illustrator, he can remain a fine artist by saving his pay to buy the time to paint. The elusive recognition of the art world becomes less important than personal commitment in defining one's status as an artist. As one artist whose work in photography began after she arrived in SoHo as the wife of a painter explained,

> It was a deliberate decision to call myself an artist. It meant a commitment to me. It means to me anyone who has this commitment—to any occupation. It means being into how a thing is done, enjoying it, self-discovery. The more official definitions of "artist" were motivated by the big egos here [in SoHo]. But some who do art are not artists. They're not really involved in it. It means a degree of exploration, of progress. You don't need to meet with any great critical acceptance.

But if some artists use a standard of personal growth to sustain them while they wait for critical recognition, others use the artistic identity to explain and cope with personal difficulties. "It is the artistic life itself that is conducive to emotional instability," maintained one conceptual

artist. "Right now, I am in the process of going crazy. It's because you
have to be open and exposed a whole lot as an artist. I have two kids
from my first marriage, and now my second marriage is falling apart. As
an artist I've made strong emotional demands upon my wife." The very
sensitivity which he sees as essential to him as an artist is blamed as the
source of his trouble. From this point of view, the existence of emotional
pain and the collapse of human relationships can be turned into a
certification of artistic identity. This artist, like many with steady and
demanding financial responsibilities eating into their commitment to art,
copes with the pressures by defining them as part of the condition of
being an artist. Since he feels that his whole existence is as an artist, he
cannot live with any other occupation. And so he cannot solve his problems. "When my kids ask me if it is worth it, I tell them I'm compelled to
do art."

The least productive assertion of the artistic identity is the claim to be
exempt from other responsibilities. Where a dealer might help to dry out
an alcoholic artist who is selling, and members of a SoHo artist cooperative have "carried" an unhelpful but artistically prestigious fellow
member, the artist who is a failure has a narrower base of support,
usually consisting of an employed spouse or lover. These, however,
eventually tire of supporting the role of artist in a roommate when it
means fulfilling all other roles necessary to the relationship themselves.

One artist responded to a career slump and a state of depression by
staying in bed all day for months at a time, reading science fiction. At
night he drank. He refused to perform any household drudgery on the
grounds that, after all, he was an artist. His wife eventually left him, and
without her support he gave up his fine-art identity. She reported that
after a few years he had become highly successful in an advertising firm.
The dramatization of the "ignored artist" role requires, paradoxically,
that one not be truly ignored. Once deprived of any audience, individuals usually soon give it up.

Marginality, Alienation, and Exile

The artistic identity elicits opposition from American society. As one
SoHo painter and full-time college art teacher put it,

> The decision to become an artist in the United States, not in
> Europe, is seen as useless, effeminate. Male art majors get a lot of
> flack from their parents, I've noticed as an art teacher. Most art
> majors drop out of art. . . . It is hard to be monetarily unsuccessful in
> this society. And also, art is a lonely occupation. The rewards are
> often in the work itself, and the products may never be seen except
> by other artists. It is the last psychological and intellectual frontier.

Such an artist can turn the indifference of the world into a prophetic affirmation of self. He is tempted to see himself as one striving to hold open a door through which a glimpse of a different reality is possible, and who finds nobody looking. It is the routinized nature of society that the artist blames. "Reality sets in; people don't care about innovation. They don't know how to read a painting. When they ask me, 'What does it mean?' they want dramatic not plastic content. . . . You don't have to suffer to make art, but you do have to be on the outside to look in."

The artistic consciousness is perceived as a condition of being out of phase with the world, and some less than successful artists cling to this condition as an assurance of their artistic authenticity. Erik, an abstract expressionist painter in his forties, illustrates this characteristic. He has been a serious student of painting since his childhood, first exhibiting and selling at age sixteen. But his style is not in vogue now as a developing tradition, and solid recognition has eluded him. He, in turn, feels the SoHo market is over promoted and faddish, too full of painters afraid to take the risks of real innovation. Styles like the popular new realism, he feels, collapse culture into the depthless present of an amateur snapshot.

Erik works as a carpenter building advertising sets and doing loft renovation for, among other clients, successful SoHo artists. He stops work one month out of three to paint on his accumulated savings. A former loft dweller, he sees SoHo as having become compromised by bourgeois culture, and he now prefers three tenement rooms in a burned-out section of the lower east side of Manhattan, a short walk from SoHo. In economic, cultural, and geographic terms, he and others like him are captured satellites of SoHo, in stabilized antagonism and attraction. The rent Erik pays is one third of that common in SoHo, but with ten robberies in the last six years, his housing is not really inexpensive. He says he stays where he is for the view. A look out the windows reveals tots climbing in and out of the cellars of demolished tenements and unboarded derelict buildings. The sun glints off broken glass and auto chrome strewn around the empty lots. The shops, all Spanish, ungate and open for only a few hours during daylight. "This is not America. It is the edge of the world. That's why I like it down here," he says.

He came to New York City and the area near SoHo because it is the center of the art world, the best location in which to study and find a market. He lives where he does because it seems not to be claimed by any world at all. SoHo proper preserved the symbolic marginality of artists and poets in the 1950s and 1960s, before legalization of the artists' residency escalated real-estate values and brought both the art market and such amenities as take-out French paté into the neighborhood. For many artists living away from the strip of art galleries along West Broadway, SoHo continues to provide a needed peripheral milieu.

Artists strive to protect their creativity from the formula traps that accumulate in their medium and from the regulations which pervade society in general. And because their artist identity is basic to their sense of self and is not limited to their occupational behavior, they may also exaggerate their conflicts of interest with institutional society.[8] In the years after SoHo was rezoned to permit artist residency, many artists remained philosophically opposed to, and in practice unwilling to cooperate with, political canvassers, the artist certification committee which was set up as residential gatekeeper, and with the organizational requirements of community action. They felt nostalgia for the days when the bureaucracies were kept away from the creative process and artists lived illegally with commercial leases, with beds and stoves hidden in the work debris around their lofts. Some continue to leave their doorbells in disrepair as they did in the days when they routinely ignored all daytime knocks to avoid city inspectors and meter readers. Sensing that lawyers and ''burghers'' playing real-estate games may be the ultimate beneficiaries of SoHo's residential regulations, some artists feel cynically justified in fabricating painting credentials for their nonartist friends and for buyers of their co-op loft spaces. They cannot believe that government regulation can serve the creative process.

Artists without obvious success feel that their creativity requires them to maintain at least a symbolic marginality, if not precariousness, in their lives. The easy references some of these artists make to suicide plans, to doubts of their own sanity, to the manic-depressive emotional cycle to which they say their creativity is tied, and the acute adolescent self-consciousness to which they refer appear in everyday conversation as incantations of marginality. Such self-description seems to enhance the existential vertigo which they feel is necessary to hold their creative edge. The family and personal lives of the successful artists, by contrast, are stable retreats from the public world that verifies their identities as artists. Successful artists may acknowledge the tensions and strains of their occupation, but they do not parade an existential precariousness or instability as evidence of their creativity.

In their flights to avoid social integration as nonartists, the least successful artists see themselves as pilgrims, traveling light. They attach themselves to a theme of exile that was popular with an earlier generation of American artists.[9] One such painter said,

> I went to Greece essentially for a supportive audience. Not an audience supportive of my particular paintings, but supportive of the quest of the painter. Those people were responsive to the adventure of trying to become an artist—or a monk or a fanatic, for that matter. And they would be the material, in a way, not really the audience. They were open to the heroic adventure of becoming an artist, the ethical decision that a sage, a fanatic, an artist must make.

This decision entails independence from the standards of society and thus secures an escape from the taken-for-granted nature of conventional perception. It is not especially fashionable in the art world to carry this decision to bohemian extremes, however, since such extremes in dress, sexual practice, and use of intoxicants no longer distinguishes the artist from the excesses of much of bourgeois society. This has been true in New York since the 1930s, when the urban middle class began to assimilate the outward signs of unconventionality that had previously had a protest value.[10]

Successful SoHo artists tend to view flagrant bohemianism as evidence of a superficial artistic talent and commitment. But even for those who enjoy the rewards of recognition, the sense of social marginality persists and calls for some form of expression. Many successful artists, sure of their place in the art world, have moved out of SoHo to nonurban surroundings. The pastoral fringes of New England are popular, as were the Connecticut farms for Malcolm Cowley's artists during the thirties. Parts of Vermont remain socially closer to SoHo than does Brooklyn. The successful artist can live among horse- and crop-talking farmers and still be within a day's drive of his SoHo dealer, the art market gossip, and his artist friends. Moderately successful artists remain tied to the city by their own and their spouse's jobs and cannot so easily make a symbolic departure from bourgeois society. The least successful artists are the most emancipated and the most in need of symbolic reinforcement of their artist identities.

Myth and Reconciliation with Society

The artists who find access to the market difficult tend to mythologize their alienation more than do successful artists. They see the artist as one who stimulates the cultural bloodstream of society, preventing its descent into triviality, decay, and death. "Self-expression is not art," explained one painter. "Art has to hit a truth discernable to some part of humanity. Perhaps only to yourself as a part of humanity, at first. The vanguard hits home to a few, but this reverberates throughout all society eventually. Without art, things would not change. It is messianic. . . . My purpose here is to enlarge meaning."

The myth of the messianic artist has a powerful hold on the artist whose work fails the commercial test. It provides a nonrevolutionary, indeed a nonpolitical, way toward eventual reconciliation between the creative self and institutional society. It defuses some of the tension between the dominant commercial and functionalist culture and the subculture of artistic response. In the myth, the bourgeoisie is pictured as preoccupied with preserving itself within the exiting social structure, which becomes its tomb. The artist, with the covert sympathy of this same bourgeoisie, alters and renews routinized social visions. In this way, the world is saved by its own artistic outcasts. "As an artist, you have a special relation to the objects you make; they subvert the world," said a collagist whose work has yet to find a market. "Art should be dangerous. But at some level our society is willing to be subverted by the artist, who changes what is, creating new forms." The notion of the artist as the savior of existing society by his power to transform it provides the possibility of a reconciliation between the artist and society and between the artist and the parents from whom he had to break away to realize his calling.

The Protest of Secular Artists

According to the messianic view of the relationship between art and society, the fine arts serve a purpose superior to that of the decorative arts or the functional crafts.

Craftspeople in SoHo feel that their social role and their products are disparaged by the artist-savior myth propagated by unsuccessful artists. It denies them the higher prestige which rewards the producer of nonutilitarian works. Many craftspeople attack the mystique of the fine artist by saying that it disguises and promotes a parasitical relationship of artists to society and to conventionally productive people. "They think that if you're born with one talent," said a weaver, "you can't have another, such as economic ability. It just helps them feel superior to the person they end up leaning on. It's a total myth to think that to produce crap which happens to sell limits your creative spark. It's a cop-out and an excuse."

Craftspeople are unwilling to concede that the magic of artistic "creativity" is a monopoly of the fine artist. They struggle against their own functionalist tradition in order to raise the definition of their work to the status of being "museum worthy" and collectible as art. Their furniture and textiles are losing their identity as useful objects and are becoming wood and fabric sculpture, some even flaunting a decadent dysfunctionality. SoHo craftspeople, intent on bridging the gap between craft and fine art, are making craft-like objects with art materials and art objects with craft materials. Either way, they reject the prosaic definition of craft as the creation of objects by hand which, while beautiful, are somehow in their essence serviceable. Status-enhancing craft journals support this trend toward making the products of woodworking, pottery, weaving, and smithing into collectible art.[11] Several SoHo galleries feature such work, and dealers report that buyers are often more comfortable evaluating evident craftsmanship than obscure conceptual statements motivating some of the avant-garde fine art. The craft strategy in SoHo is to free such craftsmanship from the assumption of utility, letting the craft object float more freely in the market.

The Religion of Art

The occupational commitment which supplies the master identity of aspiring fine artists functions also as a substitute religious conviction. It seeks to resolve questions of ultimate meaning with a doctrine of individual creativity. According to this conviction, after a period of self-discipline and practice, the creative experience occurs as a moment of harmony between the individual and a deeper reality.

According to some artists, making art resolves conflicts between the cognitive and the emotional sides of the personality, allaying their fears of personal disintegration. One described this function as a ritualized part of his painting technique.

> You have to struggle against fixations [upon abstract ideas] to get back to sensuous impulses. So I like to use brushes rather than rollers or spray. They are slower and give me more control. I buy the pigments and mix them with the vehicles, though all the colors I use are available premixed. The labor process helps me to think through the use of the color. Do I want to use it or not? I deliberate sensuously. I can't go any faster than the hand can illustrate the sensuous idea.[12]

The manual aspect of the arts and the possibility of a dialogue between painter and canvas appear to artists as a creative advantage when compared with the blank page faced by the writer. The unblocked creative process signifies the moment of cohesion when the artist feels most completely an integrated self. Libidinal pressures seem under control, made into usable material rather than suffered as compulsions. Social pressures are surmounted. Intellectual bewilderment seems resolved. In the studio it is possible for the artist to realize moments of liberation, a diffused eroticism, and a potency which is absent from his other relationships with the world. These moments of creative control constitute an ecstatic experience which can sustain the artist who is without market success.

The power of the creative experience was described by one painter as follows:

> There is a part of the self I abandon myself to, the gutsy, sensual part. But on the other side is the intellectual, the critical. All painters must switch back and forth between the two. . . . I think all kids have this animalistic inside, this subconscious. They have good color and

plastic sense. When they have to face life, the feeling for the plastic disappears. Artists have to struggle with this, to nurture the beast within themselves while they refine their intellect. Ryder is an example—he couldn't verbalize very well, but he was powerfully expressionistic. Some artists go insane quickly from this strain. They go too far in one direction.

The creative moment is one of mastery over both oneself and the world. It can hold at bay the perceptions which haunt existence in a secular civilization, perceptions that life has no higher purpose, that existence is absurd and arbitrary. When the structure of mundane routine cracks during sleepless nights, the artist can cling to the rock of his commitment to art. As one painter put it,

> Art changes reality for everybody else, and so it is a way of dealing with the awe and terror I feel about creation. That anything exists at all fills me with awe.... As an artist I can order the world in a way that in a family or on the job, I can't. It doesn't do the same thing for me. My art allows me to explain creation in a way that takes anxiety away from being alive. Why am I here at all?

The artist is a remaker of the world. The SoHo community presumes that an artist's desire to mold public reality has prima facie legitimacy, although in specific cases the community has had a difficult time trying to distinguish the aesthetic value of an outdoor mural or street performance from self-advertising. Changing the public's perception of space, form, and color, the artist feels like a cocreator of reality. This is one reason artists have the self-confidence to place their statues in apartment malls and public parks, even when their works provoke public opposition.

SoHo artists do not describe themselves as members of religious organizations. While over a dozen cooperative experiments in early childhood education have been set up by SoHo parents to meet the needs of their children, no religious services have been organized. When residents venture into adjacent Catholic parochial schools and community centers, it is usually to wait uncomfortably in line to vote on election days or to transform convenient but underutilized church spaces into daycare centers. Yet even while rejecting conventional religious answers, SoHo artists remain aware of the religious questions. Though they may think of these questions of ultimate meaning in psychiatric or philosophical terms, their artistic commitment is one of their ways of answering them.

Conclusion

All stages of the fine art career are profoundly affected by the conditions of the American market, which determine that most artists must survive for long periods on anticipation while subsidizing their art with other jobs. Even after suffering through a long "apprenticeship," they may never realize financial or critical success as artists.

When beginning his career, the aspiring artist is nourished by a home and community which orient their children to an awareness of the humanistic tradition; personal autonomy is valued, education in personal awareness and expressive skills is expected, and occupation itself is seen to some extent as a personal voyage of service to others and discovery of self. The humanistic tradition drawn on by the parents of SoHo artists portrays the choice of career as a response to a "calling" from the collective nature of reality, an appeal that is echoed in the inner self. However secularized this conversation with that reality has become in the modern world, it is a dialogue which supports the individual in contradicting mundane convention in the interest of conformity to a more elevated reality.

The humanistic perspective on career is strongest in those families where the parents' occupations give them some justification to claim autonomy, service, and identification of self with occupation. At the same time, however, this perspective is distinctly subordinate, even within the professional level of the middle class. The dominant outlook is materialistic, pragmatic, and mundane. Consequently, the aspiring artist articulates his or her ambitions in the middle-class milieu without being able to make them a rationally defensible choice.

The choice of an art career in this culturally complex context becomes interpreted as a necessary development of the self for which early artistic precociousness is taken as evidence. Lack of affiliation with youthful peer groups, adolescent self-consciousness, and feelings of being socially displaced find a resolution in the commitment to art.

The second stage in the artistic career, following motivation, involves an outward identification of the self with art, a declaration to the family and society that art has become the essential identity and the only means of achieving full personal realization. This declaration, usually made as a decision to study art at the expense of more practical courses of education, is escalated into a rebellion by parents who withdraw their psychological and material support. This rebellion is not forthright because it is not a clean rejection of middle-class traditions or a complete reversal of the priorities accepted by the middle class itself. The rebellion involves an educational commitment to art without a rejection of economic achievement, and includes the assumption of the self-image of artist as a "master identity." As a quasi-sacred identity, the self-image of artist is not usually paraded in public but awaits the external recognition which will allow the aspirant to say, "Yes, I am an artist."

The third career stage lasts from the end of formal education until recognition has been achieved, the career has been abandoned, or the artist dies. In this stage, the successful artist separates himself from the unsuccessful. The problem of this period is maintaining a career in the face of neglect by society. Those who persist through a protracted "incubation period" do so on a staple of hope mixed with moments of minor and uncoordinated recognition—a grant, a sale, a show. The successful artist is the one who is able eventually to consolidate these moments of random recognition into career momentum.

Artists in this middle period must avoid a careerist involvement in a competing nonart occupation if they are to persist. They must act as their own patrons, and having to justify this, they maintain a commitment to the ideological uniqueness of art in relation to all other occupations. The successful artist is released from this necessity; the art world confirms his identity and its market calls forth a practical and realistic series of responses to career questions, not ideological fireworks. The enduring but unsuccessful artist, avoiding a realistic confrontation with the dilemma of art versus economic success, is the main proponent of the artistic mystique. He may even come to see art and the artist in near-religious terms; the artist becomes an outcast and marginal figure who will eventually return to redeem the mundane world from its own decline into routine and from its lack of perceptiveness. The creative endeavor becomes, then, crucial to social invigoration and to the survival of mankind in truly human terms.

The perception of the artist as set apart in a cultural, rather than simply in an economic, sense is used to excuse, even ennoble, the unsuccessful artist's departure from middle-class occupational expectations. For him, social and particularly market marginality can become a confirmation of occupational purity. When success does not confirm the artistic identity, failure may be drafted to the same service.

5 The Successful Artist in the SoHo Market

The Artist-Dealer Relationship: The Path to Success

From among the hundreds of fine-arts graduates and self-trained artists who pour into SoHo each summer—most of whom leave during the
succeeding winters—only a few are able to catch hold of the market. They
comprise an elite among the three to four thousand artists working in the
community and have achieved recognition and economic success
through their affiliation with a prestigious dealer in whose gallery they
periodically show and in whose judgment his customers have confidence.

The dealer is expected to be an aesthetic counselor, a trustworthy
business manager, and an emotional shock absorber. It is the rare individual who can play all these roles for the artist. At the minimum,
however, the successful artist demands a tough sales representative, and
it is only since the 1960s that artists have been in any position to make
such a demand. Up to that time, the sales potential of living artists was
considerably less than it has since become, and artists had no choice but
to tolerate a sometimes despotic dealer paternalism. Even today, some
long-established dealers affect an aristocratic disdain for commercial
details when it comes to getting out a statement or a check promptly
after the sale of an artist's work. Other dealers lack the capital to advance payments to the artist until the client pays the bill. Since some of
the biggest clients also have a cavalier attitude toward the art transaction
and may delay payment for six months or a year, the artist may find

himself waiting for his money from a dealer who is reluctant to press the buyer. Such artists feel that they are having their noses rubbed in the market, and by switching galleries when they are displeased with a dealer's performance, the more successful among them are able to do something about it.

Successful artists seek a gallery that will advertise their work aggressively and lend it as much prestige as possible. They may find, however, that they sell better in a moderately well-known gallery than in one that is already topheavy with the biggest names. One SoHo artist, despite the critical success he had gained with his Fifty-seventh Street dealer, found that through gallery advances over the years he had accumulated a $13,000 debt which he was unable to pay because the sales of his work were insufficient. His dealer ran one of the most highly respected galleries in the art world but remained emotionally committed to the artists who had been with him the longest and through whom his gallery had achieved its fame. Consequently, he neglected his newer artists. The painter switched to a young SoHo dealer who applied to the marketing of art the salesmanship he had perfected in the printing business. "My debt is now down to two or three thousand, after a year and a half," said the artist. "This guy may be considered crude and a pusher, but he does sell your paintings."

Each artist wants the dealer's customers steered to his own work. The success of one artist may be interpreted by the other artists in the same gallery as neglect of their own talents. Switching galleries often alleviates jealousy among artists and, if handled correctly, can speed up the process of recognition. It gives an artist a measure of control in the art market and allows him to exploit opportunities to develop his career.

The successful artist relies upon a relationship of confidence with a competent dealer in order to exploit his opportunities for career development. David, an artist in his mid-thirties, is a good example of how such artists operate.

David was born and grew up in a middle class section of Brooklyn. He traveled the same social distance, from a family-based neighborhood to cosmopolitan Manhattan, as do most artists who arrive in SoHo from the West, Midwest, or abroad. After high school, he entered a well-regarded college of art and engineering as a student of architecture. When the art and architecture curricula divided after the freshman year, he said, "I discovered the only thing I was interested in designing was my own studio." David switched to fine arts. He hoped to further his childhood interest in painting and still be able to satisfy his parents' desire to see their son in a profession. Always an "A" student, he graduated at the top of his class. He commuted throughout his college years, living at home and avoiding the bohemian life. He pursued his career with the same deliberate concentration that his childhood friends employed in going on to study medicine or law.

At the time of his graduation, David suddenly realized that while he was a success as an art student, he had no immediate way to make a living. He therefore took an intensive summer course in art education and became license to teach art in the city school system. He taught for four years and designed book jackets until gradually his fine-arts career began to support him. While his incubation as an unknown artist was uncharacteristically short, he remains an economic realist.

> The reality of being an artist is, for most, pretty grim. First you think, "Once I have my first successful show, I'll have it made," That's not so. I had a very successful show, sold fairly well, and got placed in a few museums and collections. But still I seemed to stagnate. One good show doesn't mean at all that everything else you do will sell. I presume that had I gone to graduate school I would have known more about the art market. Art students can know who you are, but still, nothing really happens to you.

David was being handled by his first dealer at this point, a man he characterized as "drunk, lecherous, and obnoxious." When the opportunity arose, he switched to a more conscientious dealer who was also more ideologically sensitive to clients. This dealer was a former staff worker in an uptown gallery who had established her own growing business in SoHo. He selected her on the basis of his own impressions and the advice of a top SoHo dealer who, while helpful to young artists like David, was not yet willing to commit himself to them. David has worked out a flexible arrangement with his new dealer. Little is stipulated in writing. She handles his market affairs, including his shows in Europe and in other American cities. She collects a 40 percent commission on sales of his work from her SoHo gallery and 10 percent on sales through her network of connections to other galleries. David shows only when he is ready and takes no stipends to even out the good seasons and the bad. He regularizes his income with the help of his wife, a free-lance journalist, who does much of her work at home and is in charge of the family finances.

David has had a dozen shows in major European and American cities, all arranged by his SoHo dealer. His only complaint is that his best shows have occurred out of town. Given the focus of publicity on New York in the art world, this is a handicap. "If it doesn't happen in New York, it doesn't happen," he laments. Shows that are not widely reviewed and paintings that disappear into the hands of obscure buyers add little, he feels, to the momentum of an art career. As he becomes better known, however, more of his exhibitions are being mounted in New York.

The realism with which he approaches the market and the emotion which leads him to paint are not always easily reconciled. He feels that if he were to pay more systematic attention to his career, he might paint less. An output of fewer but better paintings would benefit both his income and his reputation. The fact that he likes to paint causes him to produce too many pictures. He's done well over 150 major paintings since college—eggs, fruit, flowers, landscapes, figures. All are large and intricately executed in a realistic mode. His versatility worries him as much as his prolificacy. It obscures the recognizability of his work. "If you see a piece in a show and can't recognize it, that's me," he laughs. However, he acknowledges that he has benefited from painting in the marketable style of sharp-focus or photo realism. Private buyers and museum curators who are seriously interested in representing this style are obliged to include David's work in their collections.

David discusses the upward movement of the prices of his work, the vital signs of his professional health, with the objectivity of a surgeon reading an electrocardiograph. Through his most recent sales in Europe he established a price range of $8,000 to $10,000, 20 percent more than his previous prices. He anticipates that, as the dollar value of his work increases, his dealer will agree to lower her commission rate to one-third.

Very good years for the sale of his work have been followed by years when nothing seemed to sell. He blames the periodic slumps in the economy and their effect on the art market. "No one sold anything in 1975." In slow periods, however, the art market reinforces the careers of artists who have already proved successful. David's dealer's contacts helped him. He coped with the decline in the market for major paintings by turning to work that could be sold as prints and by obtaining Bicentennial commissions from the Department of the Interior and from major oil corporations. "When people know you, you just get these jobs," he explained.

Creativity and Commerce

The guiding aesthetic concern among successful painters, whether minimalists, conceptualists, or realists, and indeed the central value for the entire modernist period of art, is the demand for originality. According to Poggioli: "Classical art, through the method of imitation and the practice of repetition, tends toward the ideal of renewing, in the sense of integration and perfection. But for modern art in general, and for avant-garde in particular, the only irremediable and absolute aesthetic error is a traditional artistic creation, an art that imitates and repeats itself."[1] Originality, more than a singular mastery of craftsmanship, keeps the successful artist ahead of the field of imitators. Indeed, conceptualization can be a sufficient aesthetic justification, as when a SoHo sculptor creates blueprints for work later executed by metal workers and carpenters. Technological innovations have so facilitated copying that the ability to accurately reproduce an image from the world or from a conception no longer serves to distinguish one student from another. Significant art begins with a new perspective that permits the reappropriation of exhausted and banal subjects. For example, the construction of paintings employing the point of view of the camera lens—the photo-realist technique popular in SoHo—reclaims familiar imagery through a shift to the camera's perspective and selectivity. The artist, Poggioli argues, must continually seek new ways to "deform" the existing imagery.

> The deformation is determined by a stylistic drive, which inaugurates a new order as it denies the ancient order. The motivation for this denial is very simple: modern civilization has achieved a representational technique so perfect that the artist can easily become a pedagogical monstrosity, that is to say, a disciple more virtuoso than his own teachers. The extensiveness of the artist's information and the efficacy of devices could easily put the modern artist in a position to acquire, if he wants it, a mimetic handiness that artists in other times have attained only thanks to long apprenticeship, by means of hard, day-in-day-out exertion.[2]

The modernist mandate to surpass mere technical virtuosity becomes the burden of having to sustain an independent vision. Perhaps this is an impossible burden. In any case, it has brought some SoHo painters, even some of the most successful, to the point of creative exhaustion. Unable to constantly come up with fresh ideas, such painters believe they develop creative blocks, which they may treat by therapeutically repainting old themes. Such work can prove financially rewarding for the artist who caters to an unsophisticated audience. New buyers of art, especially those who seek to enhance their status through art may be unable to detect stereotypical imagery, uninspired craftsmanship, or trivial innovation. Among artists themselves, however, the producers of such art are shrugged off as unworthy of serious attention, and painters who confuse repetition and voluminous output with genuine career progress pay in prestige.

Artists are concerned to distinguish between creativity and copying and to discredit those who meet the demand for innovation by plagiarizing the work of others. When, for example, a California artist who had been painting in the photo-realist style began to acquire a significant reputation by imitating the innovations of more successful SoHo painters, he was vilified in SoHo artist circles with the name "Double Cross" and denounced in letters to art journals. Artists are keenly interested in setting the record straight as to which artist originated which idea. Successful artists feel they must guard against lesser artists stealing their ideas because critics, left to themselves, cannot be relied upon to distinguish original work from warmed over, eclectic copies. The nonspecific influence of one artist upon another, an inevitable occurrence, is permissible when it is deferentially acknowledged. But artists, concerned as they are with the trademarks of personal styles, prefer to link themselves openly only with the deceased. In so doing, they are able to place themselves in the forward motion of art history, while avoiding living competition.

The successful artist does not confuse sales and income with genuine reputation, nor would other artists let him. Stories of mediocre artists who have become commercial successes are a staple in the SoHo art community and circulate as cautionary tales. Gossip both activates the artist community and acts as a social control. In the retelling, the vulgar success is ridiculed and stripped of any artistic pretentions. One artist, describing another, said,

> [He] has what we call a painting factory. He has a Chinese houseboy and he paints in a Dior jumpsuit. He has assistants to size—really, to *paint* the canvases, to tell the truth. He is going great guns. At a recent show in Washington, he had something like 600 tulips, 500 anemonies, 700 of something else. This is terrible. . . . He's very topical, too. At the space shot period he came out with his moons and things within a few days. I call it the "New York School of Wallpaper Painting."

According to this artist, many of the new realists have wandered over the frontier and out of creative territory. "The new realists are 'The New York School of Billboard Painting.' I sound jealous, but really, my own career is doing very well." Painters watch each other with whistles in their mouths, ready to blow "foul" when an "uncreative" painter gains a market advantage.

Investor influence on the higher levels of the market may tempt the successful artist into a casual attitude toward creativity. A collector, taken with the treatment of a particular subject, may ask the artist for another painting along the same, proven lines. The artist may comply, maintaining that he has cast the used theme in a fresh perspective. But other artists will insist that they see little that is new in the piece. A dealer often finds that his artists are linked in the minds of collectors with particular subjects, and when these sell well, the dealers try to persuade the artist to continue executing the familiar theme. This is the dealer pressure that artists in cooperative galleries congratulate themselves on having avoided. Some artists compromise with this pressure by doing a series of pictures on one subject, developing it completely, and then abandoning it. The relationship between artist and dealer reaches its most subtle plane as the dealer tries to draw out more works on a popular theme without openly contradicting the artist's ideological commitment to originality.

Role Exaggeration and Situational Trust

An allocation of roles may take place between the successful artist and his dealer in a way that allows each to exaggerate the importance of his own function. The successful artist becomes exclusively an artist, disdainful of all commercial considerations, while the dealer claims a scientific knowledge of the market that he does not have. The empathy required in the relationship between dealer and artist can erode as their roles become more mutually exclusive. The artist especially may become increasingly unwilling to share the credit for his success with the dealer.

Dealers sometimes spectacularly fail to live up to their claims of professionalism and cannot deliver the market they promise to their most successful artists. For example, in 1976 a showing of the works of a New York painter, widely known for his recycling of the imagery of mass culture as fine art, was arranged in Tehran. The Persian audience was not only oil-rich but was known to have identified in the past with avant-garde American artistic and cultural commodities. When the show opened it shocked the Tehran art world; it was composed of paintings of cats and dogs. Nothing was sold. The artist's agent had not scouted the market sufficiently and did not realize that dogs and cats are considered to be ritually unclean in Iran; neither they nor their likenesses are tolerated in the proper Persian household. Artists entertain themselves with stories of such dealer blunders in order to minimize the dealer's role and humble his posture.

Beyond having to answer for his own mistakes, the dealer often has to absorb or deflect the resentment which the successful artist feels entitled to express toward the art market and its infringement upon aesthetic freedom. The art world as a subculture gives the highest prestige to originality, which it understands to be the product of creative autonomy. Artists themselves protect this perspective by cultivating a suspicion of commercial success. Artists of all degrees of economic success share this suspicion as a basis for occupation-wide fraternalism. Although, like the belief in the sourness of grapes out of reach, hostility to the market is more noticeably the rightful consolation of the unsuccessful artist, anticommercial grousing serves the purposes of the successful artist as well. Hostility toward the market and the dealer reassures the successful artist that he has not compromised his aesthetic standards or "sold out" to get where he is. As one successful SoHo artist said, "I don't want to owe anyone. I won't take advances or stipends [from my dealer]. Dealers give you nothing for nothing. And if I fail, I have the consolation which only artists have of becoming really important after I'm dead."

The ideological conviction that the autonomous individual is the creative force in society entitles the successful artist to claim protection against that society, especially its political and commercial concerns, on higher moral grounds. "Political purposes mean the death of art," a successful photo-realist painter said. "A few could do it, like in *Guernica,* but most can't. I am into beauty. I feel I'm making a statement about landscape details that are ignored by necessity in everyday viewing. I don't feel that I'm celebrating commodity culture, though I know that some people say so. I don't consciously search out objects for their machine-cult value, even if I do end up painting planes, motorcycles, and car engines." "As a professional artist, I paint for art history," said another successful SoHo artist. "Anything less is simply masturbation."

The claims of society upon the autonomy of the artist take their most immediate form in market pressures transferred through the dealer. As a result, both individual dealers and dealers as a group find themselves the object of resentment by successful artists. Nevertheless, in order to reduce economic and ideological stress, successful artists must express confidence in their dealers. One's own dealer is treated as the trustworthy exception in a market toward which they remain wary. Having risen toward success through the layers of the art market, these artists either have personally experienced dishonest dealers or have had to show solidarity with those artists who have. Artists feel victimized by the market, but their moral indignation is qualified by prudence. They are fully aware that their own isolated market role commands little power. One successful artist observed:

> Dealers don't like to socialize with artists. It makes them nervous. They are aware that they have made a big killing at one time on the artist's work and will do so again on his future work. Dealers would rather get together with each other to show off their collections. Things of mine that I sold for $1,000 have gone up to $15,000. That's an increase of fifteen times! The dealers and the collectors get it. I'm not happy, but I'm getting used to it.

The top dealers buy and speculate in the works of their artists. They explain that such investments strengthen the artist's belief that, as dealers, they are doing all they can to increase the value of his work. Artists are aware, if not effusively appreciative, of this dealer function. "Dealers will collaborate at an auction to keep the price of a painter's work high so that their own collections of that painter do not depreciate," said one painter. "So even if photo realism became unfashionable in a year, I'm well enough established to be protected." The successful artist benefits from this commercial manipulation, yet withholds his moral approval. The very success of such efforts can be construed by an unhappy artist as evidence of his exploitation.

Commenting upon the market in general or upon their past dealers, successful artists characterize the trust relationship between artist and dealer as deliberately encouraged by the dealer for his own advantage. The artists feel that, while their access to the market is clearly limited when they pledge to sell only through one dealer, the dealer tries to avoid making his commitments to the artist concrete. "When I first came [to SoHo], I talked initially to [a top dealer] who didn't pick me up," explained one artist. "He seemed helpful and encouraging, but that was all. Later, he was furious when I began to sell and was with someone else. [He] wanted to let me develop without his taking any risk, but without losing me either, you see. I went with someone who would pay me a stipend."

Expressing confidence in the abilities of his present dealer, another artist displayed the characteristic attitude of artists toward dealers other than their own: "Dealers are more dishonest than any other businessmen because artists are so vulnerable. Not a day goes by that a dealer does not swindle an artist." This artist was not surprised when he heard the news of the Marlborough Gallery conspiracy which was revealed in 1975 during the trial of the decade in the art world. "It's only the tip of the iceberg, just a bigger example of what happens every day," he commented.

The head of the international Marlborough Galleries, Frank Lloyd, was the agent for his longtime friend, the painter Mark Rothko. Before Rothko committed suicide, leaving two minor children, he named Lloyd a trustee for his estate, which included hundreds of unsold works. Lloyd was convicted of conspiring with other trustees to purchase for his gallery over eight hundred of the estate's paintings in order to resell them at six to ten times the purchase price. The gallery would have realized an illicit profit of more than $5 million on the Rothko children's property, which it had arranged to have underappraised through collusion with another gallery.[3]

The abuse of trust exemplified by the Marlborough Gallery case demonstrates that the dealer enjoys a great freedom to maneuver in the performance of his role. Because of his obligations to present the work of each of his fifteen to twenty artists to society effectively, the dealer must remain free of the control of any one artist. Each artist wants his show at the height of the art season; each wants to be treated as a crucial member of a most important movement. The dealer needs and gets a great deal of latitude in order to balance their conflicting demands.

On the other hand, the dealer's relationship with his buyers is equally demanding and essential to the successful transaction. The artist knows that his dealer will not automatically steer each collector to his work. He cannot contractually require that the dealer attend to the artist's interests at the expense of the collector's. The more innovative and aggressive the dealer, the more freedom he requires to adjust these short-run conflicts of interest.

The selling of art is itself an art, an art of juggling a multiplicity of interests and of anticipating responses. The dealer's position at the center of the art transaction requires the assumption by buyer and seller that the dealer's knowledge and fairness will resolve the obvious conflicts, and that the long-term interests of dealer, collector, and artist coincide. The fact that dealers can accumulate personal holdings of their artists' works, in which they then speculate, shows that the art market is a web of trust based upon mutual liability. It is less professionalized than the stock exchange, where, by contrast, the Securities and Exchange Commission forbids the broker to speculate in the stocks he recommends to clients on the grounds that it would constitute a conflict of interest.

Artists have to trust their dealers as a requirement of market participation. Their relationship with their dealers is personal as well as financial. Because it operates in the realm of economic uncertainty, it seeks refuge in the realm of personal obligation. Many of the particulars of the dealer's services cannot be contractually delimited. Nor can the artist's resolve to continue to produce saleable work. The mutual and extralegal dependence of the artist and dealer finds expression in the language of moral obligation. As a show of reciprocal trust, the financial contract itself is often a verbal one and is hostage to the continued assumption of goodwill by both parties.

This assumption is a *situational* trust whose moral corollaries the artist as well as the dealer tries to exploit. Artists count on the dealer's sense of responsibility to compensate for their generic market weakness. The successful artist is tempted to prove to himself that his relationship with his dealer is one of friendship and concern by asking the dealer to cope with his personal problems. Various artists have, for instance, expected their dealers to supervise their efforts to control alcoholism, to find carpenters to renovate their studios, and to handle their attacks of anxiety about their creativity. But it is clear that dealers, too, derive advantages from the emotional as well as the financial dependency of artists. The artist who feels able to impose on his dealer with midnight phone calls for psychiatric advice is more than contractually tied to the dealer.

It is difficult to avoid presuming the existence of emotional ties and personal obligations in a relationship which requires situational trust. Feeling that the dealer wants to help him as a friend, the artist more willingly gives the dealer the flexibility he needs to coordinate the roles of artist's manager, buyer's counselor, and collector in his own right. While artist and dealer are aware of the manipulation and exploitation to which trust may be put, this awareness is displaced as a criticism of the market in general, so that the business of creating and selling art can proceed. Dealers stereotype artists as a group as being childlike and unreasonable, while artists characterize dealers as dishonest. Particular artists and the dealers with whom they affiliate, however, find in each other an exception to their respective stereotypes.

Evading the Dealer

Those few artists with the strongest market leverage and economic self-confidence hire personal agents, usually lawyers, to oversee their businesses and negotiate with their dealers and buyers. These artists are freer to indulge their feelings that the market abuses the creative artist. For the traditional trust relationship, they substitute explicit contracts which provide for such details as the reclaiming of sold work for exhibition purposes, or the claiming of 10 percent of the appreciated value of a work on its first resale. Their demands are justified by their anti-commercial indignation.

The "celebrity artists," those among the successful elite who utilize a public persona as showmen and entertainers to draw attention to their art, disparage the market aspect of fine art by seeming to circumvent it with a mass appeal. They cater to the public's uneasiness about esoteric pretentions by making their art an outrageous plaything, a spectacle that people of all levels of education in art may attend, if only they will accept the unstuffiness of the aesthetic enterprise. Like Christo's running fences and wrapped buildings and Warhol's movie-star portraits, the work of celebrity artists is grist for commentary by the mass media and seems to solicit public response rather than critical appraisal.

A few successful artists, rather then evading the gallery system, have campaigned for its reform. The highly successful New York painter Robert Rauschenberg and his business manager, Rubin Borewitz, are leading advocates of an amendment to the federal Copyright Act which would give artists 15 percent of the appreciated value of paintings at resale. They took up this issue in 1975 after one of Rauschenberg's paintings, *Thaw*, sold to the collector Robert Scull in 1963 for $900, was resold at auction by Scull for $85,000. Other well-known artists, including Carl Andre, Sol LeWitt, and Hans Haake, support artist royalities. However, not all of the artist community share their enthusiasm. As artist Judy Pendleton, a spokesperson for the royalty movement which calls itself the Artists Rights Association, said, "The country is getting used to contracts. People accept them for anything they buy—a used car, an apartment—so why not a painting? Part of the job is trying to get the *artist* to accept the contract as part of the deal."[4]

The royalty contract advocated by some successful artists has proved to be a divisive issue because it would affect the well-known and the unknown artist differently. Edward Koch, as a Manhattan congressman who identified artists as an important part of his constituency, explained this difference: "I am concerned that this proposal will inhibit art buying particularly from young artists most in need of help. Many people seek out new artists from whom to buy work at modest prices because of potential gains in the future. We must be careful not to undermine art buying incentives."[5]

So long as the power rests primarily with the dealer to decide which artists from among the flood of aspirants have the qualifications to be "collectible," the artist-dealer relationship will remain one of situational trust. The dealer, as gatekeeper to the art world, assumes the initial costs and risks of bringing unknown artists to the attention of those who review art and those who purchase it for public and private collections. The artist has no choice but to trust the dealer in this subtle promotional process. Once the artist becomes known, he can take a more active role in self-promotion by gallery jumping. The best known artists, in whom collectors and critics have a substantial investment, can use this broadened base of support to increase their share of the profits from their career success and to drive harder bargains with both dealers and buyers.

Status Awareness

All the participants in the art transaction have an interest in maintaining a clearly defined status structure among artists. Art attracts investors and collectors because the market focuses upon and validates relatively few art works. The art market requires scarcity, and it achieves this through a restriction of the artist to essentially artisan techniques, which assure that production will be limited and will end with the lifetime of the artist.

While the artist's death allows the dealer to complete the reification process, which transfers life to the collectible art works, it is the ideology of the art world which sustains the collectibility of art by the presumption of its scarcity. The art market limits itself to important original images and objects. The more that film, video, and printing processes flood the public with standardized and simplified imagery, the more the quality of originality is used to differentiate fine art. Because accuracy and inexpensive duplication are characteristics of technological processes, it has become more important that the art world structure its status system around the relatively few unique products of individual creators.

The artist climbs a narrowing ladder of status on which gallery affiliation provides the primary handhold. The successful artist is, not surprisingly, status sensitive. He wants representation in a gallery where he can show with only reputational equals. He considers the collector's confidence in the gallery to be convertible into a willingness to buy what is displayed. But the gallery system requires the dealer to present a status hierarchy rather than status equals in his exhibitions. This allows the collector to speculate on the new and the cheap, the artist to move from obscurity to recognition, and the dealer to retain an au courant reputation.

Each season the dealer selects new artists on the basis of their potential. Artists of realized reputations who enjoyed a similar trial period in their own careers may resent being shown alongside lesser lights. Dealers must solve the problem of mollifying feelings of hurt prestige. The tradition of noblesse oblige that links artists of differing reputations together aids the dealer in placating his upper-status artists. Dealers have come to rely heavily on established artists for recommendations as to which new artists to visit or try out. Known artists are encouraged to play a mentor role, which softens interartist jealousy and facilitates the gallery's search for new blood.[6]

Role Strain: Success and its Aftertaste

If successful artists are nervous about threats to their status, they are often bewildered and angry at seeing the consequences of their success, specifically, the speculative trade in their paintings. "I sometimes wonder about the strange commodity that art is," said one artist. "How is it that paintings of mine which once I could not sell cheap, say, for under $500, are now worth many times this just because of the fact that I've done other things since?"

The successful artist often feels that he is passively carried by the currents of a market over which he has no control. Such artists find that their names alone have become as much an item of trade as their art work. When investors have succeeded in pegging the prices of an artist's entire output to the rising value of his reputation, authorship becomes more important than the merits of a particular work. When the market responds primarily to the fact that a particular work is "a Rauschenberg" or "a Smith," the artist himself has become a commodity.

In addition, accidental market configurations may be responsible for much of the value of the artist's work. This dislocates the artist's preferred belief that, as a creative individual, he is responsible for what is essentially aesthetic value. "I'm lucky to be a leading member in what the critics call a 'school,'" said one artist. "It gives me a firm position in the art universe, and every show and major collector tries to get "a Hopewell" [not the artist's real name]. Just being a good painter who was one of a kind, I might be ignored."

As a market entity of considerable stature, the successful painter may find that he can no longer afford to express his communal impulses freely. "I've sent three or four things to Vietnam war protest sales in the past, and had one in the Chilean refugee show," explained one artist. "I get many requests, and I used to usually send at least a print. Now, my paintings take six weeks to complete, and sell for far more than they used to. I feel priced out of the charity market."

There is often role strain involved in sudden upward mobility. The artist who was in debt to his dealer and whose renovated studio represented all his assets may find himself relatively "rich and famous" a year or so later. His old economic habits, developed to cope with poverty, are now counterproductive. Yet such habits may still be utilized as a refuge from the pressures of success. One well-known artist spent three days chipping cement away from his bathroom drain pipes so the city inspector could approve his loft renovations. He was within a few weeks of an important show, but he acted as he had done when he first came to SoHo and had to solve his renovation problems with his own labor. Another artist, who was capable of grossing $15,000 with a single painting that might take him six to eight weeks, hired a truck and scouted the suburban lumber yards for bargain sheetrock with which to renovate his SoHo loft. He spent several weeks on this partition-building project. A third artist worked as a helper to the carpenter he had hired to renovate his loft. The carpenter reported that, despite the artist's fits of enthusiasm with hammer and nails, he was susceptible to distractions and impeded the construction work by arranging the building materials into sculptural forms.

The rise in status introduced by success also strains relationships among artists as well. As one newly successful artist explained, "I've gotten friendly with other artists who are successful. I lost friends who were less successful." Other artists make special efforts to avoid having their success disrupt their friendship with less successful colleagues, but this can spoil a democratic realtionship by the suggestion of condescension. "I respect the people who haven't really gotten anywhere," said one artist, "keeping their art a private thing while they work at something else, say teaching. The vast majority do fail, and end up doing five-and-dime paintings or the like."

College teaching, sometimes seen as an alternative institutional prop for the fine-art career, cannot deliver the art-world prominence offered by dealer affiliation. Teaching absorbs the artist into a collegiate rather than an art world, as a now well-known artist explained:

> When I taught at [a small Ivy League school], no one there saw me as an artist. It's easy to fall into the role of artist-in-residence for a bourgeois faculty, but that's not being an artist. All my life's dealings—in faculty politics and whatever—were as a teacher. I was somebody who painted on the side. I put "teacher" before "artist" on my income tax returns. I finally maneuvered it so they would not rehire me. I could not have stayed on the faculty and developed as an artist.

The successful artist feels guilty and the unsuccessful artist has his sense of failure aggravated by his contact with a more successful friend. It is difficult for such a pair to share an ideological contempt for the market's blindness to creativity. While artists strive to remain sympathetic to those who are less successful, they are drawn into increasing social relations with their market peers. The proximity of failure in their own careers is unsettling enough without the hovering specter of their unsuccessful friends. "I have a friend, a former artist, who now makes toys, mostly adult toys, and gets lots of orders at the crafts fairs like Rhinebeck," said another successful artist. "He makes dancing dolls, Nixon wood puzzles, things like that. He insists they are not art, but games. Another friend, also a former New York artist, is how having a life crisis about what to do with himself."

Self-mockery is one way in which artists adjust to an identity that has become "rich" and "famous." One successful artist, leafing through the pages of a home-decorating magazine during a conversation with friends, stopped at a picture of a living room with lush floral paintings on the walls. The paintings were his, he said. He had done them in his hungry days, not so long before, when he had taken commissions from a decorator who supplied him with the subject and color swatches to coordinate with the furnishings. He had worked under various French names which, together with a fictitious biography, had been supplied to the client with each painting. "I was once as unfamous as you can get," he said, slowly smiling.

The Nonbohemian Character of the Artistic Elite and the Rationalization of the Creative Process

Successful artists are systematic and disciplined in their work routines. As one such artist put it, "If you are going to succeed in an orderly world, you must get into being orderly." He feels that "self-indulgent" artists, who choose to work according to their moods, are note being realistic and will ultimately fail. "Some artists believe in the myth of creative frenzy, but not me," he said. He and other successful SoHo artists plan their creativity and do not trust to the inspiration of the moment, believing that it can let one down. "There is simply no such thing as inspiration," insists this orderly artist. He observes that to depend upon having a great idea as a substitute for a work routine directed toward the systematic solution of problems will eventually leave one with neither a painting program nor a reputation. He knows of only one artist of any reputation who "goofs off" by staying "stoned" much of the year. Two months before a show, this artist locks himself away and somehow accomplishes a year's work. To the more systematic artists, he is a marvelous exception.

Successful artists refer to each other as "machines," reflecting the fact that the pace of their work is like that of an assembly line and that in order to keep up they have to sublimate their more random impulses. They often feel that they are being pushed toward a nervous breakdown by the relentless pressure of precision work. SoHo's abstract painters and new realists, unlike the conceptualist sculptors who usually contract the fabrication of their pieces out to foundries or cabinetmakers, create a finished product and operate with at most one assistant. They typically can do no more than six or eight paintings a year, each requiring over six weeks of daily effort. A painting may sell for $15,000 or more. To keep the quality and rate of their production up, these artists must remain orderly and keep to a strict schedule. Tasks of taping edges or filling in color fields must be laid out and ready for assistants. While their dealers or personal agents handle sales and exhibitions, and their wives and accountants organize their finances, they remain in the studio six, eight, ten hours a day. Having adopted a method which constricts their productivity and continually generates new technical problems, they must become disciplined personalities. "Art is not an alternative culture," said a well-known photo realist. "It's just ahead of the everyday world. My father-in-law makes the mistake of trying to define art and the artist by their life style, but just like him, I go to work every day."

One artist following this life style lives in a SoHo loft with his wife and child and works in isolation in another loft nearby. The studio loft is clean and empty of all but his work-in-progress. No dealer has to phone him in the morning to prod him to get started; he would fire any such dealer, he says. By nine each morning, he is painting; he breaks briefly for lunch, and returns home in the evening, exhausted. He keeps his telephone manner brisk and to the point and discourages visitors. It may take him as much as four months of steady work to break down an image he wants to use through photographic color-separation techniques and to execute the finished painting on a ten-by-twelve-foot panel. He works from a forklift truck onto which he has built an elevating platform. This enables him to move step-by-step over the canvas surface, which is crosshatched into a huge grid. His work is intricate, thoughtful, and methodical. "Art is problem solving, much closer to regular work than people think," he says. He is ideologically committed to seek new effects, so the rhythm of his work is shaped by the problems he anticipates as well as those that occur spontaneously. His art is "a matter of getting in and out of trouble."

It is the pace more than the problems that sometimes makes him feel close to a nervous collapse. He has risen to a significant reputation through controlled intensity and imagines his mind as a short-circuiting electrical system. He projects failure and the tension inherent in his discipline as a vision of machine breakdown.

Successful artists compensate for their disbelief in the poetry of inspiration with a commitment to the prose of hard work. They set a difficult pace for their competitors. They utilize order and the elimination of irrelevance to prevent their tools and work places from distracting their attention. Their slides are filed in labeled drawers, their paint cans and spray guns are left laboratory clean. They buy prestretched and sized canvases and contract out the preparation of irregularly shaped working surfaces. Many work to loud rock music, which they use as a kind of white noise that numbs the sense of time and lifts them away from the voices and sounds of the SoHo streets. The new realists, who project photographic images onto a work surface, on which they then apply paint with the faintest strokes of an airbrush, hang blackout curtains over their windows, which enables them to ignore natural light and to work independently of the day-night cycle.

Successful painters learn to isolate themselves from social distractions. "People do not drop in on me," explained one painter. "I wouldn't allow it. A few painters do like to have a coterie around while they work, and there are always people that are looking for any diversion so as not have to do their own work. One old friend used to come around a lot, but I ignored him more or less, and he stopped coming."

These successful artists are artisans working without the standardizations and fellowship of the medieval guild system. Their vulnerability to competition and to the fickleness of the market prevents them from easing their work schedule or playing with new artistic developments in a merely random fashion. As they work, they keep a steady eye on the market. "I visit twenty to thirty galleries each month," said one very successful artist. "It takes me a day and a half."

Having foraged through the technology of industrial society for the tools which give their work a competitive edge over that of other artists, these successful artists risk proletarianizing the conditions of their labor.

And while they are committed by their ideology to the modernist search for the developmental possibilities by which they can become a part of the evolving edge of art history, their market orientation leads many of them toward the more accessible themes and images of popular culture.

The Rejection of Esoteric Imagery: The Passing of Bohemian Protest

The works of conceptualists, minimalists, and abstract painters are abundant in SoHo galleries, but the art movement most closely associated with SoHo is new realism. New realist painters reproduce images focused and composed through the camera's lens. Promoted first by the O. K. Harris Gallery and its director, Ivan Karp, it has since been aggressively and successfully publicized as the au courant art movement by other pioneer SoHo galleries, most notably the Louis K. Meisel Gallery. Meisel was among the first to call this new art "photo realism."

Photo realism has proven to be immensely popular with collectors as well as the general audience of art viewers who are drawn into the galleries on their Saturday strolls through SoHo. It is jealousy of this popularity, photo realists claim, which is responsible for attacks on them by artists and critics whose reputations are already committed to conceptually more "difficult" art. Photo realists argue that art should not be restricted to what is validated in the dialogue among critics and art historians. Nor should imagery be used merely to convey the conceptual interests of more philosophic, indeed Platonic, painters. "I've lost friends who became antipathetic toward photo realism," said one artist. "I can defend it. I favor a recognizable subject, as do most people."

While the public loves photo realism, the movement has split the artists' community as have few other art movements. Its very accessibility to the new art-buying middle class seems to some to be sufficient proof that it has betrayed the modernist requirement to relentlessly innovate. As a well-known conceptual artist said, "The very popularity of photo realism proves it to be a rehash of popular culture. No, it is not even a satiric rehash, or else it wouldn't be so popular." The producers of such art, by making a virtue of its accessibility, threaten to carry fine arts toward immediately comprehensible images which do not require the interpretive intervention of the critics. As one photo realist said,

> Critics push art which requires interpretation. There are, for instance, two types of conceptual art—the poetic and humorous, and the type pushed by *Art Forum,* serious, Platonic, about which volumes of theory can be written. The first is intuitive and so unexplainable. In the second, the link with lived experience is broken.

Art Forum hates new realism because it is totally accessible to the average person. It needs no elite interpretation.

Another photo realist agreed that accessibility was the defining characteristic of this movement, the characteristic that becomes its indictment in the eyes of the critics.

> Some call recognizability the lowest common denominator in art, and us photo realists "sell-out schmucks." I could fight this out on theoretical grounds, but usually I don't. I'm not really concerned to do so. I'm concerned with the relation of the camera to painting. Abstract people, with the stamp of approval from [Clement] Greenberg and [Andre] Emmerick, are upset. Why can't I just look at a piece and understand it, at least partially? I want my things to be accessible to those who know no art theory.

The attraction of photo realism lies in the approachability of its imagery to the most naive art viewer. There, depicted with the sharp focus of a camera lens, is the familiar world of store fronts, highway fast-food restaurants, mass-produced knick-knacks, and commercial symbols that lure the public. Any sense of historical depth is banished in mutely reflective chrome and plate glass, with which this movement is enamored, or reduced to the gritty nostalgia for a rusted forties automobile. The frontiers of visual association extend only to the dawn of graphics, to the vintage airplane. Photo realist images glitter with the dozens of coats of enamel which this society lavishes on its motorcycles—its material symbols of escape. These paintings have no need to invoke cultural reference points outside the commercial development along the highways they picture. They reveal no sense of human presence beyond that of pinup images of narcissism and unobtainable desire. It is these works that sell so well that they support the careers of the largest group of the successful SoHo artists.

The photo-realist movement owes its popularity to its ability to seize and reveal the one-dimensionality of a culture and a consciousness framed by advertising graphics. One artist spoke wryly of the avant-garde art of fifteen years ago as having been absorbed by today's society in the trivialized form of commercial designs. "Yesterday's Jackson Pollock is today's linoleum pattern and Gucci print." The new realism is a not-so-seasily absorbed revenge. It is as a nondidactic social record that these works are disturbingly interesting. In close focus, or from a photographer's middle distance, the photo realists depict the perspective of the participant in American society who is unaware than anything but a consumer's culture exists. The painted snapshot of the characterless development house, its self-consciously posed family standing in the driveway by the station wagon—this is a reification of our meanings and desires, the sentimentality of a society without a useable past. As Americans, we are shown comprehending reality in terms of the static and arbitrarily concrete imagery of the tourist wandering through the public spaces of a foreign land exactly like our own. "Here I show a bank building, people in cars, the whole thing seen through a car windshield," said an artist about a work in progress. "That's how we see the world, right? And this is the new American landscape. I'm just a contemporary landscape painter."

More than other artists, photo realists avoid commenting on their paintings. They believe that if an image is effective it is so as an image and should not need a "verbal caption." Nor do these artists indulge in unambiguous social criticism. To do so would reduce their art to a mere instrumentality, a cartoon. They are not priests and they claim to have no mystic or arcane knowledge of reality. Their strength is their sensitivity as representative social participants, as litmus paper that reveals society's dream to be just another California suburb.

Photo realists are the representative artists of the 1970s. It is not surprising that in a society which reduces the aesthetic experience to a commercial lubricant, artists would raid consumer culture for their graphic inspiration. Continuing in the tradition of the pop art of the 1960s, photo realists create a commentary on a society which digests its daily art as package design, and searches its commercial imagery for an aesthetic common ground. Rather than lampoon the concreteness of the commodity by making it oversize, or the triviality of comic-strip emotions by reproducing the comic strip as serious art—tricks of the pop artists—the photo realists rely only on a slight shift in perspective to transcend the clichés of their visual terminology. Theirs is a tough, anti-romantic definition of fine art in which the commercially immersed artist is allowed to have no heroic or humorous distance from popular culture other than that achieved by consciously making that culture an object.

In photo realism, with its philosophy of nontranscendence, SoHo has broken with the bohemian traditions which were strong in the Greenwich Village of the 1920s and persisted through the mid-fifties at such centers as the Black Mountain School.[7] Since the artist was deprived of the protection of aristocratic patronage with the French Revolution, artists have survived in bohemian subcultures in neglected pockets of bourgeois society. The bohemian artist has protrayed himself as the follower of a persecuted cult of beauty, whose central sacrament was the enactment of the artist's defeat at the hands of a vulgar, profit-oriented society. César Graña describes the spiritual basis of bohemianism, as found in nineteenth-century Paris, as follows:

> Bohemia embodies as a social fixture the burning and doomed enthusiasm for the life of the spirit, the daily battle against the powers of

the modern world. . . . Bohemia, for its part, despite all the burning bitterness of its anti-social feeling, was, almost by definition, politically powerless. What caused it to flourish was, in Dondey's words, "the arsenal of the soul," the pursuit of purely ideal engagements. Of these the most typical and the most influential historically was the religion of beauty, *l'art pour l'art,* a kingdom whose integrity was free from the secular world, whose tasks . . . permitted the gratification of the romantic need to be at the same time significant and self-centered.[8]

Such a spirit as Graña describes has reached its most diluted form in SoHo, with photo realism's antiromantic definition of fine art. Its major SoHo alternatives—abstract, conceptual, and minimal art—have defied human interaction by their opacity or their architectural cleanliness and sterility. Perhaps sensing this, the crowds have turned to the photo realists, who tease the audience with a familiarity of imagery whose reflective surfaces convey only a resounding silence about the sub-surface of everyday life. While these artists have no bohemian affectations, their attempts to objectify our plane of attention convey a marked discontent with the triumphant concreteness of commodity culture. A residual bohemianism remains as the quality of a dry irony.

Conclusion

The artists who are emerging successful in the SoHo market are those who are able to appeal to two audiences at once. First, they succeed in convincing a critical audience—one comprised of other artists, dealers, experienced buyers, and commentators all committed to modernism in art—that their work is significantly avant-garde and deserves to be singled out for attention. Second, they appeal to a less critically assured audience—those whose education and occupational mobility have made them aware of contemporary fine art, but whose daily immersion in popular culture has prevented the refinement of that awareness. This audience wants a certified fine art which is also exciting and accessible to them in nonesoteric terms. Satisfying each of these audiences involves the artist in different strategies.

The critical audience is not satisfied with well-crafted repetition, with decorativeness, or with accurate representation; it wants work that is consistently innovative in its approach to important art problems. The demand for such innovation is a burden to the artist at odds with the realities of the market, since potential customers require a certain amount of consistency or at least predictability in an artist in whom they intend to invest. The solution, for both artist and dealer, is to relegate innovation to marginal alterations within a slowly evolving and characteristic style, once such a style has found market acceptance.

Where dealers cultivate stability within innovation by promoting discernable "movements," constellations of recognizable styles, artists seek a style and a methodology which will permit a routinization of the process of art production so as to make innovation incremental. This is done in three ways: First, through their formal approach to art education, their effective use of dealers as agents, and their continuous surveillance of the market, artists try to anticipate the career consequences of their aesthetic moves. Second, by an allocation of mechanical studio tasks to assistants, by their use of labor-saving tools and prefabricated materials, and through a methodology which generates technical and conceptual problems, they are able to concentrate their attention on those aspects of the work process itself which generate aesthetic challenges. Finally, by organizing their personal relations around their career goals, they are able to enjoy emotional support and a sense of involvement with others without submitting to artistic domination by a social circle. SoHo artists are free to survey the market and art history to identify problems of their own.

The second audience, composed of the aesthetically curious rather than the fully knowledgeable, and approaching art through the modalities of popular culture, has become important in the expanding art market. But they bring in their own concepts of art. Lacking the cultural sophistication of the first audience, they bring to the gallery a familiarity with popular culture that is their most salient and powerful visual resource. Central to popular culture are the sharp, vivid, and clearly focused images of advertising, film, and illustration; these have become the aesthetic coordinates of daily life in America. The graphic depiction of commodities, widely distributed or massively scaled technological products, the clarity and lack of ambiguity of the camera-lens perspective, roadways replete with display-package architecture—these combine to form the modern public landscape and iconography.

This iconography owes its coherence and intersubjectivity to the everpresentness of mass culture, rather than to its ability to express the contradictions and complexity of human experience. It represents a taken-for-granted world in which the power of visual concreteness and familiarity discourages critical distance.[9] Like an all-news radio station, it simply repeats itself in a present without perspective. While it is sufficient as a sign system to direct the traffic of everyday life, it is unable to infuse those signs with an intimation of the human struggle to impose meaning on disorder and disappointment. Popular culture is all on a horizontal plane of message and sign, in which the questions that surround everyday life, questions that demand a symbolic formulation, are trivialized with a specious definitiveness of image. Popular culture is insufficient to locate the individual in a full-dimensional world or to enable him to peer around the edges of daily life.

The new audience approaches fine art with a sense of the insufficiency of popular images, but also with a taste for their energy, vividness, and lack of subtlety. Some SoHo artists, photo realists and a few conceptualists in particular, have been able to build careers by satisfying the needs of this new audience by appropriating the commercial imagery of everyday life and presenting it as fine art. These artists are providing the new audience with both the accessible subject matter it prefers and the opportunity to stand outside an objectified commercial culture. The photo realists' endorsement of popular culture in the vehicle of fine art, their appropriation of its graphic strength, becomes an ironic commentary on that culture's limitations.

6 The Integration of the Status Community

Membership Hierarchy

Fine artists who direct their work toward the New York market live within social rather than spatial bounds and therefore constitute what Joseph Bensman and others have termed a "status community."[1] They are drawn together socially by their shared commitment to occupational values which emphasize the central importance of aesthetic concerns in their lives and the determining position of the individual in the creative process. They rely upon a specialized set of organizations—schools of art, museums, galleries, and critical art journals—for public presentation and sale of their work. Similar training, institutional focuses, values, and economic problems comprise the basis of a subculture in which interaction occurs, a community forms, and a consensus on status positions develops.

It is the status structure of the community that channels the value commitments and ambitions of new and old members and gives the community coherence. The primary goal of this hierarchy is the making of fine art which the community itself and then the wider society will treat as historically important and as highly marketable. Those few who attain this goal are independent professionals who can devote themselves completely to their art. Beneath this stratum are those artists who, in one way or another, have fallen short of the goal. These would include, among others, the market success who lacks the full aesthetic esteem of colleagues, the market failure who retains peer or critical

esteem, the university art teacher who continues to be artistically creative, and the creative artist who supports his or her art with a job in a
commercial studio.

Any departure from the ideal of the autonomous professional is cause
for both personal concern and collective evaluation in the art community. The criticism is invidious and harsh for those who compromise
basic standards of creativity for a pseudo-avant-garde success. Because
they are successful, this type is widely known and gossiped about. But
for most other statuses in the art community the circle of concern is
more personal, and the object of evaluation is the usefulness of a sup-
plemental occupation or activity for an artist's survival and advancement. Friends, acquaintances, and artists themselves look upon these
compromises as strategies. A full-time teaching position in an art school,
known to be poorly paid, is justified to the extent that its schedule can be
compressed into two nine-hour days, leaving the artist relatively free to
do his or her own work. A fling at creating a design for a bar mitzvah
card for a wealthy client is rationalized as an exception to one's serious
work, an exception that pays next month's rent. Tenure, in a teaching
environment where many jobs are limited to year-to-year contracts,
means desired security, but at the same time it is suspect in that it
suggests that what began as a vehicle for survival has become a limit to
ambition.

In the background of these concerns and evaluations lie two re-
alizatons: First, the career of the artist matures slowly, and compromises, especially for the young, can coexist with the hope of eventually
achieving professional autonomy. Second, there is also the possibility of utter professional and personal failure. A tenured art professor,
struggling for galleried status, told of an encounter with one such failure:
"When I was in SoHo last year for my sabbatical, I ran into an old
[fine-arts] classmate of mine from Iowa. Some in our class have gone on
to become quite well known. Well, this guy was on the Bowery, sitting
on a piece of cardboard. He was too drunk to recognize me, I guess.
That's the other extreme of where our group has ended up. Me, well, I'm
where I am."

Structuring Institutions

Insofar as fine artists belong to a status community, their activities and
values are focused by means of a set of occupation-related institutions.
These include educational organizations, museums, the gallery-
marketing structure, and the critical art press. All four institutions work
together in a roughly coordinated fashion to reach a consensus and to
confer prestige on practicing fine artists.

There is, however, a major imbalance in this sytem. The marketing arrangements are inadequate to absorb and support the number of art graduates leaving school each year. The institutions of the art community do not enable more than the exceptional few to rise to recognition and to achieve substantial economic rewards. This failure of art institutions to reward the majority of artists is the result of the larger society's view of the arts as recreational and decorative rather than as socially necessary. "Some small part of 1 percent of all artists can live from their art," said one successful SoHo artist. "I'd locate myself at the bottom of that thin top layer. No, I'd never recommend that anyone go into art. It has to be something you feel you absolutely have to do." Artists feel that their commitment forces them to depend upon faulty institutions that, however correctly they may rank artists, do not serve their economic needs.

The institutions that most artists first experience and fault are the schools and universities. Irrespective of the quality of instruction they offer, art schools do not provide bridges to the art market for fine artists.[2] The student's status and achievement at school do not necessarily translate into an ability to make a living from fine art. A year's postgraduate awakening dissolves the commitment of many would-be artists.[3] "There I was, having graduated first in my class from Cooper Union, and there was no way I could earn a living," said one now successful SoHo painter. "I had to study for a teaching certificate in art to survive." Another highly ranked SoHo painter said:

> Leaving school is a very hard time. You're confronted with only you. The structure of the institution is gone; the structure of the family is usually gone. There you are, left. It's then up to you to structure, to *make* a structure. It's a matter of having to focus, to organize your life so that, between waiting on tables and answering a telephone switchboard, you still have the time and the best part of your energy to do your own [art] work.

Art schools do provide some practicing artists with teaching jobs, of which the artists-in-residence positions are perceived as the most desirable, having the maximum amount of recognition of the creative process per se and the minimum amount of interference from a bureaucratic administration or an indifferent student body.[4] But all such positions involve some compromises with the goals of the professional artist, compromises which can produce frustration and cause personal disorganization. A successful SoHo artist said of her early career:

> In the sixties nobody hired women for teaching. All my friends seemed to have these cushy jobs teaching in universities, and I didn't. Half of them have since become alcoholics, and the other half have

gone to pot in some other way. The job is too staid. I teach one course now, advanced painting, but I could never have survived [as an artist] in one of those full-time jobs. Though at the time, I wished I had had one.

Young artists who try to utilize museums of contemporary art as the primary showcases for their work also encounter difficulties. Few of these museums show the work of more than a dozen artists in their annual shows of new talent. Those who are chosen often feel that the selection process is bewilderingly arbitrary. "Of the thousands of artists submitting slides to the Whitney annual [that year], I can't really say why they accepted my work," said one SoHo artist. "My dealer sent them in, and I guess it was a fluke. And I could never figure out why anybody bought the piece, but they did. It was hung practically in a closet."

In addition, many artists selected for these shows subsequently drop out of sight. The museum alone cannot speak for the art community as a whole. "Look back at some of those old Whitney annuals," said the artist quoted above, "and see how many names you've never heard of again." The museums lag behind the galleries in the process of validating art reputations. Their first interest is in maintaining the value of the collections and building upon the aesthetic commitments which their curators have made to already established artistic directions. They have a conservative inertia and consolidate rather than initiate reputations. Artists themselves expect this institutional conservatism. In fact, when museums take on the trendy characteristics of avant-garde galleries, established artists protest that they have turned into mere amusement arcades.[5]

Commercial galleries, discussed at length in chapter 3, act by design as bottlenecks limiting the number of artists who can gain access to the market. Galleries are committed to maintaining the value of the work of their established artists so that collectors can count upon some stability in the market. Dealers must protect the limited number of buyers from the confusion of individual talent by sorting out and promoting trends and movements. As a result, artists complain of being steered, however subtly, into the aesthetic directions that are most advantageous to the dealer.[6] Because dealers channel the pressure of the market back to the artist, they cannot escape the resentment of those artists who feel that their creative independence has been violated.

Artists believe that the critics who write for the art journals and the middle-class press wield arbitrary and excessive power in the process by which artistic rank is assigned. Critics are resented for standing between collectors and the artist's work, spoiling its immediate visual appeal with a verbal filter. They are accused of muffling creativity by promoting the fear of deviation from some authorized aesthetic. One SoHo artist explained this interference by critics as follows:

> When Hilton Kramer [art critic of the *New York Times*] recommends a show, it sells out. It sells out in three days.... I've seen a couple looking at a conceptual piece—a white field with a green dot in the center, I remember. I don't understand this kind of work, personally, but I think you or I or anyone could do it. This couple looked at it and bought it, all because they had read that a critic said, ''Buy it!'' It doesn't matter what collectors like. They will spend $200 on lunch around here, and they think nothing of it, but they won't spend $200 on a piece of art, even if they like it, unless it is approved by a critic. It's not the money. It's the status of owning the thing. They are afraid of making a ''wrong'' decision. Hell, if critics approved, I could sell anything.

This artist was viewing the market from long experience and only modest success. However, successful artists also complain that critics transform and distort a visual experience into an intellectual one. They see critics as trying to limit the accessibility of art to only those who are educated and interested in abstract aesthetic problems. Artists who stress the aesthetic availability of their work to a lay audience feel threatened by critics who brand such art as unserious or naive. At best, critics are praised for pointing out to the artist facets of his own work that had not occurred to him before, thus giving him a set of linguistic tools which are occasionally useful in impressing the buyer.

Audience and Allies

Artists concur in the belief that the institutions of the art community support a status structure in which few artists are permitted to succeed. The unsuccessful artists experience this situation as chronic status injustice and have staged demonstrations in SoHo in the form of street festivals to gain government jobs for ''unemployed'' artists.[7]

Artists are able to generate contagious indignation about the lack of rewards for their profession. Members of the art audience who enjoy social proximity to artists are susceptible to the artists' feelings of economic deprivation, and they can be turned into allies of the artists' cause. One group of allies are business and political leaders who use art to dramatize their humanistic concerns. Their roles as trustees and benefactors of art institutions make them vulnerable to embarrassing demands by artists to make good on their custodial roles by steering business and public policy into line with artists' interests.

A second and much larger segment of the lay art audience is composed of the professionals and bureaucrats who share the middle-class regard for art and artists as intrinsically valuable. Parents and teachers groom this audience by communicating to them an esteem for art that is later reinforced by a liberal-arts college education. This is the middle-class that visits museums, uses art at home to express their own status, and may have childhood friends or family members who are artists.[8] This audience frequently cites the last fact as proof of their acquaintance with the difficulties of the art career and of their own social acceptance by artists. This audience is attracted to the values that they believe are exemplified by artists. Of all modern workers, artists appear to them to retain the most control over their labor, which is essentially creative and which reflects the stamp of individual personality. The artist as symbol stands opposed to the routinization of work and the submergence of the ego that characterize the bureaucratic order of society. As romantic symbols of disenchantment with the world, artists represent the possibility of work which is holistic, rewarding, adventurous, and creative.

In their role as allies, this middle class brings with them the resources of organizational expertise, occupational contacts, and professional skills. SoHo artists were able to add these allies to their own resources in order to win political victories in their community.

Social Networks

While artists in SoHo can be effective territorial actors when it is politically necessary, they usually orient themselves toward the status system of the art world and prefer to limit their social contacts to small gatherings of other artists selected along lines of rough prestige equivalence. This allows the more successful among them to maintain social distance from nonartists or lesser artists with whom they share the sidewalks, restaurants, and loft buildings. The perception that the creative community is threatened by tourists and other nonartists makes successful artists even more status conscious. "I'm upset by the decision, for example, to open SoHo to tours and festivals that bring all sorts of people into the area," said one artist. "And setting up coverage of loft living in *Life* magazine—what right did the SoHo Artists Association have to do that?"

The informal conversation of artists is often shoptalk in which they circulate useful information about market opportunities, jobs, and current art developments. Those who share the same market perspective because they have the same reputational standing have more in common and so tend to seek each other out. These social networks have a practical importance in that they help artists finance housing and locate jobs.

A young sculptor, a few years out of a college art program and still seeking his first professional show, described his studio arrangement:

> Molly and I looked individually for spaces where we could live and work before we decided to share a loft in SoHo. We would each prefer to work alone, really. But we are old friends from college, and we get along. I saw nothing any good without a fixture fee of thousands, or else the rent was $600. Molly came in on the deal after I had located this space. She pays a bit more than half the rent, since I paid the fixture fee. If we can sell the improvements to the next tenant, we'll split any profit from our renovation.

Peer social networks ease the chronic job difficulties that most artists experience when they are trying to establish themselves. Another artist said,

> It's hard to get recognition. I've published a few articles, had a few shows, but never sold anything. It's especially hard with the conceptual art I do. . . .
> My economic situation is an emotional drag. I'm always having to get work. I rely on friends, mostly. Twice, when I haven't been working, I've taken a walk down West Broadway [SoHo's main street] and asked people if they knew of any jobs—sanding floors, sheetrocking walls, painting. I always meet somebody I know, and I always got work that way. A lot of new loft owners need help in setting up.

Some friendship groups are also utilized as criticism circles, but this tends to be a pattern characteristic of students and not-yet successful artists who are status-relaxed because they judge themselves by their potential more than by their current status in the art world. Most artists observe a code which requires them to avoid damaging criticism of the work they see in progress when they visit each other's studio. An as yet unsuccessful artist explained the protocol as it applied to the artist with whom he shared a loft.

> Jack's also a sculptor. I've given him ideas and technical help at times, but I avoid art criticism with him. He feels I don't take his work seriously as it is, which is partially true. Most of my friends who are sculptors look at each other's work and don't comment. Those who do comment may be artists, but never sculptors. Artists are insecure on the question of good and bad. They don't feel secure enough to praise without negating themselves, or to criticize without leaving themselves open to criticism.

The experience of a well-known artist indicates that socializing along peer lines according to prestige extends to other status levels, and that its rules against fraternal criticism remain in force.

My best friend at Pratt Institute, after me the best student in the class, commuted with me to school every day for four years. Now we've split. I asked him what his objections were to the kind of realism I was doing, because I was writing a short piece. I expected just a comment. He sent me back thirty objections—"amoral," "historically irrelevant," things like that. That was it between us. It was a matter of ideology.

When the student status no longer provides a context for the analysis of one another's work, a context which is understood to restrict criticism to that which is helpful and constructive, friendship requires a moratorium on such commentary. The successful artist is publicly committed to an artistic direction and can be severely damaged by disparaging evaluations of his work. Such artists consider their styles to be their publicly recognizable signatures. They make efforts to keep abreast of new art developments in their field, primarily because they do not want to appear to be repeating the work of someone else. Artists say that the occasional efforts of a SoHo dealer to bring his artists together for drinks and conversation, which he expects will result in aesthetic stimulation if not cross-fertilization, have failed utterly. "I know all the other photo realists, but I'm at the point where I don't think I have anything to learn from them," said one artist.

The social networks provide material aid to artists at all levels of success, however, often in unpredictable ways. As one artist explained,

I had had a teaching job, but gave it up, and for a long time I looked for one and couldn't get one. Then, a month ago, I was at an opening and was introduced to this guy who said, "You want a job?" It was in Delaware. That's how the art world works. It runs on the basis of who you know. You try and hire your friends. I didn't take it though. I didn't want to leave SoHo.

Successful artists are constantly being thrown together by the market, particularly by the need to compensate for market randomness and by a need for occupational understanding. Their social networks serve not only as status pockets but as shelters from the intensity of the competition among them. These networks generate an empathy and solidarity which orient artists toward the market as a group, rather than toward each other as rivals. Friends attend the small celebrations that take place when each of them opens a show in a gallery or museum, and they attend the parties that frequently follow these openings. When sales are good, they share this news, and when reviews run cold, they point out the advantages of any publicity whatever, or mutually disparage the reviewers. They try to make a joke out of their competitive position with each other by such things as wearing tee shirts decorated with photo-decals of each other's work. An artist in one such group left SoHo to live in the country, but he comes back every six weeks to deliver a painting to his dealer and to reaffirm his network ties. "I find myself telling the same stories of country living a dozen times," he says. The social network is the human ground on which these artists touch base and break out of their studio isolation.

It is the stabilizing effect of the status network rather than the SoHo location that provides the successful artist with most of his sense of community. Mutual recognition is a cushion which enables such artists to view their day-to-day setbacks and market anxieties from a more personally secure perspective. Success and the artist network free the artist psychologically and enable him to use the dealer in a more deliberately self-interested manner.

> I'm thankfully free of the need to socialize with and aggressively try to sell to the gallery owners. I have prestige I never had before. Now the gallery owners come up and talk to me. I find out in talking a half hour to two or three people more than I knew about the art world in years of being on the outside—what shows are happening, who's doing what.

The population density and the degree of specialization among SoHo artists have encouraged the development of these social networks. They tend to occur where the horizontal stratification of status in the art world intersects with a particular definition of the avant-garde in art at a particular time. Due to the absence of a monolithic establishment controlling the rewards of the art world in order to support one particular style, there is a pluralism of styles, each of which is considered by their proponents to be avant-garde. While artists recognize an art frontier with many styles and mediums, they sometimes sharply disagree as to whether particular directions are authentically avant-garde. To some extent, the social network is an attempt by the artist to draw support for a collective definition of this art frontier, one which legitimates his own work.

The act of formulating and reformulating a perspective on emerging art is facilitated by the fact that network members work in the same medium and in related styles. Within these similarities, however, they seek to remain differentiated as individuals, and artists who begin to evolve in too similar a direction threaten one another's distinctiveness and render network cooperation impossible. SoHo artists, then, concentrate on promoting their own styles within a porous market, and use the milieu of the network as support for the validity of their own work. Movements, as collective assaults upon an entrenched art establishment, do not describe the ebb and flow of network life in SoHo. Status as ultimately validated by the market, and not aesthetic mission, is the dominant principle of social organization. One SoHo artist said simply, "I had lots of friends who were less successful."

Private Networks and Public Bars

As SoHo has grown into an entertainment area with over a dozen bar-restaurants, each more expensively furnished than its immediate predecessor, artists have found another reason to identify themselves with their social networks rather than with the geographical district. Little discussion of art can be heard in the bars, which tend to be similar to those on the Upper East Side of Manhattan and reflect the same cosmopolitan taste in food and decor. It is the taste of young lawyers, doctors, and accountants, rather than that of artists. The bars that are "in" for a particular season are packed to standing-room capacity on weekends and buzz with a "singles" ambiance. They are too expensive to become regular drinking spots for most artists and reflect little or no consciousness of SoHo as an artists' community. Asked if they visit the local bars often, most SoHo artists make it a point of occupational status to say no. "There's only two bars, I think, that I've ever been into in SoHo," said a painter-sculptor of some reputation who has lived there since 1967. "One of the major fringe benefits of being an artist is knowing all the cheap places to eat in Chinatown," said another artist, explaining why he usually avoided SoHo restaurants.

Artists do, of course, visit the area bars, but they are not habitués. This is a matter of work discipline, as well as economics. "I would enjoy going to bars and talking half the night," said one successful painter, "but it takes too much out of me. I can't afford to be hung over and start work late the next day."

Successful artists also avoid the bars because of the bars' dominant clientele—quasi-artists and nonartists who use SoHo as a place of entertainment and the artists as a source of environmental coloration. "I think that it is outsiders, those coming to New York with no roots here, that get into the bar scene more than local people," said one artist.

The bars have also declined as gathering spots for working artists because the nature of the art world has changed since the 1950s, when places like the Cedar Bar in Greenwich Village provided booths where avant-garde artists regularly sat to drink and argue. One successful artist explained the lack of such places in SoHo:

In the 1950s there was an exchange of aesthetics in the bars. Artists were starving then, not selling as they are now. This was when abstract expressionism first came to America. Now the conceptual aspect is as important as the execution, and loose tongues, being overheard, can mean you have lost your idea to someone else. Now, the art world is more serious about economics and concepts, and this has the result of lessening the artist's contacts.

The successful artist prefers an artist community which is organized around the studio, the gallery, the network, and the family. With the increase in possible rewards, moreover, artists see themselves as having less leisure time for casual social contacts. The stress of working long hours in isolation is relaxed within the peer network or the family, rather than in the more open arenas of aesthetic and social contention.

Cosmopolitanism

Aspiring artists come to New York and SoHo to be near other artists, art schools, art libraries, museums, galleries, and dealers. If they become successful, they remain in SoHo for its cosmopolitan qualities, which are essential to their careers, not for its neighborliness. As one successful artist said, "I've judged art shows in the Midwest. All the paintings are forty-eight by fifty-six inches. After wondering a while, I discovered that that's the largest size that will fit into a station wagon. You would never find this in New York. Here the idea governs the form. An artist here can't isolate himself and come to think he's so unique. There are fifty people in New York who do what I do. This forces me to substitute innovation for mere eclecticism. New York is the 'real world,' though it's also provincial. It thinks it's the *only* place in the world." "You have to be in New York to see what's up and so you are not repeating what another artist has done," said another successful artist. "This is as important as it is to see what's fashionable."

Because they take their coordinates from a cosmopolitan art world, successful artists do not seek to utilize SoHo as a local community or neighborhood milieu in which nearness confers the dominant sense of identification and responsibility. They express a preference for urban anonymity in contrast to the small-town visibility which many of them grew up with and escaped. As one successful artist explained, "Sometimes living in SoHo is too much community. I can't walk the dog in the morning without seeing eight people I know, and having to stop and talk. Sometimes on the way to the subway you want to say to someone, 'Fuck off, I've got to go.'"

Well-known artists view the pressures of propinquity as a burden. They express their status concerns as a realism which is incompatible with romanticizing SoHo as a residential community. Said a widely recognized painter,

> There definitely is a community down here. But there are disadvantages, too. It's noisy, the trucks start up at 5:30 A.M. It's dirty and full of rats. I once killed one with a pole in my loft. But I am always running into people I know. I know the chesse man, the gallery people. And it is good for the kid [his three-year-old son]. People here have similar affinities, problems, and interests.

Conclusion

Residents of SoHo participate in the overall status community of art through small social groups which have a characteristic pattern. These groups are occupationally based but socially centered and can usefully be termed "support networks" to emphasize their function as systems providing encouragement, stimulation, and mutual aid for individuals, who work essentially alone on the leading edges of artistic innovation. Where the status community includes all participants in the production, analysis, and consumption of art, the support network is a social unit composed largely of producers. The characteristics of these support networks include the following:

1. They are of small size, and the quality of the interaction among their participants is personal. The core of each network contains from three to twelve mutual friends. Lines of individuals, attached to the core as friends-of-friends, form a periphery of streamers, sometimes intersecting outside the core, and sometimes joined only at the core. It is this periphery that provides the unknown faces which appear at the larger parties and the gallery openings of network members and that supplies potential recruits who are occupationally qualified and personally compatible with the core.

2. They have an occupational basis. Most of the core members, with significant exceptions, are engaged in art utilizing the same medium—sculpture, dance, or video. In one case, a network of dancers shares a collective living and performing space in SoHo. Where network members are performance artists and work in ensemble, such as some dancers and musicians, they frequently work together. The majority of SoHo artists are painters and not performers, however, and do not work with others. The networks which include these artists are composed of those who are distinctly different in their approach to a common medium. Members seek to remain distinct and non-competitive in their

work, so as to lessen the tension of rivalry in what is intended to be a mutual support group. Artists who work alone may, however, cooperate in joint compositions from time to time. In doing so, they preserve their identity as individual contributors, as, for example, when an electronic composer works with a holographic sculptor and a dancer to create a work. Such cooperation may bring subgroupings of artists in different fields into the same network.

3. Each network member endorses the work of the others by attending their exhibitions, celebrating their receipts of grants and prizes, and sometimes by exchanging works of art. This endorsement connotes an evaluation which is positive and of roughly peer level, but which, in contrast to the evaluation which members make of the rest of the art market, is nonspecific. Network endorsement is not to be confused with critical diagnosis. Except in student circles, the network does not encourage analysis or pointed mutual evaluation of members' work. When one artist, perhaps in a midnight phone conversation, offers to tell another what is wrong with the other's work, a breach in network etiquette has been made and, unless repaired with tact, it results in an end to the close social interaction between the two. Artists are too closely identified with their work, too vulnerable to criticisms by dealers and critics, to gratefully suffer a dissection at the hands of friends. While the network provides encouragement and stimulation by example, it is also a retreat from an art world that is pervasively critical with a bewildering multiplicity of standards. Criticism from network peers, unless very carefully handled, tends to be taken as being ad hominem. When artists within a common network can no longer endorse one another's work, they socially disengage themselves. In a subculture where critical evaluation is constant, the network is a refuge of collective endorsement where mutual analysis is delicately tangential.

4. A fourth characteristic of networks is the rough parity of reputation among their members. In this respect, the support network can be seen as organizing on a personal basis the prestige stratification found in the wider status community of art. Because members are reputational peers, they can endorse the work of one another and identify with the successes of one another without sacrificing their occupational standards or their ambition. They are comfortable with one another because market-derived enmities and jealousies need not become devisive intrusions. In celebrating each other's victories, they celebrate their own past or future successes.

5. Members of support networks engage in a great deal of mutual aid. They trade information on job availability, sources of materials, housing, and important new work being done in the field. When in a position to do so, they nominate one another for artist-in-residence positions or for speaking engagements. They pass information on grants and

"grantsmanship" among each other and survey the art-world horizon for new ideas not only in their own medium but in other areas of art. Nonpeers are not occupationally situated to practice reciprocity in this aid, nor status situated to benefit from collective definitions of avant-garde boundaries.

6. A sixth characteristic of networks is that their cores frequently contain some individuals who are not occupationally qualified. These are the spouses, lovers, and friends of core members, who emphasize support, encouragement, and organizational assistance. Their critical commentary is valuable because it is presumed to be naive and unthreatening. The fact that they can participate in network activities indicates that sophisticated and rigorous criticism is muted in favor of social support.

By providing a large and varied population of artists in a relatively compact area, SoHo has aided in the development and elaboration of support networks among artists. While these networks differ from those of the French impressionists and the abstract expressionists in that they are not primarily vehicles of an artistic movement, they do provide the environment of protection and stimulation that encourages individual experimentation and achievement.[9]

7 The South Houston Industrial District in Transition

Growth Patterns and Land Use in the South Houston
Industrial District

During the 1700s the land that is now the SoHo district, bounded by Lafayette Street on the east, Houston Street to the north, West Broadway on the west, and Canal Street on the south,[1] was largely a portion of the Bayard family farm, which stretched over hills and meadows from Canal Street up to Bleeker Street.

During the Revolutionary War period, wooden palisades were built across the Bayard farm, and two forts were erected in 1776 on hills situated at the present site of Grand Street, marking the northern defensible limits of the city. The war left Nicholas Bayard, the farm's owner, financially devastated, and he soon after was forced to mortgage one hundred acres west of the unimproved wagon road that was to become Broadway. This tract of farm land, comprising most of what became the SoHo district, was subsequently laid out in streets and sold in lots.[2]

Development of the district as a part of the city was impeded during the eighteenth century by the presence of a swamp and stream near the present Canal Street. These emptied into a collect pond on the site of the present "Tombs" prison at 100 Center Street. As the city to the south' grew in population, the pond was made increasingly pestilent with dead animals, the refuse of slaughterhouses and tanneries. After more than a decade of dispute about the best method of reclaiming the pond and

111

swampy area, a channel was dug along the present Canal Street, the pond filled by leveling some of the hills near the present Greene and Broome streets, and for the first time an adequate stone bridge was built at Broadway connecting the district with the city. In 1802 the city corporation surveyed and set an official grade for Broadway from the Canal Street bridge up to Prince Street. By 1809 Broadway had been paved through what is now SoHo and on up to Astor Place.

Development of the area for middle-class residence then began. Broadway was made forty feet wide, laid with sidewalks of stone, and lined with poplar trees. New York officials called it "the pride of our city." Until midcentury this avenue was the chosen promenade for the city's well-dressed. Construction of handsome residences proceeded until the War of 1812, which disrupted construction in the city and caused a temporary mercantile depression. But by 1820, with the general economic recovery, Broadway from Broome Street to Astor Place had become once again the fashionable residential area for the merchant classes. Houses "of a superior description" were occupied by well-known and prosperous residents of the city, including James Fenimore Cooper, members of the Astor family, and the postrevolutionary minister of France to the United States, Citizen Genêt. Speculators in real estate, capitalizing on the fact that much of the city's housing stock had been burned during the Revolution, accelerated the northern growth of the city far in excess of real population pressures.[3]

The streets behind the Broadway frontage, many named for revolutionary war generals such as Greene, Wooster, and Mercer, rapidly filled with more modest occupants. A portion of one block of wood-frame houses survives from this period along Spring Street near West Broadway, including the oldest house in the SoHo district, number 107, which was built by a shoemaker in 1806. If these houses were at all typical of the period, they would have been run as boarding establishments by their owners. At the time such an arrangement provided the main source of lodging for even the middle class in the city.[4] In 1803 the district was first included as a part of the city and designated the Eighth Ward. Its boundaries were set at Canal Street, Broadway, Houston Street, and the Hudson, or "North," River. By 1825 the Eighth Ward contained 24,285 residents in a city of 166,000 people, making it the most populous ward in all of New York.[5]

This first residential period in the history of the district lasted until the 1860s, by which time the wealthy had moved north to Fifth Avenue above Thirtieth Street, where A. T. Steward, the dry goods merchant, was building a two-million-dollar home. During the decade of the 1850s, a wave of new construction turned Broadway from a street of elegant houses and small brick shops into "a boulevard of marble, cast iron and brownstone commercial palazzos."[6] At midcentury Broadway was the city's central business district and boasted the finest shopping. Lord & Taylor, Arnold Constable & Co., Tiffany & Co., and E. V. Haughwout had large stores in the district and conducted both retail and wholesale businesses. (Haughwout's building still stands at Broadway and Grand Street, and a wholesale textile firm conducts business there behind the rusted facade and dirty windows. The older era is still visible in the magnificence of the processional columns and deep relief of the windows of the building, a cast-iron version of a Venetian Renaissance palace constructed in 1857 by Haughwout to display his cut glass, silverware, clocks, and chandeliers.[7]) A traveler who visited the city in 1853 found its stores and hotels along Broadway "more like the palaces of kings than places for the transaction of business." The St. Nicholas Hotel between Broome and Spring Streets, which opened in 1853 to serve commercial travelers, was described as "perhaps the largest hotel in the world, and certainly the most comfortable." Its 600 rooms accommodated 1000 guests, who were waited upon by 322 servants.[8] Elaborate construction by the city's leading merchants and hotel keepers made the district less attractive to middle-class residents, and an exodus began. One fourth of the population, 10,000 people, left the Eighth Ward between 1860 and 1865.[9]

As the nation's most active port, New York City had become the center of wholesaling activity in the United States by the middle of the nineteenth century. New York merchants profited over their rivals in Boston and Philadelphia when the British, after the War of 1812, dumped an accumulation of unsold woolens, cloth, hardware, and cutlery at auction there. With the completion of the Erie Canal in 1825 the city became the primary terminal for western agricultural markets. In 1851 the Erie and Hudson River railroads were finished, giving New York the first continuous rail connections west, ahead of either Baltimore or Philadelphia.

Within the city, the SoHo district was the prime location for the establishment of wholesaling operations. The district was near the South Street docks, where information about arriving cargo was first circulated, and near the Pearl Street markets where the cargo was auctioned off. Wholesaling activity in the district accelerated the departure of its residents.

By midcentury, the traditional business practice required wholesalers to entertain their out-of-town buyers, many of whom came by sea from the southern states to sell cotton and buy provisions for their plantations. A new innovation, the business expense account, had come into use for business entertainment purposes. Buyers stayed in the major hotels of the district and visited the theaters and music halls which made the mile between Canal Street and Houston Street on Broadway "the entertainment center of the city."[10] According to the commentator

Jacob Knickerbocker, "When [customers] come to New York to purchase, most of them also expected to have a good time and looked to the salesmen to provide it for them."[11] The "amenities" serving the wholesale district included a notorious red-light trade in the houses off Broadway in nearly every street in the present SoHo area. Publishers printed guidebooks to the area's brothels for commercial travelers.[12] The transformation of the area into a red-light district was further incentive for the remaining families to move out.

During this same period, the area to the east of the district was filling with immigrants who crowded into tenements and constituted a ready supply of manufacturing labor. The Seventeenth Ward on the Lower East Side of Manhattan, a place of concentrated immigrant settlement, had a population of 72,000 by 1860. The population of all New York had increased to 700,000, more than four times greater than it was in 1825.[13]

Structural Ecology

Manufacturers rapidly took over the district in a boom of industrial construction which began in the early 1870s and lasted about fifteen years, during which the structures which presently characterize the district were built. The theaters, hotels, and retailers moved north like the middle-class residents before them. The old brick and frame houses were razed, and manufacturing buildings were constructed for iron foundries, metal shops, glass manufacturers, piano makers, and tobacco processors. These manufacturers both produced and sold their products under one roof. Buyers were shown inventories on the first floor while manufacturing proceeded on the floors above. By the 1890s, textiles, clothing, and printing predominated among the district's firms.

The district continued to be favored by its location. Goods and materials were easily transported to and from the Hudson River docks, and the tenement neighborhoods on the Lower East Side of Manhattan supplied a cheap labor pool within walking distance. The manufacturers of women's garments, in particular, depended upon the availability of immigrant women workers, a reliance which has continued up to the present time.[14]

In addition to the availability of labor and the ease of shipping, innovations in building techniques and materials played a role in the rapid conversion of the district into a manufacturing zone. In the late 1840s James Bogardus had established a factory below Canal Street to make cast-iron building components, ushering in a superior construction method that soon was widely applied in the district. Manufacturers wanted maximum natural light in a gas-lit era, both for the display of their products and for their production. The superior compression strength of the new cast-iron components allowed the walls at the front and rear of factories to be opened up with large windows. Cast-iron columns enabled floor loads to be increased. Because mold carvers could make cast iron as decorative as clients desired, it soon became the preferred facade for the factories which doubled and dressed as showrooms. Manufacturers at first erected eclectic versions of Italian Renaissance designs, later switching to copies of French Second Empire architecture. The architecture reflected the aristocratic pretensions of merchants and factory owners, who were willing to bear the expenses of an appropriate symbolism. The iron was "cast and painted to imitate expensive stone columns, arched windows, and ornamentation; every effort was made to deceive the beholder into thinking the iron fronts were made of stone."[15]

The capacity for useful longevity in these buildings, many of which are now more than 100 years old and still functioning as factories, can be attributed to the strength of their cast-iron and brick bearing-wall construction. The buildings are not large; most are 25-by-100 feet and reaching only five to seven stories. The brick bearing-walls on the long sides of these buildings are 3 to 4 feet thick at their bases and are set on stone foundations.[16] For a period lasting well into the twentieth century, these buildings were maintained to the standards of their construction, that is, as prestige symbols. "The objects of great pride to their owners, [these buildings] . . . were well kept and were painted frequently."[17]

Cast-iron building material allowed strong and serviceable buildings to be constructed at lower costs than had previously been possible because foundries were able to replicate castings of modules from the one set of molds and create entire building facades from a small number of components. This was rudimentary mass production. Clients were able to select designs already on hand from a catalogue and choose the window modules and interior columns which pleased them. The facades were preassembled at the factories, the parts fitted and numbered, then moved on heavy wagons to the site and erected in a matter of a few days. Iron buildings made in New York foundries were shipped as far as San Francisco. This was "prefabrication of a high order, a valuable addition to American construction technique."[18]

Manufacturing Decline

So favorable was the district's location for manufacturing, and so advantageous were the new building methods, that nearly the entire district was rebuilt during the last quarter of the nineteenth century. However, after the turn of the century, new developments in the transportation of both goods and the labor force worked against the district.

By the early 1900s New York had elevated steam railways in operation, and subways were being dug. The slow, horsedrawn car that had limited the mobility of the work force was replaced. Workers began to move further away from the district to uptown locations, to Brooklyn and the Bronx, and to commute to jobs in various sections of the city. Even more decisive for the decline of the district as a first-rate manufacturing and wholesaling area was its desertion by the buyers. In 1910 the Pennsylvania Railroad built a terminal for its passenger lines at Seventh Avenue and Thirty-fourth Street. Buyers, now coming by rail rather than by boat, stayed in the midtown area of the terminal. Following their customers, the wholesale garment and fur showrooms left Lower Manhattan and moved to newer lofts near the terminal. A hotel and entertainment industry grew up nearby. "This [railroad terminal] was a magnet which began to draw the showrooms, one by one, from their downtown locations." [19]

A survey of manufacturing in Manhattan conducted by regional planners in 1928 revealed that the South Houston area was in a marked decline. The district's dominant position in printing, for example, had passed to an area around Thirty-fourth Street. The number of plants in the South Houston District declined, and those remaining were small shops employing on average only ten workers or less. [20] The decline was due to the growth pattern of the city; the law firms, financial houses, and central offices to which the printing firms were linked had largely left the city hall area for the new midtown business center. [21] In the apparel business, the pattern was the same. In 1900 the district had been the center of women's garment manufacturing in both the city and the nation. By 1922 the majority of these firms had moved to an area between Twenty-third and Thirty-fourth Streets from Fifth to Seventh Avenues. [22] Fur wholesalers, who in 1900 had been concentrated almost totally in the district between West Broadway and the Bowery below Houston Street, had moved as a body to new buildings around Twenty-eighth Street and Seventh Avenue by 1922. [23] The furriers, like the fashion-conscious segment of the garment industry, settled into the Pennsylvania Station area because of its commercially advantageous location.

The newer buildings above Fourteenth Street were superior to the cast-iron structures below Houston Street. Most were built after 1890 and used a newly developed steel-frame construction which permitted greater floor areas, more stories, and increased fireproofing qualities. [24] These newer buildings are still in demand by manufacturers and have consistently supported a higher rent level than the smaller cast-iron buildings.

World War II brought peak utilization back to the South Houston District for as long as war production lasted, but in the postwar period manufacturing declined rapidly both in Manhattan and in New York City as a whole. The region around the Manhattan core was now easily reached by trucks traveling on new arterial highways, and it was much cheaper to build on the outlying land than downtown. Manufacturers, however, cited the outmoded structures in the older manufacturing areas of New York, Philadelphia, and Boston as their most compelling reason to relocate to the urban fringe. Large, low plants that could take full advantage of mechanical material-handling required tracts of land available only on the outer rings of metropolitan regions. The most competitive plants were very large, one-story buildings which could incorporate the new continuous material flow-systems. Mechanization, the key to the competitive advantage, had raised the average floor area per employee from 1,140 square feet in 1922 to 4,550 square feet in 1945.[25] The buildings in the South Houston District had become too small. Their material flow-lines were strangled at elevator points and by the complete absence of off-street truck docks. While suburban plants were accommodating block-long, continuous-bake ovens and huge rotary presses, firms in the South Houston District were finding that even forklift trucks were too large for use in thirty-foot-wide structures and eight-by-eight-foot elevators. The district came to depend upon low-profit firms which could survive with labor-intensive procedures.

After fifty years as a prime manufacturing district, it was apparent as early as the 1928 economic survey that South Houston had been downgraded to a secondary industrial area. Many of the firms were subcontractors, mainly in the garment and textile trades, who handled seasonal orders and overflow from midtown manufacturers. Doing business in the district had become dependent upon cheap rents which cushioned firms through slow periods. Nevertheless, while some firms were short-lived, others were nurtured in this environment of obsolete but readily available structures. The area was described as performing a "nursery" function for fledgling industries, even prior to 1930[26]—a role it has maintained to the present.

A survey of the district in 1962 found that the largest manufacturing group continued to be firms producing textiles and inexpensive apparel. The output of these firms was not the fashion-influenced clothing of the Seventh Avenue manufacturers, but rather "women's and children's underwear, blouses, skirts, and sportswear of standard design."[27] For about the last forty years, the district has been characterized as a location where low-priced merchandise is manufactured under congested and inefficient conditions.

A survey undertaken by the Planning Commission in 1970 revealed that industry had largely abandoned the smaller buildings with less than 3,600 square feet per floor and had been replaced by artists. Industry now occupied only 73 percent of the lofts in the district, compared to

94 percent eight years earlier. While manufacturing still showed some strength, having lost only 5 percent of its employees since 1962, wholesaling and retailing businesses had lost 37.4 percent of their workers.[28]

From 1,000 to 2,000 artists were found to be living in the district, having converted the smaller lofts into joint working studios and living spaces. Artists lived in 660 lofts in the twenty blocks surveyed, 86 percent of them in buildings with less than 3,600 square feet per floor. Still, the artist influx was not sufficient to counter the retreat of industry. A vacancy rate of 7 percent existed in the district, and 16 percent of the smaller buildings had vacant floors. Buildings larger than 3,600 square feet retained industrial vitality; while they constituted only 36 percent of the total buildings in SoHo, they contained 84 percent of the area's employees.

By 1970 a clear pattern had emerged. The smaller buildings with the least operational efficiency for industry were being vacated rapidly. Their occupants had been the least profitable firms in the district, engaged in such activities as the storage and distribution of used cartons or rag bailing. Landlords were discovering that the only tenants available to replace the departed industries were artists.

Artist and Industry: Recycling Lofts

The political turmoil that began in Europe in the 1930s stimulated an exodus of artists, dealers, and collectors to the United States. Their concentration in New York established the foundations which made this city the postwar successor to Paris as an international art center. The first school of the modern art in the United States was set up in New York in 1932 by Hans Hofmann, a teacher of considerable reputation who had emigrated from Munich two years before. It was to become an important influence on the first internationally recognized generation of American artists, a group which emerged in New York City in the 1940s. By 1939 the European surrealists had arrived in the city. They helped to make the Lower East Side of Manhattan a center for American artists arriving from around the country. Museums and galleries further stimulated the development of New York as an art center. The Museum of Modern Art, founded in 1929, and the Museum of Non-Objective Painting (now the Solomon R. Guggenheim Museum) brought the European surrealists to the public's attention. Peggy Guggenheim's Art of This Century Gallery exhibited the Europeans along side the young American artists during the war years.[29]

American economic and political domination in the world after the war reinforced the position of New York as a focus of the international art market. Two-thirds of America's better known artists were estimated to be living in New York by the 1960s.[30] The city's institutional facilities for studying art and for making a living in the fine and commercial art fields are still unequaled in the rest of the country.

Studio Space

Large numbers of students and young art-school graduates, attracted by this opportunity, arrived in New York in the 1950s and 1960s only to discover a serious obstacle to the pursuit of their careers. Adequate work space for artists was extremely hard to find. This was especially true in Manhattan, where the fine- and commercial-art institutions were concentrated, where the artist subculture thrived, and where new arrivals wanted to live.

If an artist from the Midwest expected to find the classic studio in New York—high ceilings, enlarged windows with a northern exposure, a corner fitted out for sleeping and cooking—he was bound to be disappointed. Such studios, once a feature of areas like Greenwich Village, had become "an insignificant contribution to artist housing."[31] None had been built for fifty years. As early as the 1920s, studios were regularly being demolished to make way for a more intensive rebuilding of the Village. They were replaced by one room efficiency apartments. Village realtors, anxious to suggest a bohemian milieu to their clientele of business and professional people, had taken to calling efficiency apartments "studios."[32] Remodeling and rebuilding in the Village continued in the intervening years and additional work studios were subdivided or demolished.[33]

Out of economic necessity, many artists tried to make the "old-law" tenement apartments that were built prior to building-code restrictions serve as work studios. The availability of these, the cheapest tenement apartments, accounted for the residency of many artists in areas such as Manhattan's Lower East Side. But halls and staircases were hardly more than shoulder width in these buildings, and rooms were often as small as six feet across. It was impossible to work on anything close to the large scale that was becoming popular in the 1950s. An artist could not get a large piece up the stairs, let alone have the space to step back from it and view it properly while working.

Outside Manhattan, individual houses were available for rent or sale, but even those artists with the money to occupy a suburban house did not want to live or work outside the artist subculture and its Manhattan focus. An examination of the Artist Tenants Association records for 1963 revealed that of the 662 New York artists on the mailing list, 620 lived in Manhattan.[34]

Life Amid Industry

During the middle of the 1950s, an increasing number of artists began working and living in manufacturing lofts. These lofts, even those in the smallest and oldest buildings, were huge by comparison with the working spaces of the tenements. They usually had at least twenty-five hundred square feet of unpartitioned floor space, far more than a middle-class house or a luxury apartment. Up to the mid 1960s, such lofts could be rented for $90 a month and less, the bottom of the commercial rent scale.

The lofts were large, but they were spartan in the extreme. Their only fixtures were toilets and cold-water lavatory sinks. If heat was provided, it was according to the terms of a commercial lease, that is, only during business hours and only on weekdays. Artists had the immediate necessity of having to invest money and months of their own labor, to improvise hot water systems, rig heating systems, and build sleeping and kitchen facilities. They could not even begin these tasks until after they had cleared out the decades' accumulation of broken machinery, textile or leather scraps, clots of spilled paint, and families of well-established rats.

By trial and error, artists learned how and why to vent plumbing, how to bend rigid conduit for electrical lines, and how to build partitions and storage closets. There was never money to hire licensed plumbers or contractors, and artists were not in the legal or financial position to file plans for building alterations. But as some artists discovered they were good craftsmen, a good deal of help began to be freely exchanged. Fortunately, the renovation standards of this first generation of loft dwellers ran little beyond the luxury of a working toilet, a gas connection to the stove, and electric lights. For years, many artists lived in lofts where their bath and dishwater was heated on the stove.

These early artists were a tiny residential minority, surrounded by industry, living in a district that did not reflect their existence in any way. When they opened the metal fire shutters on their alley windows in the summer, they looked directly in on the factories. Women, stripped to their underwear in the summer heat, could be seen gluing wigs on a procession of children's dolls. A floor below, workers would be removing artificial fruit from glazing ovens while milliners at long tables sewed the fruit onto hats.

The streets were nearly impassable. Trucks were obliged to load and unload at the curb and, when the curbs were filled, in the middle of the narrow streets. No off-street truck docks existed. Bales, cartons, and garment racks blocked the sidewalks in front of building entrances, and pedestrians were forced into the street to pick their way through the stalled traffic.

At night the district emptied almost completely, and an artist walking home on the deserted streets experienced a liberating anonymity. Even at night, however, the rules of the industrial district had to be observed. A Volkswagen bus left by an artist at a curb claimed by the all-night bakery would be found in the morning rolled into an intersection with its tires slashed. Some artists went onto a night schedule in order to avoid the noise of the industrial day. Working at a drawing table, they could hear the small sounds of rats scratching on the tin ceilings for scraps from workers' lunches. Looking down from their windows, artists could see police sleeping in their patrol cars, and garbage trucks from the sanitation station on Spring Street lined up, their drivers dozing or sipping coffee. As a poet living on Wooster Street in this period said: "In the beginning we would wave hello to the cops from our window. We knew ten or twenty. But later our paranoia took over and we hung black canvas curtains. We were living illegally." At night the district lapsed into nearly complete anonymity.

The Culture of Illegal Residence

The major drawback to the use of a manufacturing loft for both living and working was its illegality. Factory buildings had manufacturing or commercial certificates of occupancy, and the building owners could be cited with a violation and fined if the city discovered residents in their buildings. The building owners themselves were seldom fooled into believing that artists were not making residential use of their lofts. Artists, rebuffed by realty firms, usually rented directly from owners. A survey of the South Houston District showed that 40 percent of all the buildings had an owner on the premises during the day in 1962.[35] These buildings had been purchased by the resident business firms as protection against eviction or higher rents. Businesses often did not require all the space they owned, and leased out the upper floors. As the level of business activity declined in the district, it was these upper floors of owner-occupied buildings that fell vacant, and which artists sought to rent.

Owners on the premises knew the habits of their tenants. They tolerated illegal living, feigning ignorance, because it gave them an advantage. It meant that the artist, having signed a commercial and not a residential lease, could at any time be considered in violation of his tenancy agreement. If an owner needed a floor for his own business expansion, for a more desirable tenant, or wished to turn over a completely vacated building to a new owner to get a better price, the artist could be summarily evicted.

Renting to a residential artist gave the owner greater control of his building, and it did not add significantly to his troubles with the city.

Doing business in old loft districts required so many departures from the building code that an accommodation existed between owners and city inspectors. The worst violations such as fire hazards were corrected, and other building code departures were ignored. Building inspections were not routine, but "largely depend upon complaints or referrals."[36] Half of all plumbing jobs done in the city are estimated to be performed by less expensive unlicensed plumbers, work annually worth from $24-million to $40-million.[37] The economics of maintaining old loft buildings, even for manufacturing, made owners especially dependent upon unlicensed craftsmen to fix heating, sprinkler, and water systems. Owners learned to cope with the inspectors by hiring workers who had themselves "rented" the credentials of a licensed plumber or electrician who signed for the job. Building inspectors informally "licensed" this arrangement by imposing a fee of their own which was negotiated with the craftsman loaning the license. Explaining the system, one plumber said,

> The inspector will only take and discuss money with a plumber with whom he's worked before. Both have to have a license and a job to lose. He'll prefer to overlook what would be a violation, rather than to certify new, poorly done, unlicensed work. Then he'd have more of an out if there was any trouble. He just didn't see anything. But the work has to look good. We all assume offices and phones at the Department [of Buildings] are tapped by the City Office of Investigations.

The rate of the bribe paid to an inspector was tied to the fee paid for borrowing the credentials of the licensed plumber, but both were fairly well standardized so that the building owner still got the work done at a substantial saving.

Inspectors from the city tried to bring the new artist occupants under the terms of the prevailing arrangement. "Inspectors were always looking to get paid off," said one early South Houston District resident. "They would look around and say, 'I have a brother-in-law that can plaster around those columns.' [Exposed cast iron was in some cases considered a violation.] Inspectors would come and fish—'You need metal shutters,' they'd say." Having established the need for and cost of a repair, the inspectors would generally settle for a small bribe from artists. The artists' problems were compounded because there were several inspection agencies—building inspectors, plumbing inspectors, and fire inspectors. Although it placed them in even greater danger of eviction, many artists illegally tampered with their gas or electric lines. In order to afford to heat a drafty loft during the winter, some artists reversed the connections to their gas meters periodically, running the dials backwards. Self-taught artist electricians were always willing to help a fellow artist reroute cables around the electric meter, especially after Con Edison had turned off service for the nonpayment of a bill.

Poor artists accommodated to loft living by maintaining a low profile. They deliberately let the soot accumulate on the windows facing the street or hung black canvas to prevent the escape of telltale light at night. They did not put their names in lobbies, and left their door bells in disrepair. Between 8 A.M. and 5 P.M., the working hours of Con Edison and city inspectors, they were not at home to anyone who unexpectedly knocked at their doors.

Often an artist took elaborate steps to hide the signs of residency and loft improvements from the landlord who might notice how livable the space had become and demand more rent under the threat of eviction. "I had boxes of things, clothes, my bed, all rigged with pullies so they could be hauled away up out of sight," said one artist. Corners made into kitchens were secreted behind rough partitions that appeared to be canvas storage racks.

Underground living accentuated the sense of separation which artists felt between their own subculture and the rest of society. Even after several years in a loft, artists felt like transients. The most mundane aspects of daily life could assume dramatic significance which, while a burden, also reassured the artist that he had not compromised his unique vision for the comforts of social integration. "Getting rid of the garbage was an illegal act in itself," explained one artist. [The district, officially without residents, had no municipal garbage pickup.] "You would do it very late at night, walking to a pile [awaiting a commercial carter] put out by a factory. Once, the police followed me for several blocks, and I had to return home with my garbage."

The artist subculture operated in the interstices of industrial activity. Visitors came after dark, yelling up from the street to a fourth- or fifth-floor window. The occupant would wrap the door key in a paper bag and drop it down. The visitors would climb onto a loading dock and disappear into an unlit commercial lobby. All outward signs of residency would cease.

Artists Find a Political Voice

In 1960 a fire broke out in a South Houston building totally occupied by industry. Firemen fighting the blaze fell to their deaths through a shaft that was not clearly marked. After that, the Fire Department initiated a citywide inspection of loft buildings for fire hazards, referring other violations they spotted to the appropriate city agency. While artists were never cited as responsible for this or any other loft fire,[38] they were caught by surprise in the new city campaign. "I lived on 28th Street," said one painter. "One day I came home and found a padlock on the door. It was the Fire Department. They said the building was a fire hazard, and I couldn't even enter to get my things."

The Artists Tenants Association was founded at this time as an ad hoc group that tried to secure some official rights for artists living in loft buildings. The ATA, as it was known, estimated that a thousand artists were harassed after the South Houston fire. Many of these joined the organization, along with other artists whose landlords had evicted them for other reasons. Artists were evicted from an old furrier building on Forty-fifth Street, for example, because their landlord was selling the building to developers of a trucking garage.

The leadership of the ATA contained artists who had some understanding of and connections with the political bureaucracy of the city. One leading figure had worked on programs of the Department of Parks, Recreation, and Cultural Affairs and had access to members of staff in the office of the commissioner of Cultural Affairs. The ATA did not organize around a neighborhood base, but was a citywide organization. Their Committee for Artists Housing drew members from the liberal community of lawyers and civic activists, many of whom lived in Greenwich Village and who identified with the artist subculture. The object of the ATA campaign was to put pressure on Mayor Robert Wagner. They enlisted considerable support, including that of the press, and at one point threatened an artists' boycott of New York's galleries and art museums.

Victories and Defeats

After many meetings between the ATA and the mayor's staff, and with representatives of the fire and buildings departments, the mayor intervened and an agreement was reached in August 1961. Artists were to be allowed to occupy commercial buildings, provided the buildings had adequate means of egress and that no more than two units for artist-living existed per building. This agreement became known as the A.I.R. program, standing for Artists In Residency. Participant artists had to notify the Buildings Department, which would send an inspector to see that the residence complied with all city regulations. Artists could then mount a sign at the building entrance informing the Fire Department that, in case of fire, an artist lived on a specific floor.

The amicability between the city and loft-dwelling artists did not endure, however; most artists, the ATA found, were not registering their occupancy with the Buildings Department. On consideration, they preferred their illegal status to disclosure of their addresses and forced cooperation with city inspectors. They remained skeptical of the city's efforts to aid the artists search for housing and chose anonymity over trust in the vagaries of city policy.

The artists who clung to their underground way of life proved to be prudent. By December 1963, the city had begun to refuse A.I.R. applications on the basis of new zoning maps. Ruth Richards, an ATA official, explained, "We didn't know that M1 [light manufacturing] and C8 [dense commercial] districts were out of bounds for artist occupancy." The ATA estimated that a third of New York's artists lived in M1 zones in Chelsea, the West Village, and Lower Manhattan and could be dispossessed. "The A.I.R. program was a fiasco," said Richards.[39] Artists felt that the city had acted in bad faith and that the threats of a fresh wave of evictions constituted a betrayal of New York's artist community.

From December 1963 to April 1964, the ATA coordinated a fresh campaign to gain support for artist housing in manufacturing areas. They mailed pleas to thousands of New Yorkers, purchased advertisements in newspapers, and stuck posters on walls and subways. They were able to secure the support of Councilman Paul O'Dwyer, and met with City Planning Commission Chairman William F. Ballard, Buildings Commissioner Birns, and Acting City Administrator Maxwell Lehman.[40]

The ATA persuaded the major museums and commercial galleries to take, for the first time, a public position in support of the housing campaign of artists. This institutional support allowed the artists to dramatize the economic importance of art to the New York City economy and public life. The tactical alternative, a boycott of museums and galleries, would have been a burden shouldered by only the minority of the city's artists who had exhibition schedules and was rejected as ineffectual and divisive.

On April 3, 1964, the ATA coalition demonstrated its strength. Close to ninety commercial galleries closed for the day in sympathy. Representatives of the Museum of Modern Art and the Guggenheim Museum joined with ATA representatives in meetings with officials from the Planning Commission and the mayor's office. At the same time, a thousand artists picketed city hall, receiving extensive television and press coverage, demanding an end to the eviction of artists from lofts in manufacturing zones.

During the same month, the artists coalition succeeded in persuading the New York State Legislature to amend the multiple-dwelling laws to allow artists to live and work in commercial or manufacturing buildings in "any city of more than one million persons," the code name for New York City. State multiple-dwelling laws govern physical requirements for buildings throughout the state and had to be made compatible with local city-zoning resolutions allowing artist residency, which the artist housing coalition was seeking to have passed.

The victory at the state level was symbolically important, but substantially flawed. On the positive side, the language of the amendment, Article 7-B, recognized artists as an "enhancement" to urban life who

deserved special housing provisions: Artists find it "particularly difficult...to obtain the use of the amounts of space required for their
work" due to high rental costs and the low incomes characteristic of the
arts, conditions which "threaten to lead to an exodus of persons regularly engaged in the visual fine arts from such cities, to the detriment
of the cultural life thereof and of the state." On the negative side, Article
7-B discouraged landlords from renting to artists because it imposed
stringent fire proofing provisions and prohibited manufacturers and artists from sharing the same building (Section 277). In the ensuing years, the
ATA found that most landlords would not and could not upgrade their
buildings to satisfy the provisions of the multiple-dwelling laws that
applied to artist residence. In response, artists simply put up A.I.R.
signs to warn firemen, but did not tell the Buildings Department in order
to prevent a visit by a city inspector. Fear of sweeps by the Buildings
Department had abated, and by the end of 1964 illegal living resumed as
before.

Not having presented their claims in terms of limited territorial demands, the ATA found they could not move the Wagner administration
to allow artists to occupy vacant lofts in all areas zoned for manufacturing. Negotiations collapsed after the city refused to accept the findings of an ATA survey that showed that 28 percent of New York's
artists already lived and worked in manufacturing zones.[41] "No one in
any official capacity [in city government] was on our side, and that was
our missing ingredient," explained Ruth Richards, an ATA leader.[42]

Conclusion

The place of the artist in the space of the city can be understood if the
making of art is recognized as one in a succession of manufacturing
activities which the economy, the physical structure, and the governmental policies of the city support or retard. Art production, however, is
an uneconomical and therefore a weak competitor for urban space. It
must rely on an availability of outmoded but sound structures—the un-
expended capitalization of previous manufacturers who require newer
structures more suited to competitive technology. The availability of
buildings adaptable for artists' purposes at a time when political and
financial changes had shifted the marketing of art to New York City
made it possible for the number of the city's artists to increase rapidly.

Insofar as urban zoning patterns reflect the distribution of entrenched
economic interests, and to the extent that urban planning initiatives seek
to rationalize the use of space along the lines of increased efficiency, the
recycling of outmoded buildings so as to support emergent and noncom-
petitive uses such as art production is an unanticipated process. It de-

pends upon a lack of effective planning and a corruption of zoning enforcement. The conversion of factories into studio use in New York depended upon a political and economic climate in which local ad hoc adaptations of space were possible.

From the end of World War II to the mid-1960s, the New York artist community was a cosmopolitan status community, structured around formal organizations, a set of occupational values, and informal social networks; it was not a territorial community. As artists took over outmoded lofts spaces in manufacturing buildings, they assumed a common interest in the political as well as economic availability of such structures, and out of a perception of their shared vulnerability they established a protest organization. The art producers pressured the formal art organizations and the art public into, for the first time, taking an advocacy role in the interests of artists.

The beginnings of formal organization of the art community around the political pursuit of their needs for working space set the community in motion as another urban interest group. These first organizing efforts accomplished one important goal; it made artists aware that they had to compensate for their economic precariousness with governmental protections if they were to hold on to their spatial niche in the city, and that government protection was only to be achieved through pressure from the institutional art world and the wider art audience. Artists could not come to terms with the city government, however, because they continued to act as a spatially diffuse status community. Their program was coextensive with the scattered pattern of artist housing which existed. Had they claimed a specific share of the space in the least viable "commercial slum" areas like the South Houston Industrial District, they would have been able to ask for more limited but less grudging concessions from the city government.

8 SoHo and the Politics of Urban Planning

The Vortex of Lower Manhattan Development

In the early 1950s the Lower Manhattan office complex found itself declining relative to the Midtown area. In an office technology of air conditioning and artificial light, financial and commercial operations could be more rationally and competitively organized on the large floor areas available only in modern office structures.[1] But those in the financial district were old and built to a scale of narrow streets and small blocks laid out in the nineteenth and even the eighteenth century. The Chase Manhattan Bank, leader among the downtown financial institutions, faced a choice of either moving its operations uptown or constructing not only new downtown space for itself but promoting the reconstruction of the entire area to provide for the interdependent community of financial institutions upon which it relied. In 1955 Chase announced its decision to invest $120 million in a new headquarters downtown, and the following year it led in the establishment of a district chamber of commerce, the Downtown–Lower Manhattan Association. The purpose of the DLMA was to coordinate area-wide redevelopment and to act as the collective negotiating agency with the various levels of government whose cooperation would be essential.

In 1957 and again in 1958 the DLMA sponsored planning studies which became the basis for the subsequent transformation of the district.[2] In 1965 the City Planning Commission endorsed the direction of these plans in its own study, the Lower Manhattan Plan.[3] The essence of these plans was a conversion of Lower Manhattan from a mixed-use area—with its then declining commercial waterfront, its food marketing and distribution facilities, and its several specialized manufacturing districts—into, essentially, a base for national corporate and financial expansion. Loft buildings were to be demolished to make way for commercial offices. Streets were to be widened or closed to allow developers to create large blocks. The piers were to be replaced by landfill on which housing for the area's white-collar workers was to be built. These new residents were expected to create a demand for the retail services, the shops and restaurants, that would transform the area into a pleasant corporate location, active twenty-four hours a day.

Working in close and complex collaboration with all levels of government and interested public agencies, the financial community, led by Chase's head, David Rockefeller, realized much of its plan. The role of the Department of City Planning in this redevelopment was to act as a facilitator, offering cooperative zoning innovations and the planning aid of its staff.[4] More importantly, it gave legitimacy to the plan by setting it in a context of city-wide public-interest needs. In a persuasive and visually spectacular six volume *Plan for New York City* issued in 1969, the City Planning Commission incorporated the DLMA's goals into a comprehensive city plan. At its heart was the concept of Manhattan as a national corporate center to be achieved through the close cooperation of business and government.

> In 1955 the Chase Manhattan Bank announced its decision to build a 60-story building in Lower Manhattan—this was the turning point. Shortly thereafter, the City showed that it was prepared to back private investment with public monies for projects such as the new Civic Center, the Brooklyn Bridge Southwest urban renewal area and relocation of the Washington Market. The Port of New York Authority is spending almost $600 million on the World Trade Center. The City, State and Federal governments have committed over $47 million to urban renewal projects in the area and well over $200 million will be spent for new government buildings by the early 1970's.[5]

The Plan for the City of New York did not indicate an equal concern for the manufacturing segment of the city's economy at whose expense the corporate segment was to be publicly nurtured. The manufacturing picture was grim. In 1947 there was a peak of 1,122,000 factory jobs in New York City. By 1976 there were only 543,000 such jobs remaining.[6] For sixteen consecutive years during this period the number of factory jobs declined. Lower Manhattan redevelopment accelerated this trend. By 1976, 46 percent of the manufacturing jobs present in Manhattan in 1958 were gone.[7] Demolition of loft buildings was one reason. Nine million square feet of loft space—some 600 buildings—were lost to de-

molition in Manhattan in the period from 1959 to 1962 alone, when the
construction boom in office space had only begun.[8] That figure alone
was 5 percent of Manhattan's loft space, and lofts in areas such as the
"leather swamp" south of the Brooklyn Bridge and the luggage and
electronics district on the site of the planned World Trade Center were
yet to be demolished.

The "valley" area of low loft buildings above Canal Street, the northern boundary of Lower Manhattan redevelopment, was drawn into the
fringe of the vortex. It was reserved in the 1969 *Plan for New York City*
as a temporary refuge into which manufacturers could flee as their
buildings to the south were razed. But they had to expect to move again.

> Inevitably white-collar activities and housing are going to supplant
> manufacturing in this area, and in some other industrial areas of Man-
> hattan as well. The problem is to pave the way without losing blue-
> collar jobs. In time, the industrial renewal program will provide re-
> developed land elsewhere which can be used to rehouse Manhattan
> firms. A long-range program must be developed, however, if the re-
> location is to work.[9]

The recycling of old buildings for new uses had no place in the plan for
a Manhattan of corporate headquarters and walk-to-work housing for
their staff. The efforts to site plants in the other boroughs, an after-
thought to the Lower Manhattan Plan, were insufficient to have an impact on manufacturing job losses in the city.[10]

A Planner's Reprieve for a "Commercial Slum"

The SoHo area was available to serve as a shock absorber for the
disruption to manufacturing caused by the Lower Manhattan Plan because in 1963 the City Planning Commission had saved the area from
immediate demolition. At this time private civic groups, unrelated to the
coalition behind Lower Manhattan redevelopment, considered the SoHo
district and others like to to be lying needlessly fallow and advocated
intensive redevelopment for housing. In the early 1960s these groups
began a publicity campaign to pressure the City Planning Commission
into clearing the district and turning it over to developers. One such
group, MICOVE, claimed a membership of several thousand families
seeking new housing. MICOVE retained an architect and drew up
housing plans for nearly the entire district.

In 1962 a civic improvement organization, the City Club of New York,
conducted a survey of one block in the district and one block of a similar
area below Canal Street. They publicized their findings in a manner that
supported the MICOVE proposal and applied additional pressure on the

Planning Commission. The City Club issued the conclusions of their survey in October 1962 in a very direct pamphlet entitled *The Wastelands of New York City,* which called for the complete razing of the South Houston District.[11] The study block of 30 buildings south of Houston Street was described as typical of the entire district—a 600 building, 45 acre "commercial slum." The report found 15.4 percent of the spaces vacant, 50 percent of the buildings renting for the low rate of $0.75 per square foot per year or less, and some space available at the distress rate of only $0.13 per square foot per year. The very inexpensive lofts were used for "dead storage," that is, or long-term warehousing of bulky, inexpensive materials such as rag and waste paper bales.

The report was written by City Club president Mr. I. D. Robbins, who focused on the discrepancy between the potential value of the land to developers and its present use value as a site for inefficient industries: "[These] commercial slums are located in what are potentially the most valuable areas of the city. They have the benefits of the great capital investment which the City and the public utilities have made at the city's core. They have the best subways, the best sewers and drainage, the best police protection."[12]

According to this perspective, the present tenants and structures were less socially valuable than other potential users because they made less intensive use of the land. Therefore, they had lost their moral right to remain in an area whose resources they were said to squander. Municipal condemnation of the buildings, public subsidies for their acquisition and demolition, and tax write-downs were recommended by the City Club to ease the transfer of the district into the hands of redevelopment sponsors. "Analysis clearly showed that there are no buildings worth saving among the thirty in Area 1" (the South Houston representative block).[13] The City Club supported the MICOVE proposal which ultimately called for 5,000 apartments and laid a claim to 31 acres, or virtually the entire industrial district.[14]

The MICOVE proposals presented the administration of Mayor Robert F. Wagner with a problem. In the first place, he owed his office in part to a coalition of supporters from organized labor. They were not likely to be pleased if the city moved for the precipitous redevelopment of the South Houston Industrial Area. In the second place, long-range planning strategy, derived from the Lower Manhattan plans initiated by the DLMA, called for new highway construction to facilitate traffic flow to the financial district. Since 1959 the city's Arterial Highway's Coordinator, Robert Moses, had made the construction of the ten-lane Lower Manhattan Expressway a priority item in the city's construction plans. Since the expressway had to cut directly through the South Houston Indistrial Disrict in order to connect the East River bridges with the Holland Tunnel, and Lower Manhattan with these access routes,

MICOVE housing or any other area-wide redevelopment in the district would block the proposed roadway. While Wagner played a waiting game, withholding his endorsement of the Lower Manhattan Expressway until the political dimension of the planning picture developed, his response indicated that he was not willing to preempt an expressway held by its backers to be integral to Lower Manhattan development.

Planning as a Labeling Process

It was essential for redevelopment advocates that they attach the label "slum" to the district. The slum designation was the key which could make available the city's power of condemnation. It also unlocked federal and state funds available under Title I slum-clearance legislation.[15] This was a period when the slum clearance rationale was being used to demolish older districts in many cities of the Northeast. Planners in Boston, to take an example, labeled a vital neighborhood of small businesses and low-income residents in the West End a slum, and demolished it at the close of the 1950s.[16] The city of Boston paid $7.40 a square foot for the land it condemned in the West End and revalued it at $1.40 a square foot. The land was turned over to one of the mayor's political supporters at a rent of 6 percent of the reduced value, and high-income apartment towers were built with federally insured loans.[17] The principal defect in the old West End was not one of habitability but of geography—it was located too close to the business core and had valuable river frontage. An unsophisticated political response from its ethnic residents sealed the neighborhood's fate.[18]

SoHo, too, suffered under the liability of being close to an expanding business core. The response of its residents, however, proved to be quite different.

Advocates of the immediate redevelopment of the South Houston Industrial District were attempting to extend the definition of the term "slum" to include an area officially without residents.

> Except for public buildings and occasional monumental structures, the oldest parts of cities are often composed of degenerating property, slums both residential and commercial. Sooner or later both must go, better lives must be fashioned for those who occupy them and a better use found for the land.... For economic as well as humanitarian reasons, I have believed for many years that we should *start* on the commercial slums.[19]

The destruction of low-skilled jobs filled by minority workers in the South Houston District by building demolition was interpreted as humanitarian. The workers would be thus saved from the "low wage sweat shops" which were said to prevail there.[20]

The New York City Planning Commission, unwilling to be stampeded into supporting premature and piecemeal development, responded to the pressure for demolition by hiring planner and economic consultant Chester Rapkin in 1962 to study the district. Rapkin focused on 12 blocks with buildings and vacancy rates indistinguishable from the wider industrial area. He surveyed 650 firms and found them to be engaged in almost 50 categories of industrial activities, the largest concentration being textiles and apparel, which composed 26 percent of the firms and 42 percent of the area's employees.[21]

The Rapkin report sought to remove the "commercial slum" label and the charge of wasted space from the district by separately analyzing its industrial activity and the structural conditions of the buildings in which this activity took place. The businesses were judged to be of important economic and social value to the city.[22]

The employees were found to be particularly dependent upon the jobs available in the district. Nearly all had some claim to minority status. Overall, 40 percent were Puerto Rican, 20 percent were black, and the rest largely Jews, Italians, Irish, and Slavs. "In fact, one might be hard pressed to discover a recognizable nonminority concentration of workers in this area," wrote Rapkin.[23] Of all employees, 47 percent were women, many the main support of their families; in textiles and apparel, 70 percent of the workers were women.

Prospects for alternative jobs for these workers were considered poor, as the decline in manufacturing employment was expected to continue. The report projected that minority employees of the firms to be displaced by the demolition of the district would be left behind as additional New York City unemployed.

While the businesses were considered in the Rapkin report to be worth saving, the buildings presented major hazards in their present condition and complex obstacles to rehabilitation. Many were obsolete and inefficient and were fire hazards; deterioration in 16 percent of the buildings made their rehabilitation questionable, while 8 percent were found to be so deteriorated that they should be removed. The sound buildings, like those badly deteriorated, were not concentrated so as to facilitate upgrading of selective blocks, but were scattered throughout the district. Even the best buildings lacked off-street truck docking and parking spaces, and upgrading buildings would not free the narrow streets from their choking traffic. While total clearance would undermine the employment possibilities of unskilled minority workers, selective demolition of the worst buildings and rehabilitation of the rest was too complex an alternative to be proposed in the report or to be specifiable in a plan.[24]

The district presented the city with a dilemma for which there was no wholly satisfactory planning solution. The condition of the structures clearly required a corrective response. Yet almost any response would alter the conditions in the district with a resulting loss of jobs. Industry, even that which was sound in its present location, was precarious in that it was greatly dependent upon low rents to compensate for under-capitalization. "What attracts [industry] specifically to the study area is the large supply of space available at modest rents, averaging $0.80 per square foot per annum." There was such demand for just this type of space that there was only a 6 percent vacancy rate. But the firms and employees in many cases could not be successfully relocated because of the increased cost of other space, the disruption and expense of moving, and in some cases the advanced age of the firms' owners.[25]

Rehabilitation of the buildings for their present occupants, a solution which would cause the least disruption, appeared attractive, but on analysis turned out to be self-defeating. Resulting rents could be expected to range from $1.25 to $1.75 per foot per year after rehabilitation, only half the $2.50 to $3.50 cost of new manufacturing space, but in excess of what the district's businesses could absorb.[26]

The only planning recommendation that seemed unavoidable to Rapkin was a modest program of intensified and routinized building inspections aimed at eliminating structural and safety violations in the buildings and expected to cost landlords $5 million.[27] This was a sum equivalent to all they had spent on repair of their buildings from 1945 to the year of the study, 1962. Even this program would drive some firms out of the district because landlords would pass the costs on to tenants. "Some turnover would undoubtedly result from the rent consequences of such an enforcement effort," wrote Rapkin.[28]

The Function of Obsolete Buildings:
A Counterideology

It is hard to escape the conclusion that an essential component in the economy of a firm operating in the district was its exemption from the costs of meeting the city building codes. The buildings worked well for firms with a narrow profit margin precisely because they were *not* up-graded. A policy had been in effect in the district under which the Buildings Department did no general surveys of conditions but only investigated specific complaints. Such a policy allowed firms to economize through safety-code avoidance. Low-income artists, the next manufacturing generation that began to arrive in the district in the mid-1960s in noticeable numbers, shared this operational requirement and also found a way around the building inspectors.

While the bonus obtained through building-code avoidance accounted in part for the low rents in the district, the major economy of the area was due to the fact that the buildings were old and their construction costs amortized long ago. This is why even after rehabilitation rents would have been only half that for newly constructed lofts. The structures in the district represented significant capital value, a value imparted in construction and consumed as reduced rents and neglected maintenance in more recent years.

The value of older industrial buildings to the overall economic diversity of a city was a principle rediscovered and popularized by Jane Jacobs in 1961: "Time makes the high building costs of one generation the bargains of a following generation. Time pays off original capital costs, and this depreciation can be reflected in the yields required from a building. Time makes certain structures obsolete for some enterprises and they become available to others."[29] Old buildings have a special importance in facilitating manufacturing diversity. Their cheap rents "incubate" new enterprises by allowing the firm to get started cheaply and to enlarge its space as increased business warrants. Ultimately, a successful firm may outgrow the district of old buildings, move to a new plant, and be replaced by still newer firms.[30]

Presented in the perspective of this counterideology in land use, which stressed the value of recycling buildings, Rapkin's data provide justification for a plan by which the firms in the South Houston District could, at least temporarily, be saved. While small, averaging 23 employees, they were shown to be adding employees at an average annual rate of 7.8 percent.[31] Their business volume was modest but was up 64.4 percent on average in the five years between 1957 and 1962.[32] Rather than finding the district an "industrial slum," Rapkin found it to be an instance of an "incubator area," and he endorsed, without specific citation, the Jacobs concept.

> The small firm is typical of the low-rent area. . . . It has frequently been asserted that older industrial sections, by providing low-priced space, make it possible for the new and less secure establishments to gain a foothold in the business world. With low overhead, the recurrent burden is minimized and the opportunity for expansion and development is enhanced. It is for this reason that areas of this type are frequently called "incubators," despite the fact that the period of incubation may be quite lengthy.[33]

The Rapkin study provided the Planning Commission with an answer to its critics who had called for razing the South Houston Industrial District. The incubator theory suggested the possibilities of a capitalist drama in which small entrepreneurs take risks that bring new invigorating industry to the city, and coincidentally make their fortunes. Characterizing the South Houston District as an incubator area provided a theoretically respectable justification for leaving the district alone. The planning dilemma had been dehorned by showing that the district as it existed was playing a vital role in the industrial scheme of the city.

The arguments in the Rapkin report linking thousands of jobs for minority workers to the preservation of the district's characteristics gave the Wagner administration the ideological argument it needed to justify opposition to the immediate construction of housing in the district, housing which was not coherent with the emerging Lower Manhattan plan.

Critics, who had succeeded in raising the issue of the future of the South Houston District to the level of a public debate, were not gracefully reconciled to defeat. I. D. Robbins of the City Club accused the City Planning Commission of obfuscating the planning arguments by "waving the bloody shirt of discrimination." Robbins argued that the CPC had spent $25,000, not on an objective study, but for the purpose of "clobbering" the MICOVE advocates. MICOVE made the mistake, Robbins wrote, of "presuming to tell the Planning Department staff where it should permit housing to be built without having enough political muscle to make it stick."[34]

The Wider Planning Context

The Planning Commission, however ideologically effective it was in its 1963 report on the district, had misforecast the state of industrial employment in Manhattan and in New York City. In the categories of women's apparel and textile products, the major manufacturing activity in the South Houston District, the job loss was precipitous. Where 354,000 workers had been employed in apparel and textiles in 1948, only 163,600 remained in 1974. (See appendix 2, table 1.)

In Manhattan itself, manufacturing jobs declined by 39,000 in the five years just prior to the Rapkin survey. (See appendix 2, table 2.) Between 1960 and 1970 Manhattan actually lost 21 percent of its manufacturing jobs—ten times the estimate used by Rapkin for the city as a whole.

Manhattan was not destined to be a manufacturing center. The private office construction industry had been completing over three million square feet of office space annually there since 1957. (See appendix 2, table 3.) When the City Planning Commission approved the lower Manhattan Plan in 1965, it called for the development of at least 10 million square feet of additional office space and the construction of housing for up to 100,000 people in the area below Canal Street.[35]

The Planning Commission policy of resisting development in some of the older manufacturing areas in the early 1960s, including South Houston, was not an effort to preserve "incubator" districts as a feature of business diversity in Manhattan. It was an effort to preserve a spill-over area to which manufacturers could temporarily flee as other manufacturing districts were being razed to build the new Manhattan. Manufacturing buildings that lay within the proposed route of the Lower Manhattan Expressway were to be razed.

The Threat of the Lower Manhattan Expressway as a Community Organizing Incentive

In the fall of 1968 an internationally known artist, Sam Johnson, and his wife, Dorothy, bought a small loft building on Spring Street in the South Houston District.[36] There were no residential neighbors on their solidly industrial block when they moved in with their infant son and daughter. With trucks unloading outside their door all day, there was no place for children to find a casual neighborhood play area. The Johnsons, however, were not expecting a residential community with public parks. They found the district's conditions tolerable because the surrounding area and the rest of the city supplied them with the amenities and services they needed. The cheese and butcher shops of the two nearby Italian neighborhoods and the parks and restaurants of Greenwich Village were within walking distance. Within the district, their own building offered a world unto itself.

Sam's sculpture consisted of large-scale geometric objects, often done as a series of related pieces, and he required considerable studio and storage space separate from the family's living area. One floor of their building proved admirably suited as a separate but available working space. Dorothy had more recently become a serious student of dance and choreography. She needed an extensive area to design and rehearse her performances. With a little repair, another floor of the building filled this requirement. Sufficient space remained on the building's other floors, connected by a freight elevator, for the needs of living and child rearing. On two sides, huge windows set in a cast iron facade let in abundant natural light. The building seemed to offer all that the family required to house their complex lifestyle, and they were glad to have discovered it.

No sooner had the Johnsons moved in and renovated their building than they learned that a ten-lane expessway was to be built through the district along Broome Street, one short block away. With the additional demolition required for access ramps, it appeared certain that the expressway construction would require the destruction of their building, along with a large number of the factories and artists' studios in the rest of the district.

The Antiexpressway Coalition

A limited access road linking lower Manhattan's East River bridges with the Holland Tunnel had been called for by regional planners since 1927. Viewed as a line on a map, it seemed a logical link between Long Island and New Jersey. Robert Moses, New York City's Arterial Highways Coordinator, had announced plans to build this expressway in late 1959. With the backing of Manhattan Borough president Hulan Jack, he had proposed to build an elevated and surface route bisecting Chinatown, Little Italy, the South Houston District, several Lower East Side neighborhoods, the South Village, and the fringes of Greenwich Village.[37] Moses had stressed that while many commercial firms and 2,000 families would have to be relocated, most would be leaving run-down property or substandard tenements. For the next ten years the populations of these ethnically conscious neighborhoods, along with civic reformers from Greenwich Village, fought the planners to a standstill, ultimately demapping the road. While playing an important part in this struggle, artists south of Houston Street, such as the Johnsons, were on the stage for only the last act of this drama.

In April of 1960 the City Planning Commission approved the Moses route and determined that 416 buildings would have to be razed—2,000 housing units, 365 retail stores, and 480 nonretail establishments. From that point on, community opposition to the expressway over the issue of relocation never ceased.[38] Efforts by promoters of the expressway to raise the relocation bonuses from $500 to $1,000 per family failed to appease the opposition. Politicians from the affected areas, in particular assemblyman Louis DeSalvio, representing Little Italy, brought busloads of constituents to the first and each successive public hearing on the expressway. Elderly men and women lined up at the microphones to denounce the destruction of the neighborhoods where they had been born and where they had grown old.[39]

In February 1961 liberal political reformers based in Greenwich Village made opposition to the Lower Manhattan Expressway part of their program. At a meeting of 300 people, they chose Jane Jacobs, author and theorist of urban neighborhood preservation, as their cochairperson.[40] As the opposition organized, the Board of Estimate and Mayor Wagner found themselves confronted with a planning issue which had become highly politicized and whose costs could not be easily calculated. Using a series of engineering alterations and relocation studies to delay the date of construction of the road, the mayor stalled for time, forcing those on both sides of the controversy to make a show of their political muscle.

The opposition, while initially localized, was particularly intense. Its strategy was to promote an ideology of neighborhood preservation which had potential appeal throughout the city. The proponents consisted of the most powerful business and labor organizations in the city, including the DLMA, headed by Chase Manhattan Bank president David Rockefeller, and the Central Trades and Labor Council, headed by Harry Van Arsdale. Labor and the construction industry sought the $100 million plus contracts, which included $70 million in payrolls.[41] The downtown financial community saw in the expressway a transportation facility that would complement and facilitate their plans to redevelop Manhattan below Chambers Street into the prime location for international business headquarters.[42] Proponents appeared regularly at public hearings before the Board of Estimate and circulated glowing descriptions of the economic impact of the expressway. In 1964, as the mayor continued to vacillate and delay, the Downtown-Lower Manhattan Association organized a lobbying group to demonstrate support for the road, uniting twenty-two civic, business, real-estate, labor, and highway construction organizations.[43] Attempting to reach a wider public with its planning arguments, the DLMA in July of that year published a multicolor booklet in support of the ten-lane roadway under consideration by the city. The booklet argued that the road would be a boom to real-estate investors and a stimulant to the city tax base, and that it was essential to the city's own local traffic flow.[44]

Proponents had another argument with which to prod the mayor. The road appeared to be without any local cost, with the federal government paying 90 percent and the state 10 percent under the Interstate Highway Act funding formula. In urging the implementation of his plan, Robert Moses used his leverage as broker of the outside funding to threaten the cautious mayor and city council with the loss of federal and state support.[45]

Intense lobbying rather than planning logic by proponents of the expressway quieted any potential opposition from with the City Planning Commission. According to Donald Elliott, appointed chairman of the City Planning Commission in 1966,

We could never get answers as to the benefits of the Expressway in terms of traffic flow and whatever. The CPC was never really convinced that the road was necessary. Everybody else was convinced—Moses, the Downtown–Lower Manhattan Association. But it didn't work as a planning *necessity*. There was enormous pressure—from the Lower Manhattan Association, construction workers, construction companies. The construction workers were quite candid on the social impact. They cared nothing. They just wanted to pour concrete.[46]

Opposition Tactics

Opponents of the expressway, while without the power of strategic initiative, were not completely unarmed. The most important resource of the Citywide Coalition Against the Lower Manhattan Expressway was its knowledge of the bureaucratic procedure used in urban planning. When a relevant environmental point was buried by expressway advocates, the Coalition dug it up and made it an issue. An engineering report on traffic-generated pollution was bottled up by the city government, but the Coalition knew where to apply pressure to force its release. When road planners violated their own administrative codes, they were tripped up. When local politicians attempted to negotiate personal real-estate advantages as their price for giving up opposition to the road, the Coalition was able to successfully claim the right to search the files of planning agencies until deals were uncovered and publicized.

In one instance, Paul Douglas, a prominent businessman and chairman of the Traffic Committee of the Coalition, obtained a transcript of the testimony given by Robert Moses in Washington and compared it with statements made by Moses in New York City. Douglas revealed that, in order to qualify for the federal subsidy, Moses had told Congress that 80 percent of expressway traffic would be interstate. But, to appease New York opposition to the road, Moses had shown figures to the Board of Estimate to demonstrate that 80 percent of the traffic would be local in nature.[47] Moses's role as technical expert and fiscal broker was hurt by this revelation, and a strong advocate of the road was weakened.

The coalition had to keep a sharp eye on their own political allies in the Democratic party who had been fighting the road. As coalition leader Rachele Wall explained,

> One day I got a call that Louis DeSalvio had sold out. He was making a deal to become the sponsor of some Mitchell-Lama housing in his district. We had a hell of a time tracing the facts. We went through every file of every agency we could think of to find something. Finally Paul Douglas, the president of Freeport Sulphur, a very distinguished man, his father is the Senator, said to me, "Let's look through Moses's files." We had a right to look at them, we knew that, and Paul is a very distinguished guy, and could get through. And so one day I got a call from him. "Rachele," he said, "I have a letter here that explains the whole thing." This was a gift for us, because we discovered that the people who worked around DeSalvio never wrote letters. It was very hard to get anything, any hard evidence that they had betrayed anything. The letter we found was from Moses to Mayor Robert Wagner. Wagner, of course, wanted the expressway. We always referred to this as the "Dear Bob" letter. It began, "Dear Bob, I saw, today, the Assemblyman and a builder. They proposed eight Mitchell-Lamas in exchange for not opposing the LMX.

Although I'd like nothing better than to put this thing through, a deal of this sort could not be made.''

I had to hand it to Moses. I hated the man, but I had to hand it to him. He fixed the bastards. He put it in writing. We broke the story through my friend at the *New York Times,* Sam Kaplan, who is now an associate editor of the *New York Post.*[48]

The coalition then proceeded to work around DeSalvio, thus isolating him from the protest leadership and hence reducing his ability to compromise the expressway opposition.

Finally, in March 1968, the eighth time that the Board of Estimate had considered the Lower Manhattan Expressway, it was cleared for construction. John Lindsay, the new mayor who had been helped into office by his record of opposition to the expressway, had reversed himself under enormous pressure from expressway proponents that included a threatened strike by 200,000 construction workers.[49] With the road approved, Coalition leader Jane Jacobs led a tumultuous disruption of a hearing of the State Highway Department and was arrested and charged with second-degree rioting for attempting to rip up the stenotape record of the hearing.[50] The coalition appeared to have run out of legal ammunition.

Artists Against the Expressway

At this point the artists living in lofts below Houston Street became a factor in the Coalition for the first time. When Dorothy Johnson read in the weekly arts-community-oriented newspaper, the *Village Voice,* that the loft district was about to be scythed down to make way for the imminent Lower Manhattan Expressway, she became the center of an intense organizing drive among artists. The road was a mistake from a planning and a moral point of view, she reasoned, and she was determined not to let it happen. "My response was immediate," she said. "I called *Voice* writer Mary Perot Nichols to find out what the hell was going on. Then I called the Citywide Coalition. Finally I called everybody I knew."

The Coalition welcomed the new infusion of support. To the civic reformers leading the organization, Dorothy Johnson and the other loft artists were a culturally similar and attractive group. "My husband is an artist," explained one Greenwich Village leader of the Coalition. "I understand their problems. We had to fight the developers here to keep this house where he has his studio." The artists of the loft district also represented, in very practical terms, one more community astride the path of the expressway, a community that could be organized to fight for its life against the wrecking ball. As one Coalition leader explained, "I also knew that if we could only help establish the community down there, especially in a legally zoned sense, it would stop the Lower Manhattan Expressway forever." The Coalition thought in terms of the political power and moral value of neighborhoods. They understood that the artists' late entry into the fight was motivated by their anxiety about losing their lofts. "It's always a matter of whose ox is being gored," said this Coalition leader. "That's how average citizens get involved in these reformist campaigns. They're being gored."

Dorothy Johnson, working with the advice and support of the Coalition strategists, took on the task of organizing the SoHo district. Her husband's high status in the art community gave the campaign respectability and opened doors to potential supporters to which nonartists had no access. The artists' protest itself observed the etiquette of status. "Sam did a lot of the thinking," Dorothy explained of her husband's role, "but he hated phoning."

Dorothy was not without a prior appreciation of the power of organization and the importance of information and publicity in a protest movement. A native New Yorker, she had grown up in a Quaker household with a strong tradition of moral dissent. Her father, a professor of philosophy at an elite college, served as both a model of strength and of self-righteousness against whom she had learned to defend herself. While a student in fashion illustration, she had organized a peace march during the era of protest against the war in Vietnam. Like other young SoHo residents, her opposition to American involvement in Vietnam helped her develop a confidence in her status and moral convictions that allowed her to challenge political figures and technical experts without backing down or feeling intimidated. In marrying Sam, she acquired additional status based on his artistic success. She was able to move through the art world challenging curators, dealers, politically influential patrons, and apolitical artists to act to save the loft district's studios. As her work with leaders of the Citywide Coalition Against the Expressway intensified, Dorothy discovered that she was receiving an education in pressure politics. "They were all so very sophisticated in this sort of thing. I was invited to meetings and led along. They led me to organize a constituency without my quite knowing it. They were clever."

The Johnsons rounded up artists who had previously faced the demolition of their lofts in silent isolation, and created a small core of activists. They also sought celebrity and institutional support from the wider art world to give their organization legitimacy and visibility. "Sam and I drafted a letter at the first meeting we attended [of the Coalition] and mimeographed it there. Richard Feigan had a branch of his gallery in SoHo, a warehouse, really, where he would bring clients at times. We spoke to him and he said the first thing we needed was a fancy letterhead."

At this point the SoHo group adopted a name, Artists Against the Expressway (AAE), for media recognition, and set about collecting well-known names for a "sponsoring committee" with which to embellish their letterhead. The AAE contacted widely known artists, dealers, and critics, people with influence and recognizability which extended beyond the art community itself. In response to the name of Johnson or of Richard Feigan, many responded cooperatively.[51] "We put Stella, Rauschenberg, and Bennett on the letterhead; we tried to get the biggest names." Many hadn't the time for personal involvement, but drafted letters of support and sent them to the mayor and other officials designated as targets by the AAE. Many lent their prestige. The very successful painter Robert Motherwell, for example, wrote to the AAE to say, "I am in accord with your opposition to the proposal for the Lower Manhattan Expressway. If you want to use my name in relation to it, please do."[52]

Organizing a Housing Class

Members of the AAE who did the routine work of knocking on doors and circulating appeals were those artists faced with the imminent destruction of their buildings. Their first task was to contact every artist residing in the loft district, pass along the information gathered about the expressway plans, and enlist support in writing protest letters and attending public hearings on the issue. As they made the rounds in December 1968, the AAE discovered that they had made the first census of loft dwellers in the district. They found 12 buildings owned by individual artists, 14 artist cooperatives, and 107 rental loft units used by artists—in all, a total of about 270 units with one and frequently more than one artist in residence, a few with their families. The AAE, then, was knitting together a territorially based community through a common housing interest.

Once revealed, the loft dwellers were not allowed to slide back into individual isolation and anonymity. The AAE drew up charts of the loft district, mapping the location of artists' studios. These maps were kept current with recently discovered addresses and were presented at public hearings throughout the spring and summer of 1969 as evidence that a vital loft community existed and was facing the threat of grave injury in the form of the expressway. The AAE badgered the area's artists into abandoning their inconspicuousness and anonymity. But by projecting the housing situation of artists in the district into the debate over the expressway, the AAE was raising illegal loft dwelling as an issue in itself which, sooner or later, the City Planning Commission would have to address.

Appeals and Allies

With a base organized in the district, the AAE next turned to the institutional structure of the art world. Appeals were sent to all the New York museums, personally addressed to trustees and curators. The art directors of over forty out-of-town museums were similarly contacted as the search for support extended. The chairpersons of the art departments of major American colleges and universities were informed of the plight of SoHo artists, as were major museum directors in Europe and Japan. Seventy collectors and critics were contacted. In a strong show of support, the art world responded to the appeal with telegrams directed at Mayor Lindsay and the several planning agencies involved in the expressway, urging them to stop the project and consider the consequences to contemporary artists. In a representative letter to the mayor, a Dutch publisher of art books wrote:

> As an art collector and publisher who has come to New York many times, I do not see the slightest progress in destroying the living and working quarters of many artists who have turned New York into the vital center of mid-century art for a ten-lane expressway. A decision like this would be an irreparable loss to the art world and to the City of New York. I have no doubt that among American urbanists and architects there is enough imagination and foresight to find a solution which serves both traffic and—first of all—the man in a great living city.[53]

Beyond mobilizing the art community, the AAE appeal provided the opportunity for lay members of the arts audience to constructively dramatize their involvement and concern. Their organizational work with artists moved them a step closer to the professional core of the art world, and it proved socially rewarding. Work with the AAE gave non-artists a chance to go backstage.

One important group of allies, headed by an architect, formed its own committee, Architects and Engineers Against the Expressway, and made its professional expertise available. It produced an analysis that showed that the expressway project did not fit into any "comprehensive plan" for the city's transportation needs, and that the costs would be not the projected $150 million, but closer to $500 million.[54] This allied committee carried out extensive research which pointed out that the tunnel section of the expressway, devised to minimize political resistance, would contain serious engineering faults. Dug far below the water table, the tunnel would have a tendency to float upward because of the pressure of ground water. When these facts became known, the Lindsay administration developed a plan for housing and public buildings to be built above the tunnel to weigh it down. The refusal of the federal government to pay for this additional construction under the 90 percent reimbursement formula available for interstate highways, blocked the mayor's freedom to maneuver and dealt the expressway a significant blow.

A second group of nonartists working closely with the AAE formed themselves into the Scientists' Committee for Public Information and dealt the expressway another blow. This group consisted of a core of environmental scientists working at Rockefeller Institute. They drove a car equipped with air quality monitoring devices along the route of the proposed expressway during rush hours to record pollution levels. Their research indicated that air quality was already dangerously low because of carbon monoxide concentrations, and that the increased traffic generated by the expressway would raise pollution to a level dangerous to health.

The publicity which surrounded this finding gave the Citywide Coalition a desperately needed point of leverage for a new attack on the roadway. The Coalition had by this time, the summer of 1969, exhausted their legal ammunition, and the leadership felt that without a dramatic new issue they would be unable to prevent the start of construction. "We felt," said one Coalition leader, "if we could really get something stunning, we could stop the whole damn thing. Otherwise, it was going to be built." The premilinary studies on air pollution by the scientists working with the AAE supplied the required new issue. The Coalition moved quickly to exploit it. According to Rachele Wall, a Coalition leader,

> I called a friend of mine in Washington to see if, by the terms of a new environmental protection law that had just passed Congress, the City had done all that was required in their environmental impact statement. [My friend, a newspaperman,] got into the files down there and found that an impact statement had been done, but by an engineer who just built roads and knew nothing about the environment. This engineer had simply done a number on us. There was nothing to it.[55]

Rachele Wall, using a network of connections to city leaders developed when she had worked in public relations, contacted Carol Karnheim, assistant to the commissioner of air resources for the City of New York. Rachele Wall personally knew that this official was committed to an honest and effective air quality standard in the city. She was given the pollution data on the expressway and the facts concerning its inadequate environmental impact statement. Together with Assistant Commissioner Karnheim, the Coalition approached the New York office of the federal Environmental Protection Administration, the agency charged with enforcing compliance with antipollution legislation. The EPA consequently ordered the city to make an adequate environmental impact study of the consequences of building the expressway, and Karnheim and the agency head, Commissioner Heller, were assigned by the city to make the report. Explained Wall:

It was Carol [Karnheim] who called them [the EPA] on it, and through them, her boss [Commissioner Heller]. The two of them did the report and it was a stunner. It was more powerful than we expected. Our problem at that point was that we couldn't get it out of Lindsay's office. Lindsay was suddenly changed. After getting elected opposing the expressway, he had now decided that he wanted a Lower Manhattan Expressway.[56]

The Coalition contacted Manhattan congressman Edward Koch for help. Koch, later to become mayor, was then a Reform Democrat who had first won elective office as Greenwich Village district leader against Carmine DeSapio, the regular or Tammany candidate, in 1963. The issue then was a Robert Moses plan to extend Fifth Avenue through the middle of Washington Square Park and on south. The reformers behind Koch saw this as a destruction of a viable neighborhood for the profit of those with an interest in the appreciation of land values near the extended avenue. Opposition to the Fifth Avenue extension welded together a Greenwich Village constituency of liberal Democrats who viewed proposals for urban renewal and highway construction with great suspicion. As a leader in that reform movement explained:

We were afraid to go home at night after our meetings. We were being threatened. The *Village Voice* was started at that time, and it was one of the few places we could get an ad attacking the Fifth Avenue plan. That's where it all began. To fight that road, a new political party was formed, the Village Independent Democrats. They knew they had to get DeSapio out. That was the reason the reform movement began. The road was the crucial thing. We realized that those who had political control could do anything at all to us.

Koch had been kept in office by this liberal Democrat constituency. When the Citywide Coalition called on him to help them release the pollution report on the Lower Manhattan Expressway, he responded. According to Ms. Wall, "Ed Koch went and sat in at Lindsay's office until they gave us the Heller Report."[57] The technical conclusions of the report were seriously damaging to the case of the expressway advocates, but in the forum of urban policy debate, the impact of those conclusions depended upon an essentially political effort. For the duration of the expressway debate, the coalition kept those conclusions alive.

The Artist Lobby

While the Citywide Coalition picked up the pollution issue raised by the scientists working with the SoHo artists, the AAE continued to create political pressure along its own specialized front. "Through Rauschenberg, Leo Castelli, and Don Judd," explained AAE leader Dorothy Johnson, "we had a 'token-artist' friendship with some politically important people. Don and the others would go to their parties as 'token artists,' and so we had a friendship with Marion Javitts [wife of New York Senator Jacob Javitts]." Marion Javitts took an AAE delegation to see commissioner of transportation Constantine Saidamon-Eristoff, a key advocate of the expressway whom the artists had been unable to get to see on their own. "I got a taste of their special kind of arrogance," said a delegation member, "and her [Marion Javitts's] special kind of clout. Even so, we didn't convince him. Only one of their engineers, and there was a bunch of them there, would occasionally concede a point to us. Since then, I've grown more used to this treatment from bureaucrats."

The gains were intangible at this stage, but the artists kept trying to wear down the bureaucrats with personal confrontation. The self-imposed isolation of the expressway architect Shadrach Woods especially infuriated the artists. An AAE activist said,

> Woods had an office on Broome Street [in SoHo] but *never* did he venture into the communities he casually labeled as "slums." He had a huge amount of intellectual arrogance. He would gesture toward Little Italy and refer to "that slum," never having been to the restaurants there, let alone in the houses with their windowsills painted fresh each year. I read Jane Jacobs in that period, and she meant a lot to me.

Despite the ideological and practical support from the Greenwich Village reformers, the artists felt very often as if the issues of art and artists' welfare did not matter in the decision-making process. With the lesson of their own political weakness in mind, the AAE sought to develop allied issues, such as the pollution issue, whenever possible. Saving the cast-iron facades of the district buildings was another dovetailing issue. Said an AAE activist:

> Everyone with an important voice saw this as a deserted area. When we drew up as best we could and brought with us a mapped indication of everyone living here, it didn't seem to have much impact. No one cared about artists and lofts. The issue that had some bearing was that of cast-iron buildings. Bill Woods [an architect and AAE ally] went up to Columbia and got James Marston Fitch, their

architectural preservation expert, to get involved. Through him we got cables sent to the mayor from all over the world begging that the area be preserved.

The SoHo artists, then, by beginning the drive for the preservation of cast-iron architecture in the district, linked up with and benefited from an already established constituency. Each constituency further amplified the opposition of the artists.

Public Relations

The AAE highlighted their efforts to put art-world pressure on the sponsors of the expressway by organizing a meeting of 250 artists and their supporters and allies at the Whitney Museum in June 1969. Among the representatives of art institutions who were present, Arthur Drexler, director of the Department of Architecture at the Museum of Modern Art, and Henry Geldzahler, chairman of the Department of Contemporary Art at the Metropolitan Museum, spoke in support of the artists. James Marston Fitch of Columbia University's School of Architecture attacked the expressway as a threat to the nineteenth-century cast-iron buildings south of Houston Street. Other allies of the artists, such as William Woods, spokesman for Architects and Engineers Against the Expressway, denounced the planning inadequacies of the expressway, and Max Snodderly, speaking for the Scientists' Committee for Public Information, said the road was incompatible with the city's air-quality goals. All constituencies in favor of the preservation of the district were given the microphone, in the manner of agendas at Vietnam war protests.

The artist Barnett Newman delivered the most emotional speech of the evening. He was distraught by the fact that one of the most powerful figures in the institutional art world had refused to champion the welfare of artists on this issue, and so had betrayed his role as patron and steward of artists' interests. The man was David Rockefeller. The AAE had first tried to hold the protest meeting at the Museum of Modern Art, but according to the AAE, "The MOMA refused us; there were Rockefeller connections on their Board of Trustees, and David was very much for the highway." Indeed, Rockefeller was the chairman of that Board of Trustees. This experience had only sharpened Newman's attack. After describing himself as a refugee from two previous lofts torn down in Lower Manhattan for Rockefeller-sponsored urban renewal projects, Newman characterized David Rockefeller as "the most vocal advocate for the expressway." "Let us not forget," Newman continued, "that the strongest forces against artists are the art lovers. [Let us challenge Rockefeller] to declare to us personally where his loyalty lies.

He should have the opportunity to declare whether he has some feeling for the artists who make the art as well as for the art itself. He should use his good offices on our behalf, rather than in our destruction."

The art community provides no institutional mechanism which allows artists to hold their patrons responsible for the effects of their policy making. The AAE could only try to embarrass David Rockefeller as a civic steward. The bitterness of the artists at being unable to move Rockefeller was in proportion to their inability to exercise political and economic leverage independently.

The Whitney meeting did result in favorable press coverage of the artists' plight. Grace Glueck, a cultural affairs writer for the *New York Times* and a friend of several AAE artists, had covered the protest movement previously, but the Whitney meeting became an opportunity to tell the loft artists' story comprehensively.[53] This in itself was a victory. One AAE leader said, "We got an article in the *Times* from the Whitney meeting. Up to this point the antiexpressway forces had not been able to get publicity in the *Times*. Grace Glueck was able to justify an article then. I was deliriously happy." If some allies like Rockefeller subordinated their patronage roles to their business interests, others, including members of the press, had shown themselves to be the bridge by which the artists' message reached a new and wider audience.

The artists living south of Houston Street, then, played an important tactical role in the citywide effort to stop the expressway. According to one Coalition leader, the AAE leadership "did a marvelous thing at the time. [They] gathered together all these famous names. . . . They were able to get across to officials by getting all these distinguished people involved. That was terribly important, in my opinion."

This campaign to defend their lofts had taken the artists a long way toward establishing the territorial community of SoHo. The Citywide Coalition saw the formation of a neighborhood in the loft district as the ultimate source of the artists' strength in resisting the expressway. "The good part of it," said Rachele Wall, "was that the artists were already living in the SoHo area. It wasn't SoHo then, but as a matter of fact it was at [the AAE's] meeting at the Whitney that it was first called 'SoHo.' "[59]

On July 16, 1969, Mayor Lindsay announced that the Lower Manhattan Expressway was "dead for all time."[60] Having lost the primary race in his own Republican party in June, Lindsay had been forced to turn to the Liberal party and to the Reform Democrats for support. Ten years of fiscal engineering and political maneuvering around the expressway issue came to an end. The Liberal party and the Reform Democratic clubs, the latter organized as the New Democratic Coalition, demanded a list of concessions in return for their support of the incumbent mayor, and Lindsay had no choice but to agree. At the top of the list was the scrapping of the Lower Manhattan Expressway, the symbol of a nieghborhood-razing pattern of urban renewal and planning which the reformers were united in opposing. Not content with the promise of an end to the expressway, they demanded and received the legal demapping of the route from the official city map in August.[61] In its place, "SoHo" had emerged on the sociological map of the city.

Conclusion

The SoHo district as a geographic focus for a residential community originated in the effort of a cosmopolitan community of artists to utilize and defend a concentration of old buildings that was, for them, an irreplaceable occupational resource. The development of a territorial interest had several consequences for the status community of artists.

1. The defense of loft space against the demolition plans of the expressway advocates generated a core of specifically local activists, the potentially dispossessed, who promoted the organization of district residents as neighbors with a common interest and responsibility. In doing so, these activists facilitated an alignment of artists as local residents. Consciousness of locality was legitimated by the public support given residents by the wider art community. SoHo was held to be important to all New Yorkers interested in art. When, however, influential segments of the wider art community proved to be uninterested in the needs of working artists if that meant they had to oppose the expressway, the residents promoted specifically territorial and occupational interests under their own local leadership. The status community, utilized to amplify the voice of the SoHo residents, was perceived to be compromised in its institutional leadership.

2. The perception that their problems as artists were inextricably involved with the preservation of a specific locality brought SoHo residents into active cooperation with groups outside the art world—the Italian and Chinese communities and the politically experienced Greenwich Village activists who functioned as·a bridge between the art audience and urban political structures. For SoHo artists whose political interests were ideological and national, if they existed at all, the fight to stop the Lower Manhattan Expressway became a crash course in city politics.

For those without the leverage of large economic or political organizations, coalition is essential, and locality is the key to coalition. Not only surrounding residential and business communities, but special constituencies such as cast-iron preservationists, antipollution environmentalists, and theorists of a decentralized, neighborhood-based city had, with artists, an interest in the retention of the structural character of

SoHo. Working with these constituencies, artists learned to handle political publicity, to pack public hearings, and to mix appeals for the justice of their case with claims that the retention of SoHo was important for workers, industry, and the vitality of the entire city.

3. The defense of their interests in SoHo made artists a more militant and self-confident occupational group, within the perimeters of middle-class activism. As challengers to important economic interests and public planning policy, artists brought with them the expectations of the middle class and the well-educated; they assumed that government bureaucrats were to be used as a resource and that they themselves could understand and, as part of the public, judge planning rationale. When they discovered that officials were intransigent, that data was withheld, and they they were patronized rather than informed, they were not intimidated or mollified. Their expectations were outrageously contradicted. They turned their anger, not into a depressed apathy, but into a campaign of doing their own research and enlisting the aid of their own experts. A spatially differentiated artist community, having learned the lessons of sparring with city city government, was prepared to take the initiative in securing its existence in the struggle for SoHo zoning changes which quickly followed.

Looking south across the "valley" of SoHo toward
Lower Manhattan

Galleries along West Broadway, SoHo's commercial center

A SoHo gallery interior. Large open spaces and track lighting allow an open aesthetic and a flexibility in the display of art. A nonintimidating relationship to art is encouraged.

Selling art alfresco on a SoHo street

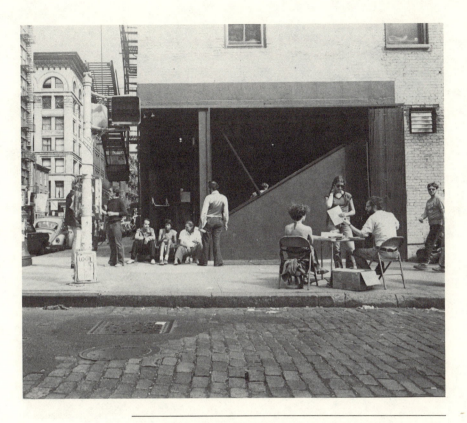

Street life in SoHo. The surrealistic windows belong to a
popular bar and restaurant.

Moving art into a loft studio

The clean simplicity that is the mark of a painter's loft. The work area is to the right, and art is stored behind the screens.

A SoHo artist teaches his son to fly cast in the studio, while an assistant works on a routine task at the left

The SoHo Center, with its cast-iron facade and, on the side wall, a trompe l'oeil. Artists without gallery affiliations keep slides of their work on file here for potential buyers. To the left, in what was formerly a pizza parlor for industrial workers, there is a reference library for fine and commercial artists.

9 The Achievement of Territorial Community

Cooperatives as a Housing Solution for Artists

The precedent for establishing artist-owned cooperatives in industrial buildings originated with Greenwich Village reformers and housing activists in the early 1960s. With friends, neighbors, and in some cases spouses who were artists, these activists were sensitive to the lack of suitable working space available to New York artists. They recognized in the covert residential uses of manufacturing lofts a basis for a programmatic solution to the space problems of the city's working artists that would also result in the creation of viable neighborhoods.

These civic activists had successfully defended their own blocks of owner-occupied brownstones and walk-up apartments against a series of high-rise development proposals and had become convinced that the health of neighborhoods required the maximum degree of building recycling, that is, the renovation of old structures for new uses and new occupants. Recycling allowed a neighborhood to infuse new life, new purposes, and new people into its buildings, while preserving the older residents from the catastrophic encroachment of development projects. Rachele Wall explained,

> Now we're in a period of survival. We should have been in a period of survival a long time ago. Many of our problems come from a politics and a real-estate outlook that says, "Turn things over and make money." Look at the destruction of our city. They created a

"co-op city," and they drained off the Grand Concourse, and down it went. You can't do this to neighborhoods. . . . SoHo is booming. The Village is booming. These are the areas that have fought hardest to stay alive and that are growing organically. . . . They're creating something in these places, they're alive, growing. Whether or not they're great, they're alive.[1]

The activists were convinced that renovation was the cheapest way to secure housing. It was slow and piecemeal and resulted in a neighborhood that had great economic variety and a diversity of life styles. The need of residents to coordinate the activities of daily life resulted in vital neighborhoods. Diversity and cooperative involvement, the ingredients of a viable urban life, were linked to building recycling.

The Greenwich Village Precedent

In 1963, Wall, Jane Jacobs, and other Village residents noticed a sign on a building at Greenwich and Twelfth streets indicating that the building had been seized for tax arrears and was about to be auctioned. The building was illegally occupied by artists. Joining some art patrons from the business world, they formed Citizens for Artists Housing (CAH) and sought to get the building legally into the hands of working artists. Wall remembered,

I knew [Mayor] Wagner from our housing battles in the Village and from the years when I worked in public relations. His brother was an artist, and that helped. We talked to him and he agreed that when the thing came up for auction the city would hold down the knock-off price to $45,000. We had quite a time getting the building. The real estate interests were bidding against us, and we were very thankful that we could pull it off the $45,000. It's quite a building, with twelve lofts. We convinced the Mayor that this was to be a pilot project, what I call "The Renaissance Act," which would show that a person can live where they work in New York.[2]

The $45,000 was secured from industrialist Jack Kaplan and made available through his philanthropy, the J. M. Kaplan Fund. Kaplan's philanthropic interests turned to the support of experimental housing programs for artists when his daughter married an artist for whom Kaplan helped secure a loft studio. Kaplan felt that the Greenwich Street project would have better stability if the resident artists owned their own lofts, and the CAH agreed to this cooperative venture. Kaplan provided an additional $60,000 for renovation work on the building and set up a fund from which artists with no capital could borrow a $4,000 down payment and pay it back over an extended period. The maintenance fee was set at the low range of $75 to $125, depending on floor size. The

Artists Tenants Association (ATA) helped handle the crush of applicants, more than two hundred for the twelve spaces. The ATA and the CAH made sure that only working artists were accepted. "Now they own a little piece of New York, and a lot of them are truly poor," said Wall. "Ownership added stability, and people care very much about the building."[3]

With Mayor Wagner behind the project, the city's Department of Buildings approved the remodeling plans in 1964, and work was completed. The next obstacle to legal occcupancy lay at the state level. The multiple-dwelling laws, which set health and safety standards statewide on residential buildings, had to be relaxed to accommodate the notion of living and working in one space. Two Village lawyers working with CAH drafted the needed legislation, and Carol Greitzer, councilwoman from Lower Manhattan, negotiated it through the State Assembly in Albany with bipartisan support from local legislators. The legislation, Article 7-B, was a concession to a local interest and applicable only to New York City. While it was narrowly drawn to apply only to lofts in commercial zones, it established an important precedent. The language of the bill held that the cultural life of the state and its large cities was "enhanced" by the presence of artists, that their low incomes made it financially impossible for most of them to maintain separate residences and studios, and that they therefore had a special claim on buildings found to be obsolete by commercial tenants. Accordingly, artists were allowed an exclusive right to live in certain industrial lofts. The legislation recognized that a definition of "artist" was needed. "As used in this article, the word artist means a person regularly engaged in the visual fine arts, such as painting and sculpture on a professional fine arts basis and so certified by an art academy, association or society, recognized by the municipal office of cultural affairs or the state council on the arts."[4]

The problem of filtering out the consumers of art and the artist life style from legitimate artists was not difficult for this first Greenwich Street building. The cooperation of the city's commissioner of cultural affairs had been secured for a monitoring program, in case other projects were to follow. Article 7-B, utilized only for this one building before subsequent amendments broadened its scope, established the principle that loft living could be made legal and responsible, and that working artists held a special priority for this type of residence. The Greenwich Street building demonstrated the feasibility of cooperative ownership. Loft living and cooperative ownership proved to be contagious ideas among artists.

The Fluxhouse Cooperatives

In 1966 George Maciunas, an artist working in the dadaist tradition of anarchistic and irreverent art, became entranced with the idea of artist cooperatives as a vehicle for the emancipation of artists. Beyond residences and studios, Maciunas hoped to establish collective workshops, food-buying cooperatives, and theaters to link the strengths of various media together and bridge the gap between the artist community and the surrounding society. Maciunas concretized his utopian planning impulses with endless and minutely detailed projections of renovation costs and the advantages of wholesale purchases. He had the conviction, essential in a social catalyst, that legal prohibitions and entanglements could be overcome, and that the first priority was to get on with the living experiment. Maciunas established himself as the president of Fluxhouse Cooperatives, Inc., in order to "perform all the organizational work" involved in "forming cooperatives, purchasing buildings, obtaining mortgages, obtaining legal and architectural services, conducting work as a general contractor for all renovation and [handling the] future management if so desired by the members."[5]

With preliminary buying agreements with several SoHo building owners and with speculatively based but convincingly detailed renovation estimates, Maciunas approached Kaplan for backing. Kaplan had formed a joint venture financed by the J. M. Kaplan Fund and the National Foundation for the Arts. Not only did this provide a source of capital, but it enlisted new and important interest groups to back Kaplan's experiments in artists' housing. According to a foundation consultant, Henry Geldzahler, the joing venture with Kaplan was designed to break through the city's M-1 zoning designation, which excluded residential occupancy in areas of light manufacturing. "The M-1 zone, now forbidden to artists-in-residence, embraces areas of downtown Manhattan where light manufacturing has declined and many buildings now stand empty," said Geldzahler.[6] The Foundation and the Kaplan Fund, with a contribution of $100,000 each, were looking for a test case where artists could challenge the M-1 restriction. Maciunas appeared at the opportune moment, and Kaplan agreed to fund his Fluxhouse program.

By the end of 1966 Maciunas had picked out the first of the SoHo buildings that he was to promote as artist cooperatives, 80–82 Wooster Street, and was taking deposits from buyers of floors and half-floors. In the summer of 1967, with $20,000 from the Kaplan Fund and the Foundation, Maciunas was able to make the cash down payment on this $105,000 building. As was to be the pattern with other SoHo cooperatives, the former owner assumed the mortgage for the balance owed. With $20,000 in grants, Maciunas was able to offer spaces for only $2,000 cash down per shareholder, using the money for renovations and charging initially only $205 per month maintenance for 3,300 square feet. By August 1967, 80 Wooster Street was fully subscribed and undergoing basic renovations, and Maciunas was lining up buyers for a second building, 16–18 Greene Street. This time he had $5,000 from Kaplan and the National Foundation to hold the building. But serious setbacks had occurred in the Fluxhouse program. The Federal Housing Administration, which Maciunas had counted on to take over the mortgages as buildings were established, in order to free the Kaplan seed money for new purchases, had refused to become involved, citing fire hazards in the area, referred to by a series of city fire commissioners as "Hell's Hundred Acres."[8] In addition, the National Foundation for the Arts and the Kaplan Fund had embarked on a project of their own, the sponsorship of a conversion of the old Bell Telephone Laboratories in Greenwich Village into a huge artist housing complex, and had therefore lost interest in the Fluxhouse venture.[9] With the withdrawal of the legitimating momentum of philanthropic and governmental sponsorship, Fluxhouse residents were acutely conscious that they were occupying buildings that had been illegally purchased and illegally renovated. Without philanthropic sponsorship, they had no leverage to get required zoning variances from the Board of Standards and Appeals or the occupancy permits from the Department of Buildings.

Maciunas, however, relied upon a different basis of legitimacy for the occupants, a pattern of building purchases and conversions that involved enough people to make the city hesitant to enforce its own residency codes. In September 1967 he advertised shares in three buildings at Grand and Wooster streets at prices ranging from $2,200 to $5,000, or roughly $1 a square foot. Within three days the buildings were 60 percent subscribed, and by December Maciunas had the $50,000 necessary for the down payment.

Maciunas moved from block to block throughout SoHo, tracking down owners who were closing their businesses and anxious to sell their buildings. His method was to hold buildings with deposits, then to line up shareholders to provide the down payments. Maciunas balanced his increasingly complex financial arrangements with a continuous flow of new cash deposits. By June of 1968 he had sponsored cooperatives on Prince Street, Broome Street, and along West Broadway, a total of eleven cooperative units involving seventeen buildings.

The city's planning policies indirectly aided Maciunas. By casting the depressing shadow of the Lower Manhattan Expressway over the area for so long, the city planners had driven down building values and undermined the real-estate market. As early as 1963, local real-estate interests whose properties had been rendered unacceptable as loan collateral had filed suit in a fruitless effort to force the city to either buy their buildings or abandon the expressway.[10] Maciunas was operating in a buyer's market, purchasing in an area many feared would become an industrial slum. Shael Shapiro, an architect-resident in one of the first Maciunas buildings, and later a consultant for many cooperatives and an active civic leader, agreed that the city had inadvertently aided Maciunas. "The Lower Manhattan Expressway made this [Fluxhouse project] possible. It depressed values throughout this area. The day after Lindsay announced the end of the expressway, real estate along Broome Street went up 50 percent."[11]

The Emergence of Vested Housing Interests

The cooperatives, which Maciunas envisioned as a numbered series of affiliated "Fluxhouses," quickly became autonomous and resident controlled. The shareholders had become restive under Maciunas's single-handed directorship, and they felt fully competent to take over building management themselves. All residents were artists under the broad Fluxhouse definition (which included writers and composers along with visual artists, "events" artists, architects, and in one case, a flower arranger), but many, especially the writers, college art teachers, and architects, were experienced with legal and financial matters and were comfortable dealing with the city bureaucracies. These co-opers were not bohemians desirous of protection from the harsher realities of their situation.

The cooperative food-buying schemes were the first to collapse. "I can remember sitting in my loft surrounded by dozens of loaves of Russian black bread," said an early resident. "George thought this kind of buying would save us all money, and he just went out and bought what he liked. We ate it for weeks." Another time it was oranges, and then toilet paper. Cooperative buying soon ended.

Residents faced the chronic problem of undercapitalization stemming from the fact that Maciunas's cost estimates were always too low, and because the shares had been sold at prices that attracted artists with very little money. Residents repeatedly found themselves having to pay special assessments for unforeseen plumbing costs or to make up a low fuel bill estimate. For a time, this condition was not attributed to deception on Maciunas's part, but rather to his alleged warmhearted incompetence. "We were all smart enough to know that George was totally unrealistic in his expense estimates," said one resident, "and we allowed for it." But as the levies continued, many found they were financially overcommitted. Their access to capital, largely through modest loans from their middle-class families, had been exhausted, and more assessments were due. Individual buildings had to resort to independent action to save themselves from default. In some cases only the exceptional connections of one or two residents saved their buildings from bankruptcy. One resident, a painter and his building's first president, explained,

I have a Harvard education, and so I have connections that way. We bought this building with a mortgage almost due [one of three], and it was immediately called. We were really about to lose the building. I had been to every bank in the city and been laughed at. You couldn't get a mortgage on anything. At nine in the morning of the day the mortgage was due, I had the idea of calling the father of a girl I used to date at Radcliffe. By one P.M. I had the money.

I knew he was in real estate, but it also turned out he was chairman of the board of the [N] Bank. Uncle Jim, we used to call him. He simply directed the head of the branch bank to make the new mortgage. He said that had it not been for him, we would not have been able to get an appointment with the secretary to the branch manager, with the kind of building we had. . . . [B] was another dear friend. I just happened to be mentioning the building's situation one day, and she offered five thousand dollars. She said it was probably made by exploiting someone anyway, and she had no doubt clipped a coupon to get it. But she offered it interest free to us for five years.

Residents solved their financial problems as a unit, giving some members grace periods on debts, taking loans from others, and using the borrowing ability of a select few. But they could not assume responsibility for the financial problems of cooperatives other than their own.

At first, however, George Maciunas handled the deposits and bank transactions of the cooperatives on a different basis. One cooperative in the formational stage found that he had lent $26,000 in members' deposits to four other cooperatives also being established, all without the depositors' knowledge. Maciunas was unable to calm the irate shareholders with this explanation of his accounting methods, published in his *Fluxhouse Newsletter*.

The reason for such disposition of monies is my principle of collectivism—running the cooperatives not necessarily in a legalistically correct way, but in a way to benefit the collective good. When a particular cooperative is in danger of losing a building to foreclosure of lien, every effort—all the funds, go to the rescue. This has worked well without detriment to anybody. Not one of the 4 closings we had so far was delayed by this principle of a "collective chest." It would not have delayed the closing of 465 West Broadway either had it not been for the interference of the "shadow kitchen."[12]

The "shadow kitchen" consisted of shareholders who did not trust Maciunas and who were eager to take over their own building affairs. They believed that his financial control and manipulation of deposit accounts enabled him to speculate at their expense. The president of one early Maciunas cooperative pointed out,

George sold the garage on the ground floor of our building for a ridiculously low price to a friend of his. It's now a theater, and a very valuable space. We saw collusion, with his friend working behind the scenes in partnership with George. When we protested, this guy rented the space to a company that parked garbage trucks there, just to spite us. Maciunas was dishonest from the very beginning.

Cooperatives found, contrary to Maciunas's reassurances, that they could not get their deposit money back from other co-ops when their own closing date for purchase arrived. One cooperative reported having to pay an interest rate of 25 percent a month to borrow two thousand dollars from another Fluxhouse in order to forestall the foreclosure of their mortgage. In another instance, a cooperative found itself sued by the bank which handled its deposits because of Maciunas's policy of shifting money from account to account. Individual cooperatives quickly discovered that if they were to survive, they had to fend for themselves in financial matters. Maciunas was hurt by this turn toward economic self-interest on the part of the cooperatives and by the criticism of his leadership which he felt had inspired it. In a letter in which he relinquished all managerial connections with two Fluxhouse units, Maciunas explained the dispute from his side.

I did not mind doing all this [managerial work] free of charge if it was going to advance the selfless spirit of collectivism. Unfortunately, it did nothing of the sort. As soon as opportunity presented itself, the collective spirit fell apart—members selfishly promoting their own interests at the expense of the cooperative and separate cooperatives promoting their interests at the expense of the entire collective. More specifically, . . . the Grand St. directors saw no reason why their temporarily excessive funds should have been used to save Wooster St. from disaster and Wooster Street's treasurer saw no reason to reciprocate this good will by returning this borrowed money or part to save Grand Street from disaster. Members showed their distrust in me, or envying better spaces of other members, actually entered those spaces to remeasure and recalculate the spaces so as to increase other's and decrease their own monthly rents. Etc., etc., ad nauseam. . . . Furthermore, since several members expressed dissatisfaction with my methods of management and accounting, a few even suspecting me of making a fortune (!), I decided to stop wasting my selfless interest which is unappreciated anyway and become just as selfish as everybody else.
THUS: . . . I will stop giving free time and advice on all matters relating to architecture, electrical engineering, mǎnagement, accounting, carpentry, building code, contractors, supplies, etc. . . . I will charge . . . for my past work in management, general contracting and accounting at the low rate of $40 per week. . . . Any further time

spent by me on any of the above matters will be charged to you at the rate of $10 per hour (which is the rate I received at the time I quit my job).[13]

Maciunas continued to sponsor cooperatives, but only as individual ventures and for a fixed fee. The Fluxhouse phase in SoHo was over by late 1968. In the absence of any overall financial resources, the problem of survival had individuated each cooperative. Financial anxiety and the recourse to purely personal resources available to the individual shareholders made self-management for each cooperative a necessity. A secularizing monetary fear had washed away any illusions about the bonds of a gemeinschaft between cooperatives. Nevertheless, it soon was to become apparent that the larger problem of resolving the artists' illegal residential status would require an area-wide organizational approach. The territorial district itself evolved as the basis for a functionally important form of community in the next phase of development.

The SoHo Artists Association

Since its beginnings in the late 1950s, residency in the district had been dependent upon the artists' ability to reach an illegal accommodation with the inspectors from various city departments, especially the Department of Buildings. The artists avoided drawing public attention to themselves and bribed the inspectors who inadvertently stumbled across them in the course of performing their duties. In general, the system worked well enough. "After all," said one artist, "if the inspectors had been honest, we would not be here now." The inspectors were not under any departmental pressure to clean up the situation, and the artists were able to keep their housing niches.

But with the spread of cooperatives and the public awareness of residency in the area generated by the artists' opposition to the Lower Manhattan Expressway, the fictions that maintained the accommodation wore out. The rate of graft had been held down by the willingness of artists to move on if they had to. But the members of cooperatives were hostages. "Inspectors wanted $100 a floor at most up until about 1968," said a long-time resident, "but then their greed drove many of us to go for legalization to stop the graft." The bribery system imposed an escalating financial and psychological tax that co-op members found difficult to bear on top of their other expenses. With each new payoff or renovation assessment, they found themselves trying to salvage an investment that looked increasingly precarious, and their anxieties mounted. One resident's experiences convey the sense of entrapment that many felt.

We bought into the co-op through George Maciunas. George said $3,000, and everybody went along. It went to $5,000, then $7,000, and finally $9,000. My parents gave me a loan by taking out a second mortgage on their house. The lawyer we talked to laughed. The whole deal was illegal, and there were no papers to speak of. There were supposed to be shares, maybe, years from then. And the lawyer kept saying, "You're throwing your money away." After we bought, we kept hearing people say that George was a swindler. We had no sense of being squatters then, and trying to change the law that way. It was more that we thought that the city wouldn't bother us. There were influential artists here, and that would cool the city out, we hoped.

There were always money problems here, and this colored the atmosphere. We were never current with the bills. The plumber was always needing money. We survived only by payoffs. If it had been a less bribable system, we would have died. There were inspectors all over. George was supposed to have had an in at the Buildings Department and gave them a $1,600 bribe. But we still had trouble. . . . Of course, the plans for our building had six floors, but the building had seven.

In this system you try to be invisible and you may get away. The structure of illegality was never clear. It could be the wrong guy you were talking to, and maybe you could and maybe you couldn't get away with a bribe. . . . After we got into it, George's socialism was certainly not an operating reality. Only survival was.

In the spring of 1968 the system of illegal accommodation began to unravel. The Fluxhouse cooperative at 80 Wooster Street began to have insurmountable problems with building inspectors. A moving-picture theater had been constructed on the ground floor of the building, but the theater manager could not secure clearance to open. The fact that his project involved public assembly permits and that eleven artists lived illegally above the theater complicated his problems. The interests of the theater owner and those of the residents seemed on a collision course. One resident recalled, "He said, 'I'll give [my theater] to a foundation and make a big fuss,' but we told him, 'You'll have to buy us out first.'"

To resolve the dispute, the artists in the building decided to hold a meeting of area residents to discuss the ramifications of their illegal status. The cooperatives were in touch with one another, and six sent representatives. Other residents of the district were reached through a less systematic method. One of the meeting's organizers explained, "We walked up and down the streets at night looking for lighted windows or flowers and tacked notices to the door." Soon afterward, they combined their list with that of the Artists Against the Expressway organization and created a comprehensive mailing list of residents.

Fifty people came to this initial meeting of area artists. The immediate problem they faced was what to do about the theater and the building inspectors. An area collection of bribe money was proposed and rejected. It seemed to make them all vulnerable to uncontrolled future extortion. "Some suggested that we try to get the building a zoning variance, even if we had to bribe to do it," recalled one participant at the meeting. "But this was not really possible, and if it had succeeded in the one case, it was still only a stop-gap. This led to a second meeting, where the aim changed to getting the *area* legalized through political action."

This second meeting was smaller and was held in the co-op loft of a SoHo architect. The debate centered on what form legalization of residency in the district ought to take. Some, including those artists who, along with nonartists, were active in the antiexpressway coalition, favored unrestricted access to the area's lofts and opposed an "artists' ghetto." Co-op members were interested in restricting occupation to artists, as one explained:

> Artists were here because of their studios. There was a legitimate reason why artists should be allowed to live here. If we talked about wanting unrestricted use, it would lead to the neighborhood being torn down. Most of us were artists, and we felt we had to assert our legal right to work, so we felt a change to a completely residential area had to be avoided. If not, it would destroy itself. And the truth was, we never could have gotten rezoning to residential.

The goal of legal residency restricted to artists became incorporated into the organization's name, the SoHo Artists Association (SAA). According to one member: "'SoHo' came up as a name and stuck. The basis for the name was that we were a viable community and a neighborhood. All the others in the city had names—like Cobble Hill. . . . The decision to create the SAA as an 'artists association' was deliberate and political."

The meeting rejected the idea of a formally structured organization and official titles, although negotiations with the city soon required that the activists assume normal bureaucratic positions. "I was chosen," the first SAA president explained, "because I was the only one in SoHo who owned a black suit." Power was held by an executive coordinating committee, elected at the second meeting. Decision-making was determined to be a collective responsibility of this small group of activists, whose involvement with the issues had provided them with the necessary understanding, and whose work for the community gave their opinions weight. Further elections to the committee were not found to be necessary. As new personalities emerged in the district, people who seemed to be articulate and able to follow through on tasks, they were absorbed into the loose Coordinating Committee structure. Others who felt they had done their share—indeed, that they had been overworked—resigned at periodic intervals, usually at the end of a crisis in the protracted struggle.

The role which emerged for the SAA Coordinating Committee consisted of six distinct but overlapping functions:

1. They were an information net, sensitive to new developments that threatened to alter the artist-in-residency basis of the community. Their extensive contacts with the city planning staff and Community Board Two, the advisory planning board within whose jurisdiction SoHo fell, were converted into antennae. The placement of SoHo residents on Board Two, an early objective, was an outgrowth of this need for contacts and information.

2. They formulated the issues which posed a danger to the community in terms which allowed residents to respond. They called, chaired, and set the agenda for community meetings and posed the alternatives upon which residents voted from time to time.

3. They were the negotiating arm of the community. A group of five or six artists from the Coordinating Committee communicated the proposals of the residents to the city planning officials and carried back to the residents a sense of what was realistically possible. As they became knowledgeable in planning politics, they educated the community, moderated its more excessive demands, and made themselves a channel for those planning officials who sought an accommodation with the artists.

4. They conducted the community's public-relations campaign. This included frequent and friendly contact with planning liaison staff, contact which gradually won the staff over to support SoHo's point of view. It included conducting loft tours for press, public, and city officials which demonstrated that safe and healthy living, as well as creativity, could take place in renovated factory buildings. Supportive relationships with journalists were cultivated, and finally, a three-day street festival and open-loft sale and celebration was held to publicize the existence and jeopardy of SoHo.

5. The Coordinating Committee worked with various professionals who, as allies, carried out the economic and legal research necessary to support the community's position. They also worked with special interest groups—for example, the Friends of Cast-Iron Architecture, whose concerns reinforced those of SoHo.

6. They periodically called upon the community to demonstrate or to testify at planning hearings. Such events were not only occasions for favorable media coverage but also aided in neighborhood-building. Every meeting and demonstration was, of course, an opportunity for the Coordinating Committee to relay information to the residents. But it was also a chance for the residents to affirm and strengthen a communal relationship with each other. Since artists worked, and often lived, in isolation, they were continually surprised to learn at these meetings who their neighbors were, or that someone they knew in the art world was living around the corner. SoHo's population was both growing and

transient. According to the estimates of some SAA leaders, a third of those artists in the community in 1968 were gone by 1970. While the co-ops had a relatively stable population and provided the means to integrate their new arrivals, the Coordinating Committee integrated the community as a whole at public meetings. The explicit purpose of these meetings was to discuss the latest city proposals or some other crisis, but the SAA leadership usually gave a synopsis of SoHo's history and the district's relationship to the city and the surrounding populations and concrete survival advice about renovating techniques and the building code. After an airing of divergent, and often idiosyncratic, opinions and problems, these meetings would end with a consensus on the most pressing issues and an enlivened sense of community. The SAA published a community newsletter, mailed to residents as the need arose, which continued this community-building function, with analyses of issues, advice on dealing with landlords, and news of local events, such as a fundraiser for a cooperative day-care center in the district.

These varied functions emerged gradually and were clarified by the flow of events. The speed with which the situation changed between 1968 and 1970 required that the Coordinating Committee act with a great deal of latitude in its representation of the community. Their executive initiatives were ratified at irregularly scheduled community meetings, which coincided with the sudden need to mobilize for a particular crisis. Because they had no independent source of information, residents were reluctant to second-guess the leadership at these meetings. More than feeling ill-informed, those who hadn't worked on a problem felt they didn't have the moral foundation on which to criticize those who had voluntarily put in long hours. The community's problems required that its leadership cultivate sympathetic, knowledgeable, and essentially personal relationships with city planners, lawyers, and architects. This put a value on continuity in leadership and predicated a mastery of a large amount of technical and chronological detail. Residents with only a passing interest in the issues could not play a constructive part. Thus, those who did pay the price in time and energy to become sufficiently involved—time and energy they felt to be stolen from their real work, their art—developed a sense of moral righteousness which justified their leadership and its style in their own eyes and in that of most residents.

The Coordinating Committee depended for its legitimacy with area residents upon more than its evident, and at times paraded, sacrifices. It had developed real expertise. While the city was not obliged to collect garbage in a nonresidential area, for example, the SAA was able to negotiate collection anyway. Committee members were constantly answering phone calls from distraught residents unable to cope with individual problems—the fumes from a neighbor's studio, or inability to obtain building insurance. Despite feeling over-worked, the committee serviced these complaints. The residents, for their part, freely imposed on the leadership. As artists, they were culturally disposed to recognize the "patron aspects" of a relationship when they saw them.

Most importantly, the cultural homogeneity uniting the community with the leadership sustained the SAA's legitimacy. The leaders, too, were artists and loft dwellers. Their self-interests and values could be trusted to be the same as those of the other residents. Furthermore, most of the leaders were co-op residents, known and accepted as competent actors within their own buildings and united in their property interests with the most active of the district's population, the other co-op artists. Thus, the personal confidence of the members of the SAA Coordinating Committee and the legitimacy of their authority in the eyes of the community were sustained by the fact that they were representative members, and particularly competent ones, of overlapping territorial and occupational communities. The basic foundation of the territorial community rested on the common interest of the loft dwellers in the preservation of their homes, their working spaces, and their property.

Owners and Renters

Despite sharing a common occupational culture and the hazards of illegal residency, artists in the district did not all agree that legal occupancy would be more desirable than the existing covert accommodation. This political disagreement grew out of the different housing situations faced by renters and by cooperative owners. As one SAA activist and co-op member explained,

> From the beginning there was a schism with the renters, though it was often unspoken. Had we all been renters, of course, we would have moved out when the harassment reached a certain point. But the core of our support was the co-ops. Owners did most of the [SAA] work, though some renters were a help. We always denied the existence of the schism, but it was there.

Renters, the majority of the residents, comprised a housing interest group divergent from that of the co-ops. Even in the period when Fluxhouse lofts could be secured for three or four thousand dollars down, many artists did not have access to this amount of capital and therefore remained renters. Some artists bought into cooperatives but found they couldn't keep up with the special repair assessments and moved back into rental lofts. In some instances, renters were already living in buildings which were converted into co-ops and were told that since the building needed operating capital, they would either have to become owning partners in the cooperative or move out.

A small number of artists with substantial incomes from art sales or jobs also chose to remain renters. They did not want the imposed neighborliness often characteristic of cooperatives, where one's own work was frequently and unpredictably interrupted. In co-ops, it seemed that there were always oil-burner repairmen to be supervised, a work detail to join, and building financial meetings to attend. Some did not want this distraction and could afford to avoid it. These privileged artists referred to the co-op activists as "burghers" and felt the SAA was an association of property owners rather than of artists, an opinion occasionally voiced in anger by the poorer renters as well. By preserving a distance from the affairs of the territorial community, these renting artists were able to emphasize the security of their ties to the cosmopolitan artistic community. They could afford to be disdainful of such parochial issues as zoning changes.

Most renters, however, were simply artists who could not afford cooperatives. On the whole, renters had become dependent upon inexpensive housing and the system of payoffs that made it possible. The illegal status kept down the competition for lofts and, therefore, the rental rates, because many people who wanted lofts would not take them on illegal terms. Nevertheless, the renters spoke for a population of low-income artists whose housing culture was rapidly becoming obsolete. "There were a lot of people very much against legalization," explained an original Coordinating Committee member. "They felt it would drive up rents, and expose us to more inspectors, perhaps those from the Fire Department. And they felt that if we succeeded, which they doubted, we would only attract the hangers-on in the art world, the psychopaths. But their objections were never vocal enough to be legitimate. They tended to be renters." Their political tactics of avoidance failed to reflect the new reality, that loft living had been exposed as an issue and was on the agenda of public planning agencies. The problem was no longer one of hiding but of finding ways to influence that planning deliberation.

The SAA tried two tactics to meet the objections of the renters. First, they set up a renter's committee to channel dissent into the formulation of proposals which would be a part of the negotiation. It was hoped that committee work within the SAA would draw renters out of their isolation and opposition and get them to appreciate the new community situation. The renters who responded were those who accepted the co-opers' definition of the situation; two bought into the next available cooperatives within one six-month period. The less property-mobile among the renters were difficult to persuade, but their own disdain for formal organization prevented them from ever becoming a second force in the community. What became known to the SAA activists as the renters' apathy soon became an issue in itself and had the effect of invalidating the renters' sporadically voiced complaints about the negotiations with the city. SAA newsletters continually mentioned the difficulty of involving the renters: "The Association invites (again) all of its members—again—to join its working committees. The Renters Committee in particular, which could have such a powerful effect on the condition of SoHo's renting majority, has had hardly a single volunteer."[14]

The second move made by the SAA to accommodate the renters, a move strongly endorsed by the SAA's ally, the Artists Tenants Association, was a call for rent control in residential lofts. This proposal, however, did not hold up beyond the early stages of the Coordinating Committee's negotiations with the city. City planners refused even to consider an extension of the existing residential rent control into commercial and manufacturing buildings. An SAA negotiator said,

> We worked out a reverse rent control to stabilize the area. We would have allowed unrestricted market rentals for business—rentals at any price—but to artists, only as a percentage increase over the previous tenant's rent. This was an ideal way, but they smelled rent control at the city. Rent control would open a big argument, and the city had a landlord bias and orientation. Elliott [City Planning Commission chairman] forbade it.

While it appeared in the first SAA proposal submitted to the city in June of 1970, rent control was dropped from subsequent proposals.[15] The SAA postponed pursuit of rent control until legalization of zoning had been achieved. Another Coordinating Committee member explained:

> The split with the renters got very outspoken at the time the city sent a proposal to us from the CPC and we countered with our own proposal. Renters felt we were selling them out. But rent control, which is what they needed, was an issue too large to fight out in this arena. Besides, we felt that the certification [of all residents as bona fide artists by a city agency] would limit the area to artists and so keep the push factor out of the rent situation in the remaining lofts. We were naive. But we were right at the time.

The SAA had to negotiate on two fronts: first, as the representatives of a united and vocal community before the city planners; and second, as realistic advocates of the possible before the SoHo community itself. To accomplish this second task, the SAA used area meetings and newsletters to educate the community about the relative feasibility of various proposals. At a point near the successful conclusion of negotiations with the city, an SAA newsletter addressed the rent control issue as follows:

There still remains, however, the criticism of [the lack of a] rent control provision. It is absolutely correct. The proposal does not really provide for rent control. The reason is this: rent control can only be established by the Department of Housing and Development, and they won't talk to anybody who isn't legal in their tenancy. So write, show up on the [hearing date], and get legal. Rent control, including roll backs, is the next battle.[16]

There is no question that the renter's interests suffered in the negotiations. The most vigilant monitors of the negotiations were those with a co-op investment at stake, and they dominated the SAA organization. The city took this factor into account in their own proposals to the community. City Planning Commission chairman Donald Elliott agreed to support zoning changes allowing residency in buildings no larger than 3,600 square feet because these were far less useful to industry than the larger buildings. But some artists already lived in larger buildings. In the exchange of proposals and counterproposals, the SAA was able to secure Elliott's agreement to exempt the existing oversized co-ops from zoning prohibitions, but it could not do the same for the oversized rental lofts. Thus the city accommodated only the articulate portion of the community with which it had to negotiate.

The pattern of agreements and concessions followed, indeed emphasized, the contours of the housing divisions within the community. The SAA, which had the function of preparing the community to vote a response to the city's offer, could only stress the intransigence of Elliott as a fact to which the community would have to resign itself. Recapitulating the negotiations, the SAA wrote:

SoHo argued that renters who were in buildings larger than 3600 sq. ft. as of September 15 should also be legalized, because the right was extended to cooperatives and therefore would not change the basic concepts behind the proposal. Don Elliott responded by saying that, to the contrary, the oversized co-ops violate the concepts and in reality should also be excluded. The co-ops were included, Elliott reminded us, because they had made building-wide changes that rendered the buildings unfit for the industrial usage for which the over 3600 sq. ft. buildings are reserved. These radical changes, the Commission believes, were not made in rental buildings.

SoHo responded that this was an unfair threat because two wrongs would not make a right. Elliott responded that the Commission had discussed this point at length and decided that *under no circumstances* (emphasis Elliott's) would they yield on this point. Elliott pointed out that the Commission believes it had made an extreme concession with possibly dangerous future consequences for the welfare of the blue-collar employing industry of the area; that no other city has made such extensive or such unique concessions to a single group; that in a city where space is at an all-time premium, this concession will prove embarrassing to them in the future; but that they are making it because they recognize the need and importance of artists. As a result, Elliott said, he did not see that the further concession of the 47 oversize rented lofts, which he declared *would* damage the proposal's principles, is possible. Under further pressure from SoHo, Elliott reiterated his stand, but promised that *the 47 artists would have a year of grace from the date of the passage of the proposal.* After that, he said, they would have to take their chances. He did expect that the Buildings Department would enforce the new zoning. Under further pressure, he stated that if SoHo made the passage of the proposal conditional on this point, the CPC would drop the whole proposal.[17]

The SAA was thus faced with the choice of a partially satisfactory agreement or none at all.

As SoHo illustrates, members of status communities have spatial and locational needs which flow from their occupational concerns. These needs led some members to make territorial claims which could only be defended politically if they were represented as an expression of the needs of the entire status community. But the territorial focus created new lines of stratification among artists, arranging culturally homogeneous residents into real-estate groupings tactically at odds with each other. Renters and housing-cooperative partners can be conceptually regarded as "housing interest groups." Their antagonism is contained within the framework of an underlying common community. Confronting urban society at large, the territorially based status community of SoHo behaved as a "housing class," as John Rex and Robert Moore define the term.[18]

The Recruitment of Advocate Planners

The first area artists' meeting in the spring of 1968 had led to the establishment of the SoHo Artists Association and its Coordinating Committee as the community's forum and political instrument for securing a zoning amendment that would permit artist studio-residency alongside of the existing light industry. But the means to this goal were far from obvious at the start of the campaign.

At this point a junior staff worker for the CPC, Mike Lewis, was sent into the SoHo district to investigate planning alternatives.[19] As a young graduate of planning school, he had been the liaison between the CPC and Local Planning Board Two since 1967. Within a few days of having contacted and spoken with the SAA leadership, he found himself nervously standing before a specially convened SoHo community meeting trying to cope with the hostility and suspicion the artists directed against anyone from the city agencies. "Mike said he felt like he needed a bodyguard," recalled one SAA leader. Before very long, however, his working relationship with the artist leadership developed into friendship, and Lewis came to consider the artists as his real planning constituency. For the next two years before rezoning was achieved, he acted as SoHo's advocate within city planning circles. He was the artists' trusted counselor and informant, a guide to their bureaucratic antagonists. Without his help, all the SAA leadership agreed, the artists' negotiations with the Planning Commission could not have been successful.

Lewis's adoption of SoHo as his own planning cause could be explained partially by the working conditions at the CPC itself. The staff was demoralized. Young planners, having gone through college during the decade when campuses were organizing centers for civil rights marches and anti-Vietnam War protests, refused to accept a merely instrumental role as technical advisors to a planning commission they criticized for being politically subservient to vested real-estate interests. They felt the need for a populist cause to legitimate their professional functions. They considered themselves to be "advocate planners," experts whose job was to enable those groups traditionally unrepresented in the planning process to find a voice in land-use policy. The artists seemed to qualify, along with the poor and the unorganized, as an ideologically suitable constituency. These planners hoped to build their careers by fashioning planning solutions to meet needs defined by grassroots constituencies.

In February 1969, just before Lewis began to work on the SoHo problem, four rebellious staff planners from the CPC contradicted their commissioners' recommendations in a public hearing. They were organized in a group called the Urban Underground, and were supported in their protest by a petition signed by twenty-five of the twenty-seven CPC staff members. The point at issue was a proposal to increase zoning densities on Manhattan's West Side, which the staff felt would lead to the demolition of sound low- and middle-income housing and the construction of high-rise luxury apartments. They based their opinion on an area survey conducted by Lewis and a second employee, Paul Barker. In a pamphlet subsequently published to clarify the press reports of the confrontation, the Urban Underground explained its views and commitments:

> People who work in this society have few ways to control the sense and purpose of their work. Society tells some of its workers that they have an expertise, a skill that they can use that distinguishes them from other workers who only work, after all, to make some bread. But that expertise is a deception. We have the concrete examples

here today of city planners, whose skills are supposedly orientated towards working with the people in this city towards the creation of a human, livable environment. But what do we find? When it comes to the question of rezoning Manhattan south of 96th Street, the city planners are lied to and manipulated in the interests not of effective planning or for community interests, but for the sake of the needs of the real estate interests, the city government, and anyone else who stands to make a profit out of people's real needs. If in our actions, analyses and exposures of what goes on in this city, such as the rezoning, we make institutions like the City Planning Commission uptight, that's only the beginning. . . . The Urban Underground will analyze, expose, and develop a movement that can contest the very roots of power in this society.[20]

The conclusions of the area survey were overruled by the commissioners for what the staff understood to be corrupt reasons. Barker said, "Commissioner Elliott told us, 'We have to reelect John Lindsay, and we need the support of real estate.'" The most outspoken staff members, including Barker, either quit or were fired during the months subsequent to the hearing. The Urban Underground collapsed. Lewis, who did not testify, found in the SoHo issue the opportunity to practice reformist advocacy planning, and he seized it.

The qualities of the artists themselves were also a part of the reason planners could identify with the community. Artists were articulate, educated, and engaged in the kind of creative and personal labor attractive to bureaucrats caught up in routine work. "Mike was the best," explained one Coordinating Committee member. "He was cooperative, he drafted things for us, he attended our meetings. He was young and gung ho on the idea of advocacy planning and the possibility of rezoning the area to feed into the cultural milieu of the city. He was fascinated with the area and with the culture. We all got socially friendly very fast." While having an artist constituency glamorized the planning job, the planner's bureaucratic skills were precisely what the artists came to realize were indispensable.

The second staff planner who became a SoHo advocate at the CPC was Alicia Pool. As a student of architecture and planning at the University of Pennsylvania, she had done summer work with Chester Rapkin's survey group on the South Houston Industrial District in 1962 and had since become an economic researcher with the city. In 1970 she was assigned to the economic development section of the CPC, which prepares advisory studies on the economic impact of zoning proposals for the commissioners. Since SoHo was an industrial zone and within her specialty, she was assigned to write a report on the SAA's proposed rezoning. Primarily a statistician, Pool, like Lewis, came to SoHo without any prior exposure to artists and the art world. Pool said of her initial contacts with the community, "There was pressure for the SoHo issue to come before the commission. My own concern was about the possible loss of jobs in the area, and I realized that I couldn't decide without a full study. I wanted to keep detached, and people in SoHo resented this."

Pool attended her first SoHo meeting in midsummer 1970, and she was received with consternation by the artists. It seemed to them that her attitude, even her conventional appearance in high heels and skirt, in no way suggested a sympathy with the artists. The news circulated around the room that in private conversation she had said, "Tear it all down and put it to a better use." The Coordinating Committee held a secret caucus, and coping with Pool and her announced study was made the special responsibility of a filmmaker and SAA activist, Noah Halliwell. "Everyone disliked her immediately," recalled Halliwell; "she was so unforgivingly negative. I felt hopeless. And she was to teach me how to help in the survey of the community."

Out of the need of the SAA to have some input into the survey of their community began a strange collaboration in which Halliwell led Pool through the neighborhood, interviewing residents and trying to cultivate her sympathy for the SAA's proposals. The artists they talked to were not particularly concerned with Halliwell's public-relations management. A third of them, largely renters, simply responded, "Go to hell!" when the survey team knocked on their door. Few other artists made themselves available to help out, and Halliwell and Pool worked against a deadline until they were exhausted. Slowly and despite setbacks, mutual fatigue and Halliwell's concentrated attentions began to have an effect. As Halliwell explained,

> I would front during the survey, trying to put people at ease by saying, "Hi, I'm a neighbor." Then Alicia would go right to the essence of her questions—"Do you have a bathing system here?" The people were often stoned, bare breasted, or obscene. Some were taking drugs, you could see that. And [she] began to break down to the humor of it all. When she found herself stepping over dogshit in a loft inspection, she began to find it amusing. She started referring to what she saw as "light party drugs." All in all it was an arduous summer.

For a planning technician such as Pool, the bohemian fringe dramatized the "otherness" of the artistic subculture, while SAA activists and the majority of SoHo residents impressed her with their aesthetic seriousness, their ease of communication, and their middle-class notions of domestic respectability. Gradually, she was converted to the artists' point of view. "I had a hippy stereotype of artists," she said, "but most turned out to be like me. They had traveled, been to college. I could easily deal with them. I saw Noah as brilliant. He was very aggressive

and anti-city, and to the artists, I was the city first of all. By mid-
September I was pro-SoHo.''

The SAA, as it had proceeded in its campaign, had discovered that a
powerful potential attraction existed between planning bureaucrats and
artists. Planners, as the products of middle-class socialization, were
imbued from childhood with a respect for individual creativity which
must often be subordinated to organizational conformity and more bureaucratically tolerable forms of ambition.[21] The seductiveness of contact with artists lay in the fact that it reactivated postponed desires for
work that was an expression of individual creativity. The result was a
personal dilemma for planners. This was resolved through their adopting
a protective and custodial role toward the artist community and champi-
oning it with the professional tools available to them. Their midwifing of
the SoHo revitalization enabled these planners to gain personal satisfaction as well as professional recognition for having had a hand in the
creative shaping of a community.

Pool was often called to clarify matters for the commissioners during
the fall of 1970. They met periodically with their various section staffs
and requested detailed assessments and technical judgments. Among
themselves, the commissioners translated these judgments into the language of political-planning realities. ''I was 'Miss SoHo' in the economic
development section,'' explained Pool. ''Eventually, I was seen as partial. My section head allowed me a lot of latitude, and he accepted my
word for things. He became a partisan advocate of SoHo, too.''

From the artists' point of view, Pool had become an honorary member
of the SoHo community, and she reciprocated with a fierce loyalty that
has endured despite the conclusion of the legalization battle and her
reassignment to planning work in other boroughs of the city. She
supplied the SAA with information and documents otherwise unavailable to a community group. The artists felt at times that they were
negotiating with more information than was available to the planning
commissioners themselves.

Broadening SoHo's Base of Political Support

In addition to presenting a sound planning argument, the SAA realized
that it would have to make its case politically palatable. Lewis pointed
out to them the importance of Community Board Two to the artists'
rezoning efforts. Community planning boards operate in sixty-two local
planning districts in an advisory capacity to the CPC. Board Two, including Greenwich Village and the SoHo area, has been in existence
since 1951. A CPC staff member attends every board meeting to act as a

channel for information both to and from the City Planning Commission, reporting local sentiment as well as formal decisions. Lewis, as the liaison with Board Two, was able to introduce SoHo representatives to those of adjacent communities in the context of the board's meetings and so widen the base of support for SoHo's zoning challenge. Since the mid-1960s, Board Two had been dominated by a coalition of reformers who had ousted the regular Democratic party from power in Greenwich Village, and therefore it could be expected to be in sympathy with SoHo. Members of the board had been among those who had perfected the art of citizen involvement in planning through their coalitions, which had defeated the extension of Fifth Avenue through Washington Square Park, numerous high-rise housing projects slated for the Village area, and, most recently, the Lower Manhattan Expressway.

Lewis convinced the SAA that Board Two was a strategically important body on which to be represented. As an information crossroads, it served its members and their constituencies as an early warning system, alerting them to all pending real-estate variances and proposals. It also lent authority to the requests of members for city records that could provide vital information. Finally, as an advisory body to the CPC, the board was entitled to hold public hearings on local matters and was thus a forum in which SoHo could present its case. By 1970 Board Two had voted to give strong support to SoHo's planning proposals.

Appointment to the board was based ostensibly on an open application from residents to the borough president or to local City Council members, who passed on the applicant's record of public service and civic involvement. In fact, explicit political sponsorship was necessary as a condition for attaining membership. The SAA knew this and applied to Leon Becker, head of the downtown Liberal party organization, for two seats on the board. Becker, an influential party leader who subsequently became a judge, had already made supportive moves toward SoHo, donating money to the SAA, in hope of enlisting area residents as members in the Liberal party. While the SAA would not commit themselves to a formal political alliance, they did assign an artist to maintain friendly contacts with the Liberal party, and the effort was a success. As this artist explained, "Through the Liberal party we were able to get two of our SoHo people onto Community Planning Board Two.... [One] had great credentials as a leader in the Artists Against the Expressway. The board position gave us the chance to unite with other groups, especially the Villagers."

The Liberal party connection also enabled the SAA to forestall the evictions of any artists in SoHo and therefore to negotiate without the immediate pressure to compromise. Due to Liberal party influence, to which the mayor, approaching reelection without the firm backing of his own Republican party, was particularly sensitive, an unwritten agreement was worked out so that the Planning Department and the Department of Buildings would honor the status quo on artists' residencies for the time being. Of course the artists, for their part, continued to form cooperative buildings and build their constituency.

Lewis made the artists aware that their greatest difficulty at the Planning Commission level would be over the effect of their residence on the jobs and businesses in the South Houston area. Chester Rapkin, by then a commissioner, still viewed the area as a vital source of manual jobs and as an "incubator" for new business activity, as did his colleagues. In collecting evidence to support their proposal, the artists took special care to refute these arguments and to neutralize any potential opposition from business or organized labor.

First, they tried to enlist the support of local businessmen for their zoning proposals. While at times they succeeded in getting as many as six businessmen to sit down with them while they explained their plans, in general the artists found business to be uninterested and unresponsive. "They were complacent, and anyway, they felt nothing could be done—they still don't see that because of us they are still here," said one artist. The single exception to business apathy was Robert Perlmutter, head of Pearl Paint, one of the city's largest vendors of artists' supplies. Located on Canal Street, he saw the growth of SoHo as an opportunity to combine humanism with good business. He gave the SAA money, testified at planning hearings on behalf of the artists' cause, and in the postlegalization period, subsidized a community lecture series entitled "Artists Talk on Art." With one articulate business representative behind them and the rest of the business interests unorganized and unable to express divergent opinions, the SAA felt safe from at least one source of potential opposition.

The local chapter of the Warehousemen's Union posed another problem. The downtown Liberal party organization was very worried that the warehouse workers would attack the SoHo proposals and the Liberal party for sponsoring them. The artists went to the union and argued that legalization would save the buildings from wholesale condemnation and redevelopment and thus preserve marginal businesses and laborers' jobs. The artists found the unions to be another organization without any interest in the local planning situation. "One would have assumed that they world be for legalization," said an artist who had attempted to persuade them, "but they were neutral. But this was enough. We realized, though, that our base of support had to be much wider than the Liberal party."

Commenting on the lack of local opposition to the SAA's proposals, Planning Commission chairman Elliott recollected,

There was no countervailing force claiming the neighborhood. The Lower Manhattan Expressway had prevented land assembly and kept the traditional developer out. . . . Industry never came to the hearings. The landlords wanted no restrictions at all, and had no vested interests in incubator industry. Business had a nineteenth-century structure, with no corporate sense. They had no trade association, they paid their workers no overtime, they were close to the law in the conditions they provided for their workers. They never defended their rights.[22]

During late 1969 the SAA acquired its most important ally, Doris C. Freedman. The SAA did not recruit her; rather, she volunteered and made SoHo one of her projects. Freedman was a member of a wealthy real-estate family and an energetic patron of the arts whose concern with artist housing had begun in the early 1960s with her work for the Artists Tenants Association. She had helped them to implement the Artist-In-Residence (A.I.R.) program which enabled residential artists to rent in commercial zones of the city. Mayor Lindsay had appointed her commissioner for cultural affairs. As such, she had official access to the planning commissioners, as well as social access to the backers of the mayor within the cultural community.

Freedman worked for SoHo on two fronts. Within the administration she exerted her influence directly and repeatedly on the office of Commissioner Elliott in support of the maximum demands of the SoHo community.[23] Working in an unofficial, but equally important, capacity, Freedman organized and led a revitalized Citizens for Artists Housing. The CAH acted as a lobbying group, recruiting important people in New York's art world as supporters of the SAA proposals. These CAH members included such well-known artists as Lichtenstein and Rauschenberg, such dealers as Castelli and Paula Cooper, and such collectors as Robert C. Scull. Freedman also enlisted politically connected art patrons into the CAH, including Mrs. Jacob K. Javitts, Mrs. August Hechshir, Mrs. Irving Mitchell Felt, Mrs. Albert A. List, and Joan Davidson. At social engagements, they were able to raise the subject of SoHo with individual planning commissioners and argue that the city should try to meet the needs of artists.

As commissioner of cultural affairs, Freedman was able to solve a problem on whose outcome the legalization issue depended—the restricting of SoHo to artists only. The Planning Commission demanded this restriction, and the SAA agreed that nonartists would have to be kept out if the limited number of lofts were truly to serve the needs of space-starved working artists. In any open competition with nonartists, the SAA knew, all but the most successful artists would eventually be priced out of the district. Freedman volunteered her office as a clearinghouse to handle the screening of residents' credentials both as bona fide artists and as persons whose work required space of loft proportions. The SAA incorporated Freedman's offer into their first zoning proposal, enabling them to meet the planners' skepticism with a seemingly workable system for keeping loft demand down and the pressure to vacate off industry.

The Steps to a Zoning Accommodation

The agreement of the mayor's office and the CPC in April 1970 to a moratorium on the eviction of SoHo artists for illegal residency marked the first change in the city's position. After a year of contact with a small negotiating group from the SAA and pressure from the political friends of SoHo, the city shifted from ignoring the situation to actively searching for a solution to artists' housing problems. Whether an accommodation could be reached and on what terms remained an open question.

Acting on the advice of the CPC field workers who had identified their own personal and professional interests with the survival of SoHo, the SAA tailored its arguments and evidence to what it had learned were the major concerns of the planning commissioners. As an SAA member central to the negotiations explained, "Mike [Lewis] told us the 'glory of art' argument is nonsense. The commissioners are philistines. They have to see vital economic factors. It was Mike's strategy to get the huge amount of information we collected and give it to the CPC. And we put out our White Paper."

In 1970 a video artist and co-op resident, Ingrid Wiegand, compiled a White Paper that was a comprehensive defense of SoHo in planning and economic terms. Accepting the CPC's 1969 Master Plan, which had seen Manhattan as being essentially a corporate-headquarters location for international business, Wiegand argued that art production, and hence SoHo, was an essential ingredient in the realization of this plan. Her argument that artists deserved a place in New York City was essentially economic. "Their economic value," she wrote in her summary, "lies not only in the volume of trade and employment in the art industry— some $100 million worth—but also in the fact that their presence contributes to making the City an attractive place to be. This 'glamour' attracts, among others, the office and executive elite, whose exodus would disintegrate the healthiest elements in the City's economic structure." SoHo was depicted in the White Paper as a "self-generating art center" into which galleries as well as artists were moving, creating a prestige market "suitable to the City's status as the art center of the world."[24]

The artists based their arguments on Rapkin's 1962 study and contended that they were not pushing industry out but simply taking over vacant buildings, "giving the traditional incubator area a new industry to nurture and a new reason for being."[25] The SAA made sure that their White Paper was distributed to all the relevant city agencies, including the Cultural Affairs Department, and it was read to the community at a special meeting. They felt it was important that the line they took be consistent and widely publicized.

In May of 1970 the SAA formulated its first proposal for legalizing artists' residences, a position which was endorsed overwhelmingly by a vote of the community in June. This proposal reasserted that SoHo, as a "multi-use complex of industry, residence and commercial activity," would revitalize the district and "contribute in a positive way to the Master Plan's goal of strengthening New York City as a national center."[26] At the same time, it admonished the CPC for its urban renewal policies: "City policy was clearly responsible for the destruction of hundreds of thousands of square feet of cheap, ideally located industrial space that can never again be duplicated."[27]

From their own reading of city-planning documents and from the information supplied to them by the CPC field workers, the artists knew that city policy was balanced between the long-term goal of replacing Manhattan industry and the immediate need to stem the flow of blue-collar jobs away from the city. In reference to SoHo, the Master Plan of 1969 said, "Inevitably, white-collar activities and housing are going to supplant manufacturing in this area, and in some other industrial areas of Manhattan as well. The problem is to pave the way without losing blue-collar jobs. In time, the industrial renewal program will provide redeveloped land elsewhere which can be used to rehouse Manhattan firms."[28]

The SAA realized that in preserving the industrial character of the district for as long as possible they would be maintaining a protective cover for themselves. The strongest argument for legitimating their presence was that art and industry were symbiotic. The artists were moving into the smaller buildings, useless for industry, thus maintaining a healthy real-estate situation. Artists were not a presence in the larger buildings in which more than 12,000 blue-collar workers were still employed.[29] It was in order to preserve this harmony of interests that the SAA volunteered to restrict residence to bona fide artists certified by the New York City Department of Cultural Affairs. They proposed further that "to insure that no industry is displaced by a studio-residence occupancy, the owner of a new space to be occupied shall provide an affidavit from the previous tenant that the latter's occupancy was terminated of his own volition, or that the space has been vacated for at least six months."[30]

The artists felt that they were fully accommodating industry, and that if the CPC wouldn't agree to let them live in the district, it was only because the city had explicitly abandoned, even as a secondary goal, their Rapkin-originated policy of preserving marginal industry. Thus, the SAA made their SoHo policy a test of the city's intentions toward older industry. The argument was well placed, because at least an outspoken minority of the planning commissioners considered blue-collar unions a part of their political constituency and were committed to preserving Manhattan manufacturing for as long as possible. As it happened, the plans to provide a vast acreage of industrial land into which Manhattan firms could be moved foundered because of a lack of city money.

To hold the city to their earlier Rapkin-study vision of marginal industry, the SAA had to compile survey data on the district to show that industry was still an important employer and that symbiosis with artists was possible. Throughout 1969, working with Lewis, SAA surveyors visited every floor of every building in the forty-block area where artists' residency was concentrated. Their findings, substantiated by Lewis for the city, showed on the one hand that artists had extensively penetrated the district. They revealed that there were a total of fifteen artist co-ops housed in twenty-two buildings and seven additional buildings owned by individual artists. More than two thousand people lived in 660 lofts in the forty-block area of the greatest residential concentration, and five to six thousand lived in surrounding areas north of Houston Street, south of Canal Street, and east of Lafayette Street. In the forty-block district, 34 percent of the buildings included artists, 19 percent of the floors were residential, and a total of 10 percent of the square footage of the district's floor space was occupied by artists. Moreover, residency had increased 10 percent between 1968 and 1969, and another 11 percent by 1970.[31]

On the other hand, however, these figures were qualified by the restrictive pattern of artists' occupancy that they revealed. Artists were concentrated in the small lofts. Of the buildings with artists, 86 percent had less than 3,600 square feet per floor; and 47 percent of all buildings of less than 3,600 square feet per floor had artists in them. Industry, which provided 27,000 jobs in the forty-block area, was shown to have the larger lofts. Eighty-four percent of industrial jobs were found to be located in buildings with floor spaces greater than 3,600 square feet, and industry remained the dominant area use, occupying 86 percent of the district's floor area.[32]

Industry, however, was shown to be less healthy than in the 1962 Rapkin survey. Manufacturing jobs had declined by 5 percent since 1962, and wholesale jobs by 37.4 percent. But vacancy data indicated that the artist incursion had not been responsible for this industrial decline. Five percent of the total floor area remained vacant in 1970 despite the artists in residence. Within a central twenty-block area, there had been a 51 percent increase in vacant floors from 1969 to 1970. The large buildings concentrated along Broadway, however, maintained merely a

3 percent vacancy rate, again testifying to the continued industrial use of buildings with over 3,600 square feet. These Broadway blocks had only 10 percent of their floors occupied by artists.[33]

By September 1970 the Planning Commission had drawn up counter-proposals based on the data in the survey. The CPC split the building stock at the 3,600-square-foot point and offered to support rezoning which would allow certified-artists residency in buildings of this size or less, providing that at least one artist was in occupancy as of May 1, 1970. The CPC was trying to limit the influx of artists. But more importantly, the CPC had responded to the SAA's criticism about the city's lack of support for Manhattan industry by assuming the position of industry's protector. They had accepted the concept of artist-industry symbiosis, provided that the artist-residency momentum could be checked. Finally, they had accepted the definition of the community's extent at forty-three blocks, less than the SAA had claimed but far more than they had expected to get.

As the SoHo community studied it in the fall of 1970, the city's offer began to look less and less satisfactory. Speakers at a planning hearing on September 23 objected that the number of lofts available to artists under the plan had been frozen at too low a number and would cause residential competition that would result in greatly increased rents. There were also forty-seven artist-occupied lofts in the larger buildings which would remain illegal, as would artists' residences outside the forty-three block area.[34]

The SAA negotiators went back to the commission and received a number of new concessions. SoHo was to be divided into an inner twelve-block area, labeled M15-A, and an outer M15-B area. Prior artist residency was dropped as a condition for occupancy of buildings in the M15-A section, opening up all buildings of 3,600 square feet or less to artists. This doubled the number of legal lofts from 300 to 600. In the M15-B area, the prior-occupancy date was moved forward to September 15, 1970, and oversized buildings which were artists' cooperatives by that date were granted zoning legality. These provisions were ultimately enacted into law. In addition, artists above and below SoHo, in areas coming to be known as NoHo and Tribeca, were given a concession. They were made CPC study areas, and evictions for illegal occupancy were waived for at least a year. The commissioners held out the possibility of eventual rezoning to permit residency for artists in these areas.

But while they were anxious for a settlement, the planning commissioners knew that a threat was a useful part of the negotiating process. They reserved four blocks, previously conceded to be a part of SoHo, for possible demolition and redevelopment as a printing complex. Much of this property, unlike the rest of SoHo, had been assembled by one developer, and the proposal was a very credible threat to the SAA.

The SAA negotiators found themselves looking at the bulldozer. If four blocks could be leveled now, they reasoned, the precedent would have been established to clear more of SoHo in later years. The artists would then have been reduced to temporary placeholders for a more comprehensive redevelopment scheme. Commission chairman Elliott told the SAA, "The Commission would prefer to buy, raze and develop the area, and [we] are only prevented from doing so by the lack of City funds."[35]

The majority of the SAA's Coordinating Committee responded to the threat by recommending to the community a speedy acceptance of the new proposal as the most favorable that could be negotiated. A small minority held that renewed negotiations would improve the package. At the end of November the community met and voted to approve the new proposal, but many remained troubled by the exclusion from SoHo of the four blocks. The razing of those blocks would result in the ousting of 80 artists, 30 businesses, and 600 jobs. As a result, the SAA negotiators continued to meet with the CPC concerning the restoration of these blocks to SoHo zoning protection.

Managing SoHo's Public Image

From the beginning, the SAA had been aided in its struggle by the fact that in New York City artists were objects of sympathy to the press. Artists occupied all the favorable roles in the moral drama of media stories. They were unthreatening underdogs, only trying to improve the city with their SoHo proposal; they were a lively and creative force, about to be crushed by an unimaginative city bureaucracy; and they were a positive symbol of renewal in a historical period characterized by a depressing war in Vietnam and a smoldering racial problem. The media rushed to "discover" the transformation of a bleak factory district into a colorful artists' neighborhood, and the artists did their best to prepare a welcome.

Inquiring journalists phoned the SAA and were referred for interviews and photographic opportunities to a list of responsible artists, known to be politically knowledgeable about the area issues and having impeccable artistic credentials. Their art work and their loft-living style made an attractive background for press coverage. The art reporters from the *Village Voice* and the *New York Times* were, in any case, a part of the city's art community and were anxious to publicize SoHo as the most significant expression of the vitality of art in New York at this time. Art writers for the city's press became channels through which SAA spokesmen could reach the public. Grace Glueck, writing in the *New York Times*, was a consistent champion of SoHo and enabled such community leaders as Bob Wiegand to express their version of what was at stake for the city as a whole in the SoHo issue. "After all," she quoted Wiegand as saying, "the atmosphere we create is what attracts high caliber people here to live and work; they'll wake up when New York becomes a cultural desert."[36]

There had been some early reluctance among SoHo residents to publicize their illegal residencies, which might compel the city to take some premature action against them. This concern became moot, however, in March of 1970 when *Life* magazine featured loft-living in SoHo in a five-page photodocumentary.[37] Artists played and relaxed in full color amid their paintings and sculptures in showcase lofts. Since the SAA didn't control the decision to print this story, and couldn't have stopped it, they chose to cooperate by giving the *Life* team access to several of their members' studios.

The *Life* story taught the SAA that if their image of the community was to be communicated, they would have to take an active part in publicity. "The *Life* magazine story on the chic loft-living down here blew our cover, so there was no point in laying low," said an SAA official. "We wanted to set the record straight. It was a house-beautiful spread. A Village person did the research, and we couldn't talk them out of it."

The SAA went ahead with its own plans to acquaint the public with SoHo through an area festival. This was an elaborate coming-out party featuring tours of selected artists' lofts, art sales, and street performances. A festival organizer explained the SAA's motivation: "The CPC was saying, 'You don't have bathrooms, so we don't want you to live there.' The festival was our way to put pressure on the CPC. We invited the commissioners to come along with the public to see that we lived like human beings. We stressed the middle-class virtues—like hygiene, and the city's definition of a bohemia got radically altered."

The whole community, renters as well as co-opers, turned out for the SoHo Artists Festival in early May 1970. For many this was the high point of the legalization campaign, in terms of communal catharsis and enthusiasm. They created nearly a hundred loft- and street-events for the public—jazz concerts, multimedia rock shows, fountain sculpture that created mist and water environments, and the chance to see dozens of artists at work in their studios. According to festival organizers, between 70,000 and 100,000 people passed through the area's lofts. Ten pieces were sold, and several artists received future commissions. The press coverage was enthusiastic and included television teams from Germany as well as local stations.[38]

The fact that the festival was held during the national Vietnam Moratorium Weekend, in which tens of thousands demonstrated in Washington and other cities, gave the events a serious resonance.

Rather than cancel their celebration, the artists decided to go ahead and to weave in the community's feelings of opposition to the recent invasion of Cambodia and the death of students at Kent State University and Jackson State College. Funereal street dances added a tone of poignancy to the occasion. But overall, the SoHo Festival seemed an affirmation of life in a weekend of national anger and depression, and the press seized on it. SoHo's position with the city emerged greatly strengthened.

Legalization

On January 6, 1971, a second CPC hearing was held on the SoHo issue, but the outcome had already been decided. The planning commissioners had been converted to the view that SoHo was an inexpensive asset to the city, a political advantage rather than a liability. In deciding to endorse the unplanned and unanticipated process of rehabilitation which the artists had undertaken, the City Planning Commission resolved its dilemma by becoming enthusiastic sponsors of the inevitable. Commission chairman Elliott admitted in later years,

> The problems of moving against buildings privately acquired was insuperable. No one would have moved out, so this prevented the setting up of an industrial renewal program. Any new industrial construction implies the need for a huge subsidy from the City, but with SoHo, the City lost no revenue. . . . The laws were being flaunted there, and the City was embarrassed by this. The flaunters produced an inequity, and there were complaints, and the petty corruption of inspectors and city services. In the long run, how could we not enforce laws in SoHo that we were trying to enforce in the rest of the city? And we also felt that the illegal living was a real cost to the residents psychologically.[39]

To the commission, legalization meant that the city could score an impressive planning victory at no fiscal cost. The CPC could, in effect, become not merely a custodian over future developments in the community, but claim to be SoHo's creator. SoHo acknowledged the formative role of the CPC and especially of Elliott. In handing out thanks to its allies and benefactors following the zoning legalization, the SAA wrote: "And strange as it may seem, SoHo's legalization is greatly due to the support and advocacy of the arch fiend himself, Don Elliott. Without his backing, Lindsay would never have come out for us, and we would not even have gotten a hearing, let alone a vote."[40]

The period of antagonistic contention with the Planning Commission was over. The SAA sought to encourage an attitude of protective benevolence on the part of the commissioners for which the artists were prepared to pay in public gratitude. As the SAA leadership knew, the community would need the help of the Planning Commission in resolving the zoning challenges they felt were sure to come.

The final CPC hearing itself was warm with mutual congratulations. The commissioners had already reached their decision to sponsor SoHo, and the hearing became a forum in which they manifested their parental concern. There was a large contingent from SoHo, and the artists limited their criticisms to urging that the four blocks slated for demolition be returned to SoHo zoning protection. Artist Robert Wiegand showed a videotape of SoHo, and Congresswoman-elect Bella Abzug and commissioner of cultural affairs and CAH chairwoman Doris Freedman praised the CPC's proposal as evidence of successful participation of communities in the planning process. They too, however, urged the commission to leave all of the forty-three originally proposed SoHo blocks intact. One CPC staff member who had worked closely with the artists said, "It was a show, a circus."

Television and the press were there to witness the marriage of planners and "ordinary" citizens. It was news, and it was good public relations for the city. One SAA activist described the appeal of the SoHo issue to the media as follows:

> There were television cameras and reporters all hanging around and waiting for our turn in the commission chambers. The group ahead of us was black, from Bedford-Stuyvesant, and wanted more apartments built with many bedrooms in public housing. But all the TV lights were off and the reporters' notepads remained in their pockets. There had simply ceased to be any news value in their kind of problems, while we were fresh, glamorous as an issue. Our so-called painting life-style was intriguing. We were news.

On January 21, 1971, the CPC voted to legalize the residential use of lofts by artists in the full forty-three blocks of SoHo, thus returning the disputed four blocks to the community. Eight days later, a very short time as these matters usually go, the Board of Estimate, the final legal authority in matters of city legislation, gave its unanimous approval.

One hurdle remained—approval by the state legislature of changes in the multiple-dwelling laws that would facilitate industrial and residential use of the same building. An architects' committee of the SAA undertook to draw up this legislation as a series of amendments to Article 7-B, the 1964 law allowing artists to convert the Greenwich Street building. The committee included Shael Shapiro, a SoHo architect, and Olga Mahl, a lawyer working with SoHo through a legal service program called Volunteer Lawyers for the Arts. They worked closely with Freedman, whose political influence smoothed the road. Their amendments to Article 7-B liberalized the fire-protection and building-occupancy restrictions for converted lofts, making them subject to the standards applied to converted buildings rather than the tougher standards used in new residential structures. The changes provided safeguards through which residential use could be safely made to coexist with light manufacturing, and also facilitated artists' certification by authorizing the New York City Department of Cultural Affairs, among other groups, to certify artists. This gave the required legal foundation to Commissioner Freedman's program for SoHo certification.

With Commissioner Freedman's help, the committee got Republican assemblyman Roy Goodman to sponsor the bill in Albany. By lining up approval for their bill from the New York City Department of Buildings and the Fire Department, they were able to go to Albany with the city's support behind them. Like the entire SoHo issue, the bill met resistance and its fate was uncertain until the last possible moment. "When it got stuck in the Senate, Goodman and the City's representative helped push it through," explained Shapiro. "Albany saw it as crazy. There was a memo from [Majority Leader] Bridges sent around, finally, that said, 'Let them live in unsafe buildings if they want to.' The bill passed on the last day of the 1971 session and was signed by the governor on the last day prior to a pocket veto."

By finessing their very modest amount of political influence and seizing the initiative, the artists and their allies had won. They had created a legal territorial basis for SoHo on which the community was to continue to evolve in the subsequent years.

Conclusion

SoHo developed as a local community—a spatially organized system of interaction among neighbors—out of the cultural and organizational resources of a preexisting metropolitan occupational community. As artists, residents shared a basis for potential empathetic and moral solidarity with one another; they shared patterns of interaction as members of informal support networks based on occupation; and they had access to a public whose identification with art could be utilized as political leverage for obtaining housing concessions from government. But as a city-wide occupational community, artists had developed an individualistic housing culture, one in which residents used their own ingenuity and the help of their social networks to obtain lofts surreptitiously. Despite its occasional political activism, this housing culture was essentially fatalistic about the possibility of a collective and governmental solution to artists housing needs and faced the residential dilemma in the paralysis of individual isolation. The surreptitious housing culture was ineffective on the collective level.

SoHo residents, benefiting from residential density and common interests provided by the housing co-op structure, developed sustained patterns of neighborly cooperation on housing issues. Most importantly, the experience of co-op renovation and resident interaction—fixing the boiler, forestalling a mortgage foreclosure—provided for the evolution of leaders whose initiative in the solution of common problems was respected and legitimated by the consent of less active residents. With the co-ops, public activity emerged alongside informal networks as a salient organizer of personal relationships.

Co-op investment and extensive renovation were not speculative for these early residents, but they led them to a highly personal involvement in their lofts as psychic investment and property. Owners were more closely identified with their spaces than were renters. Having invested their entire capital, they were less mobile than renters, should they be evicted, but they faced eviction with stronger legal tools. Co-op partnership supported a collective determination to protect and secure the housing and working space that was essential for each occupant. City initiatives to enforce the nonresidential stipulations of the zoning law catalyzed the attitudes of co-op residents, in contrast to those of renters, into an aggressive housing culture.

Four elements are important in the consolidation of this occupational community as a local residential community:

1. Although political activity was seen as a burden and a distraction from the "real work" of art, residents organized swiftly and effectively because, as artists, they shared a common cultural perspective and set of material needs. Occupation communities are incipient, homogeneous territorial communities.

2. Because their occupation is structured along prestige lines and shares a value commitment with a large urban audience, artists have a public sensitive to their appeal. This public was already aware of various roles by which a nonartist audience could actualize an identification with artistic values. Nonartists could and did become patrons and militant defenders of SoHo artists in the political arena and were rewarded by artists through established patterns of gratitude and social intimacy. Other housing constituencies, the ethnic and racial poor, for example, could not, as readily as could artists, offer the incentives and structured means by which outsiders could identify and aid them.

Those engaged in occupations as social custodians, planners in particular, found in the appeal of the artist constituency the chance to humanize their own professional tasks, which they often found to be defined in narrow political or economic terms.

3. The development of a territorial community among SoHo residents was the result of a redefinition of the housing situation—the creation of a new housing culture—based upon a common set of real and compelling

interests and sparked by a credible threat to the housing status quo. The new housing culture was promoted by residents who learned to define and execute common local responsibilities as partners in co-op buildings. This segment of the population mobilized rapidly, assumed the leadership of an assertive localism, and formulated a strategy of negotiating with the city officials, coordinating the art public as a pressure group, and educating the residents to accept realistic objectives. The development of a vocal and visually prominent local community was pursued as a deliberate objective by the leadership in order to provide a concrete and appealing focus for press relations and a stable constituency for legitimating artist spokespersons.

4. Urban housing cultures organize instrumentally and expressively to seek material concessions from government and from other urban interest groups. They act as "housing classes," since all residents and all potential residents are not in a position to benefit equally from spatial concessions. Once a local community is achieved, it creates divisive cleavages in the metropolitan occupational community—renters versus loft owners, SoHo residents versus those who find themselves outside the boundaries of an achieved zoning protection. The community system based upon locality is primarily political and instrumental, and is never congruent with the occupational community which gave it birth.

10 Family Life in SoHo

A New Basis for Community Integration

With the achievement of zoning legislation in January 1971, the basis of the social integration of SoHo was altered. Nearly every member of the original SAA Coordinating Committee had resigned by February. As their projects were seen through to completion—first the antiexpressway efforts, then the SoHo Festival, and finally successive phases of the planning negotiations—the activists who had taken charge announced to the community that they were going back to their art work. Their investment of time had been enormous and their resulting expertise had made it difficult for them to disentangle themselves earlier. Now a stopping point had been reached. The purpose of political activism for these artists had been the narrowly instrumental one of securing a space to work as artists. The status rewards from community service or political brokering never rivaled those available from the occupational structure of the arts to which the community was committed. Artistic prestige was an entirely individual achievement. Thus each person was anxious to be reabsorbed into his or her own art projects.

A network of experienced community leadership, developed over the previous two years of struggle, retired into the privacy of individual career concerns. Some leaders retained an advisory contact with a newer and less widely known generation of activists who took over what all residents hoped would be merely routine political chores, simply housekeeping. The need for regular community-wide meetings ceased.

Publication of the *SoHo Artists Association Newsletter,* the organ of district consciousness and communication, gradually lost any claim to regularity. At its inception, the *Newsletter* had been hand delivered to every loft in the district as a basic organizing tool. As the SAA matured and achieved a period of regular funding from members' dues and fund-raising events, the *Newsletter* had been machine addressed and mailed. It was expanded during this period of engagement to include social announcements as well as a staple of political analysis and exhortation. But social notices—there was only one birth announcement that ever appeared in the *Newsletter*—proved to be inconsistent with the districts' perception of itself as an organized entity.[1] Formal community consciousness, up to this date, rested on the necessity of meeting a common threat to the residents' occupational identities—the loss of their loft studios. Community awareness had not been built out of the shared stuff of domestic existence. Now the common threat had abated. As a defensive territorial community, SoHo was largely demobilized.

When the zoning crisis abated, the continued integration of residents at the district level became the function of new institutions which were crystallizing around, not occupation, but the family and, in particular, child-care needs.

SoHo residents did not revert to the anonymous style of life which had characterized their illegal phase of loft dwelling. That style of local withdrawal had been exaggerated by the residents' political vulnerability, their poverty, and their reputational obscurity as artists. The early housing culture, when residents had furtively hidden the signs of their presence from outsiders, had splintered when the co-op owners linked their occupational anxiety to a property defense. The political struggle to defend their property had swept anonymity away. In the legal phase of their residency, artists were able to build on the experience of having formed a collective political presence. Co-op residents especially had confronted and solved common loft problems and had found their relations with those around them to be often neighborly. The presence of children and the new set of needs that children bring to households was to weave these threads of neighboring into a new, purely local community fabric.

Early Obstacles to Family Formation

The accommodation to illegal living had caused many couples to defer child-bearing, and an unsatisfied demand for family life built up. Children were understood to require an increased investment in safety and sanitation improvements for the loft well in excess of that required by adults and working artists. For young artists, this extra cost was prohibitive. In addition, children increased the risk that the studio itself would be lost. In a loft leased for exclusively commercial purposes, it was impossible to conceal the presence of a baby or, when confronted by an inspector, to explain that presence. Children simply gave away the game of illegal residency.

The early demographic pattern of the district had been an additional obstacle to childrearing. While the artist population had remained sparse and scattered in rental units, neighborly ties had been nonexistent. In such circumstances, raising children in a factory district that lacked any stores, parks, or schools was prohibitively difficult. Couples who pioneered the move into SoHo were characteristically loft veterans in their late twenties, experienced in the arts of survival. They had resigned themselves to repressing domestic life. Once the trail was blazed, younger couples, also childless, began arriving directly out of art school. None started families at first. It was not until 1968 that the rise in the artist population and the development of artist-cooperative buildings made residents available to each other for a steady exchange of neighborly services that lessened the isolation of couples. With these ties to build on and their housing more secure, those artists who had waited to have children now had them. The increase in children was accelerated by the fact that buyers of new co-ops now included those with infants and even school-age children. They created a demographic ripple.[2]

Loft living with children has become a subculture of its own within SoHo. When one mother described SoHo as "just like a suburb, complete with children, washer-dryers, and the family sheepdog," she was describing this subculture and, incidentally, taking a shot at the cosmopolitan pretensions of some artists. But living with children is a minority way of life within the larger adult-centered community. Many co-ops have established unwritten "no children" rules. Because loft floors are without any sound-absorbing qualities and seem to amplify the noise of footsteps overhead, many visual artists consider running children to be only slightly more desirable than musicians.[3]

The Lessening of Occupational Obstacles to Family Formation

SoHo remains essentially adult centered because, for most artists, children are not easily compatible with their parents' careers. The higher living costs associated with children mean that artists usually find they must take on increased outside job obligations and neglect their art. For these artists, children and art comprise an "either-or" choice.

In the early 1970s, however, increasing numbers of new arrivals and older residents felt they could escape this dilemma. Their optimism stemmed from the fact that they were members of an artistic generation coming into career maturity with the art boom that had developed in the

1960s. This expansion of the market had the result of shortening the incubation period for some artists from a matter of decades to a few years. Many expected to duplicate the rapid success of the few.

Artists were finding it easier to live in the early 1970s. As the market expanded, so did art schools. In the short run, this created new jobs for artists as teachers. Part-time and free-lance positions were also readily available with the design studios connected to the New York advertising industry, many of which practiced a letting-out system to lower their overhead. The increased number of contemporary art galleries and their concentration in SoHo meant that more artists than before were able to forge promising affiliations. They were making progress in terms of accumulating contacts, if not always making sales. Thus a career optimism pervaded the district, extending from artists on the threshold of significant recognition down to the less successful. Many artists in each category went ahead and had the children they hoped would enrich and stabilize their lives.

These artists, it must be remembered, were not in a generalized revolt against all aspects of their own relatively advantaged childhoods. Their deviation from their parents' values had taken the quite specific and limited form of a career choice, a decision which they reinforced with a reliance upon disciplined work and technical skill rather than bohemian display. Most accepted an essentially traditional definition of domestic life as providing an emotional resource for them in an occupationally stressful world.[4] Children both enriched this family life and provided a bridge by which a reconciliation with their own parents was sometimes possible.[5]

At a community meeting called to explain the particulars of the new housing laws in early 1971, the speaker was interrupted by a resident who asked, "Does all this mean that we can have kids now?" The audience exploded into empathetic laughter. The remark was not a non-sequitur. As a SoHo mother of two explained the mood in the community at the time, "Kids were very public, and as long as SoHo had been reclusive and low-profile, many of us were afraid to take the step. In 1971 we were ready."

Marriage Roles and Domestic Patronage

The Artist Myth

Family structure among artists, whatever its impulses, has had to come to terms with the pressures of the art market. In this market, art is a deficit activity and marriage a form of patronage support.

The boom in the art market has not altered the fact that the income of most artists remains low and continues to be derived piecemeal from sources other than the sale of art. It remains true that most artists must sustain themselves on erratic sources of outside income throughout protracted periods of career development. Professional recognition may never come. If it does, more often than not it is an isolated event, not tied together by the market into a ladder of accumulating reputation. Artists live in an emotional climate in which their expectations of career take-off are alternately encouraged and dashed. Thus many artists are in the position of continuing for as long as they can, drawing on the energy of their inner convictions, spending the capital of their self-confidence, and supporting their art as an avocational calling. They act as their own patrons as a matter of course.

The lover or spouse of such an artist is asked to share this burden of financial and emotional support for a career which the market will not as yet sustain. Thus the obligations of love become intertwined with the expectations of patronage. There is no lack of volunteers willing to share their lives with artists and to assume the consequent supportive roles. Both marriage and joint living take on the characteristics of domestic patronage for the art career of one of the partners. It is women rather than men who most frequently assume the burden of domestic patronage, which requires the subordination of their own desires for personal expression or historical recognition to that of a partner.[6] Women are more frequently patrons because domestic patronage is similar to parenting, a role which women have been socialized to accept as especially their own. Domestic patronage provides a shelter in which conformity to the demands of a market society can be deferred beyond adolescence. Often, wives take over the functions of parents who have refused to support their artist-children any longer.[7]

The figure of the artist, in its pure form the fine artist, has become one symbol of the theme of self-expression in middle-class socialization. The artist figure in pursuit of "art for art's sake" was originally a creation of the nineteenth-century middle class.[8] It has been given subsequent life by contemporary generations who protest the social rationalization and market forces for which they supply the technical labor and into which they fear absorption.[9] Sustained as an ideological fixture rather than a utopian possibility by their parents, the figure of "the artist" is a symbol readily available to middle-class children to give form to their rebellion against what they regard as the hypocrisy and compromises of their parents.

The goal of autonomous individuality, realized through identifying with "the artist," is the ideology which recruits not only artists but also their supporting admirers. The example of April, a SoHo wife, is characteristic of the situational elements which underlie an identification with artists.

April grew up in suburban New Jersey in a comfortably well-off household. Her father was a CPA, and her mother took care of the house and the children as her exclusive work. In conformity with the expectations of their mother, April's sister married a lawyer. The couple live in another commuter suburb of New York City with their own children, whom April's sister, a housewife, drives from school to music lessons. April sought not to follow this pattern of life. "I never really felt like conforming as a kid," she maintains. "I was the only girl in my class not to have her nose bobbed. . . . By the time I was eight I had read every book in the children's library, and I made them give me an adult card. I spent a lot of time by myself."

To escape from what she called a "boring suburban existence," April spent her weekends during high school "hanging around" in Greenwich Village. "I was always puzzled as to why the Village was so attractive to me, a suburban kid. It was the only place where you could see interracial couples and blatant homosexuals."

At fifteen she started going with a young art student. Her parents were appalled and tried to break up the romance. "He was Jewish, so that part was okay, but he was not professionally oriented. And his parents weren't rich. In my parents' eyes, he was just the wrong type for me." After her graduation, April's parents sent her to an out-of-state college in order to break up the romance. For April and her high-school girlfriends, college was not part of a career preparation. It was essentially a means of social entrée. "I chose to be an English major, mainly because it was easy for me to get good grades in literature with little work. College was the place to go to be popular, to find a husband, and not to work too hard."

In her junior year she prevailed against her parents and transferred to a college near New York City to be near her boyfriend's art school. After graduation, the two were married. The marriage turned out to be a late concession to April's parents' expectations. "I'd been seing this guy for five years, and my parents were really pressuring me to get married."

He husband established himself in the field of commercial design, a decision which also pleased April's parents. His regular and well-paid employment removed some of the stigma of his being an artist.[10] The couple had two children, took a SoHo loft, and April settled into the tasks of running a household of her own and caring for the children. She soon found that her husband used his provider function and artist identity to claim an exemption from domestic duties. In addition, April had to provide continuing psychological support for her husband, whose sojourns into fine art were continually unrewarded.

April's experience is characteristic of an artist's spouse. Expectations associated with an alternative life-style are aroused and then disappointed by the prosaic realities of the job market and married life. The husband's artistic identity encourages him to demand an exemption from parenting and household responsibilities. The wife begins to wonder if she has not chosen a life that is as flat and conventional as that of her suburban counterpart. At this point she may begin to demand her own chance to realize an ego-expressive ideal.

Occupational Failure and Domestic Tensions: The Bohemian at Home

Artists who neither achieve a modest success nor ease into more lucrative vocations, but who persist in the face of a prolonged occupational failure, pose special problems for the spouses or lovers with whom they live. They need an intensified form of support. With an artist identity as their essential self-definition, and this identity refuted by the market, they are tempted to emphasize the extramundane qualities of their commitment to art by exaggerating their inability to hold regular jobs. They abandon the role of coprovider and often that of parent. Their dependence upon their spouses or lovers increases.

Such artists defend themselves with the claim that their art leaves them no time or energy to hold down a pedestrian job, while their sensitivity and the importance of their work legitimates their exemption from routine household chores as well. Lacking the objective confirmation that they are the special and gifted persons they want to believe themselves to be, they increase their practical helplessness and exploit their dependency. Their friends and especially their spouses become the essential audiences to whom they play the part of "the artist." Often, only the collapse of the marriage relationship liberates such artists from belief in their own debilitating stereotype. When outside support is withdrawn, the downward spiral comes to an end. The experience of Beth, a secretary and a commercial fabric designer, illustrates the pattern of regressive dependence which can occur.

My old man, Gerry, was a Cooper Union student. He drank too much, and eventually I came to realize he was self-destructive. While I worked in an office, he was "the artist." *Being* an artist was the important thing for him, even if he read science fiction in bed all day. He was the most important person in our relationship, and for two years I supported him. He refused even to take the dirty clothes to the laundromat. He was an artist *all* the time. He had no time for that kind of thing. He was sensitive, so he couldn't deal with the outside world.

Eventually Beth "put her foot down" and forced Gerry to get out and get a job. He achieved considerable success as a manager in an advertising firm, much to the surprise of both of them; but the domestic relationship, forced onto an egalitarian plane, ended. For Beth, the artists' claim to an occupational incapacity for economic self-sufficiency is a debilitating illusion.

They all think they're Jackson Pollock, helpless geniuses. But boy can they hustle foundations and galleries. They have to grow up and stop acting like whiny geniuses out of control. They *can* function in the real world. You should listen to some of them talk real estate in SoHo. But they load this incredible shit on their wives, and the wife acts like a caretaker.... They lean on other people.

The over-dependence of the artist on a spouse or lover, a response to market neglect, is supported by an ideological system shared by both artist and domestic patron alike. This system contains several assertions which the wife tends to find less and less credible. The first is, "Since I am an artist, wholly an artist, you can't find fault with me for not knowing how to make money." This is a rationalization based on the objective market situation faced my most artists, a conversion of their poverty into a validation of the artistic identity. The second premise is that to turn one's talents in a commercial direction, especially to do advertising work or "to turn out crap," as it is described, extinguishes one's creative spark. This belief perpetuates the monopoly of compensatory status honor claimed by fine artists over craftspeople and commercial artists. It also insures the status subordination of those whose mundane jobs pay the studio rent. Third is the premise of artistic spontaneity. "What makes me creative also makes me drink," is how it is sometimes put. The artist without market support is tempted to portray himself in the image of an unbridled spirit, extravagant, undisciplined, and profligate.

This view of the artist originates with the Paris bohemians and is a pseudoaristocratic assertion of disdain for the marketplace. The artist defines himself as the foil of the bourgeois personality, but it is the bourgeois qualities of sobriety and reliability that such an artist depends upon to complement his talent and inspiration if he is to function at all. Scorned by the artist himself, these qualities are sought in a spouse.[11] The artist who copes with failure through a bohemian persona sets up his wife as the bourgeois upon whom he relies and whom he incidentally seeks to scandalize.[12] The bohemian ideology inhibits the spouse's criticism of the artist she is obliged to look after. Her rage tends to increase over the years, especially because rational self-criticism or "a cure," such as might be pursued through psychotherapy, is rejected by such artists as an effort to "normalize" them. They take normality to be an uncreative, vegetable state.[13]

Artists who pursue the self-destructive caricature of the bohemian relinquish the discipline and objectivity employed by all systematically successful artists. Since success in the arts is more of a possibility now than it once was, however, the bohemian persona is not widely popular in SoHo. It exists as a recognizable type and tendency among a minority of less successful artists.[14] Such artists express not so much a positive commitment to their art as a negative fear of being revealed as simply ordinary people.

Marriage and the Successful Male Artist

The successful artist has a better case for spousal support than has the failure, with all his sufferings. With success comes, unquestionably, the identity of "an artist." The wife's role in the relationship is that of managing the household economy, often including the details of the artist's sales and taxes, and assuming primary responsibility for the children. If she has a career, it must not rival that of her husband in its demands for support. It should be different in kind and in seriousness from his, either more routine or more amateur.

The artist husband is usually willing to reciprocate to some degree, and will support his wife within the spirit of their unequal role division. He will encourage her to go back to school or to take up an art of her own, so long as neither threatens his centrality in the household. Under exceptional and limited circumstances, he will take over child care. But he is unwilling to relinquish in principle the primacy of his occupational commitment. He needs to feel that he can, if he must, mobilize all the available emotional support in the household to see him through an artistically stagnant period or a frantic preparation for a show, or to free him for a trip to a gallery abroad.

To the extent that the balance of emotional payments and moments of ego primacy approach equality, it is the result of a determined effort by the wife. Episodes of revolt by wives complicate the lives of male artists who would prefer not to be distracted from their preoccupations with their market positions and their aesthetic problems. Revolt takes the form of a withdrawal of role cooperation at crucial moments—when a dinner must be prepared for an important collector—and also an ideological offensive. Wives argue that since creativity and self-development make life meaningful for the husband—and indeed these are the values which both expect their children's schools to sustain—then why shouldn't they apply to the wife's life as well? Why shouldn't she be able to enact, as well as merely support, artistic values? The struggle for a more equitable role divison can provide the substance of the household drama for a protracted period. It can also lead to an abrupt divorce.

Successful male artists are slow to concede their role prerogatives. Marriage, they have found, works for them. Nearly all of the successful male artists in SoHo are married, and most have the children which intensify traditional role divisions. They had these children after their careers were established, generally beginning their families or moving into SoHo with established families after the period of residential uncertainty has passed. Some adopted their children, while others married women with children from previous marriages. The urge to acquire children, prudently acted upon, has been a consistent characteristic of successful male artists.

Having established their careers, male artists are usually willing to make some adjustments within their occupational roles in the interests of their families. But these compromises are typically seen as concessions rather than adjustments of equity. Fatherhood means a distinctly minor share of parenthood responsibilities for them. The home studio, dangerously close at hand to family life, must be deliberately defended as a place where domesticity may not freely intrude. This means that the wife must see to it that child rearing is not overly disruptive to the resident artist. One artist explained the male point of view as follows: "I have a child two years old named Dan. It is kids that tie you into what's going on here in SoHo. But the family infringes on the studio. I take some opportunities to help out, but it's more a thing that meals have become a social occasion, not just a quick hamburger. Now they're a family thing. It would be better for my work if my studio were isolated. If I could, I would get a separate living arrangement and keep just a working studio. At 3:30 Dan comes home from nursery school and things stop around here." This very successful artist continued, wistfully, "Before the kid, Pat and I had breakfast out every morning. That got us both going. My wife would go on to work, and I could spend the whole day painting."

Traditional Family Patterns and Homosexuality

The patriarchal pride and protectiveness with which these artists treat their children allows them to articulate their preference for traditional male roles. The family role-set stabilizes self-employed artists for whom institutional role props are missing. Artist-fathers are quick to distinguish their own way of domestic life from the more loosely or unconventionally structured lives they see in some new arrivals to SoHo. The subculture which combines support for the arts with a dramatized homosexuality draws particular condemnation from artist-fathers. The self-discipline and domestic tranquility which they regard as a requirement for success is threatened by blurred sex roles. While tolerant of individual homosexuals and ideologically committed to self-expression, they nevertheless view sexual self-advertisement and experimentation as a distasteful substitute for authentic creativity. More to the point, it is destabilizing to the family way of life which provides them with a refuge. One successful artist said, "I'm very upset with the kinky sex on the scene down here. Did you see those ropes and whips hanging on the Chinese screen at B's party the other night? I hope my own kid will be a mensch. Are you Jewish? That means a person, a real person."

In fact, many serious artists in SoHo are homosexual. They have in some cases established relationships which mirror in length and stability the marriages of heterosexual artists. In these relationships too, the creative role of one partner usually contrasts with the conventionally professional responsibilities of the other partner. Lacking children, however, homosexual couples appear more equalitarian in their role allocations.

Artists who are homosexuals are aware than an open dramatization of their sexual preferences may mark them as less than serious artists in the eyes of some "straight" residents. But many make a game of eliciting this condemnation, which the liberal code of the art community requires heterosexuals to repress as bourgeois. One artist who is gay holds an annual party at which nude male "slaves" are sometimes to be found "hanging" from chains. Straight artists are invited to these events and often attend, as these are the most lavish parties in SoHo. Their responses, either of outrage or of participation in the spirit of things, are equally causes for humorous comment by the gay artists.

The Child-care Burden

SoHo parents are especially concerned about the education of their children and about providing them with social experiences with other children. The latter is not easy to accomplish in an area where the streets are full of trucks and where there are no places for children to casually meet and play. The nursery school, of which more than a dozen have been established in SoHo since legalization, solves these problems and provides day-care facilities that allow both parents to work, either away or at home, undisturbed. In choosing one facility over another, parents frequently visit several to observe the interaction of children and teachers. Successful artists, having the widest options among tuition-charging facilities, are especially careful. Said one, "My kid goes to St. Anthony's school for three year olds.[15] We checked out all the childcare facilities here. A has a popular group that's very free and easy going. But we're middle class, straight. She's into drugs and hanging out. So we rejected her school."

Many of the nursery schools are cooperative and require a substantial investment of the parents' time. Even the commercial schools have begun to set up schedules for parent volunteer days amounting to a day or two a month. This parent involvement with the nursery school leads to parent involvement with each other. It is especially true in the system of after-school cooperative child-care groups that exist in SoHo. They occupy the child from the time that school ends until the time the parents arrive home or end their work in the studio. These are entirely voluntary day-care groups of six to ten children cared for by one or two parents on a rotation basis in their various lofts. With the addition of a swing or a rocking horse, lofts become easily suited to indoor play. Provided one parent is free to bend his schedule, a family can participate in such a group without fee. The parent interaction and friendship which these groups foster seem to come easiest when the parents are all artistic peers. As one successful painter explained, "All the kids in our afternoon group are the children of successful artists. Most of them are also at the B morning nursery school as well. We each rotate having the kids in our loft, a week at a time."

While both parents are involved in the child-care decisions that affect their children, it is the mothers in the families of successful artists who do the work. The artist quoted above continued, "Husbands never seem to take it. Nor is a single husband ever the parent assistant at [the nursery school]. [My wife] has done it for us all year."

The wives of successful male artists, while often working at home as students or writers, accept the primacy of the burden of child care as their own responsibility. Their other work fits in around the edges. One male artist said, typically, "I don't take care of the baby, as a rule. I do very little with the co-op nursery either. I'm under heavy pressure this year. And besides, my offers are not taken up. When [my wife] just can't take it any more, I take over with the kids. I do rank myself as more helpful than most husbands, though. And she's more organized than me; look at her desk!" His wife's desk was clean and neat, with a Rolodex index for important phone numbers. The jars of paint and the boxes of slides in his studio were, however, just as neatly arranged. He continued, "She does the periodic checkups on the kids. But in any emergency, I would do it with her."

This artist's wife elaborated on her husband's helpfulness: "In the last few years we do seem to do less and less together, like the laundry and shopping. He does what I tell him, but he doesn't see that there may be no cat litter. I run the house." In addition, she works 15 to 20 hours a week as a free-lance editor.

Less successful male artists, by contrast, spend more time performing child care because their wives usually work outside the home full-time. Their marriages appear less stable and their role allocation less traditional. This is partly a result of the economic stresses on the unsuccessful male artist.

Jake, who was once an art teacher, illustrates the contrasting family pattern of the less successful artist. He continues to sell his work, but slowly. His promising career appears to have peaked out. He now makes his income by doing carpentry work in and around the lofts of SoHo. A flawed career deprives Jake of a strong claim to an artistic exemption from parenting chores. He regularly picks up his daughter from school and watches her during the late afternoon. His wife is a dancer, whom he married when he was a young painting student. With no money for outside help, she nevertheless insisted on continuing her career. "She said all I did was go and paint whenever I wanted to, while she was stuck with Leslie."

The marriage fell apart, but Jake retains a shared responsibility for their child. He subsequently established a relationship with another woman. She became pregnant, and when twins were born, Jake moved out of his studio and in with this second family. By deliberately complicating his family obligations, he seems to have foreclosed any chance he might have had to succeed as an artist. At the same time, he acquired new roles at which he can succeed.

> The question of what I do is kind of funny. I do a lot of things. If I was being written up in a show, would they say, "He does paintings, makes wine, makes children, does carpentry work, and fishes"? I would like things in that order. Being a parent is a trip, though. Leslie is in the third grade now. I was born into an unchallenged, unspokenly male-dominant household. This is no longer true, even in the well-off suburbs where I came from. I have to learn the parent role. It truly is a role. It is equal to anything you do, and it's valid to say it.

The adjustment has not been easy.

> Of course, it's problematic financially. Carpentry and electrical work are the saving grace for me. I need to work only three days a week, so my woman is stuck only those days. There's no money for babysitters. The earning of money would have to be equal to fulfill the equal-parent thing, or resentment builds up. I resent it. I don't like always to be working for money. And she feels resentful about her lack of a job.

Successful male artists are able to bargain more effectively for stability in their home lives and for the traditional sex-role differentiation that provides it. They are not as willing to share the artist identity with their wives. In the words of one successful artist, "Living with another artist would be difficult. I have a problem with women artists anyway. We artists have delicate sensibilities. Some little thing can happen to fuck the whole day up." When "something happens," it is the wife's role to be there to handle it. Successful artists are able to command the energy, affection, and support of their spouses. It is easier for the male artist to succeed than the female because he is in a position to benefit from both the privileged status of being an artist in this subculture of the middle class, and to reap the advantages of being a male exempt from child-rearing responsibilities. The decision of male artists to have children can be seen as having the effect of reinforcing traditional family-role allocation.

Unsuccessful artists are unable to make their career the focus of their wives' attention for a prolonged period, especially when the wife has the educational and the aspirational basis of an artistic identity of her own. This can occur when young couples meet in art school and find that their careers continue to unfold in parallel. In this case, each may retain equivalent ambition. Then the husband cannot successfully assume primacy as the creative center of the household and may have to accept a more equal share of the housekeeping functions as well. If the couple has children, these functions will include child care. However, with the intense competition and protracted incubation period associated with the fine-arts career, the spouse who is not somewhat exempted from parenting and an early provider role is severely handicapped in the race for success.

The Wife's Career

A turning point in the relationship between male artists and their wives occurs when the wives demand that their own jobs, whatever they are, be treated as equally serious careers. The values of the artist community are such that the wife who supports her husband's artist role experiences a certain social invisibility. In one form or another, wives come eventually to demand recognition. A photographer's wife, the mother of two children, who is now working on a newspaper, said,

> I resent having status in SoHo only as an appendage of my husband. Sometimes I feel like an Air Force wife in the PX with shopping privileges. What happens when there's a divorce? . . . I would extend the legal privilege to live in SoHo to all cottage industries—to women working at home quilting, making pies, to anyone who needs the space. Some photographers don't need the space here. They could have a darkroom in an apartment.

The derivative social identity of the artist's wife is accentuated by the fact that all SoHo residents are required by law to be artists or the family of artists certified through the New York City Department of Cultural Affairs. While this rule is widely evaded, nevertheless, by January 1978, sixteen hundred individuals had presented their credentials to the Department of Cultural Affairs and received certification. Both formally and informally, the status system which prevails in this occupational community is one which honors fine artists.

This status system, in which individuals are ranked in accordance with their achievements as artists, motivates wives to seek a professional and often artistic identity of their own. Since coming to SoHo, the wife of one painter has written a novel about the art world; the wife of a sculptor has become a choreographer. Other wives have opened clothing boutiques or become fine-arts photographers. One wife and mother has left work as a medical technologist to embark upon a doctoral program in physiology. A substantial outburst of talent and ambition has characterized SoHo wives. This has usually begun when their youngest child became old enough for placement in a preschool or day-care facility. Nursery school teachers in the community report that this is the same time that divorces among the parents of their students seem to occur.

While the wife of an unsuccessful artist is likely to end her marriage relationship at the time she adopts a new and serious career identity, the wife of a successful artist more often works out her new career within the marriage by adjusting the role relationships. Joan, the wife of an exceptionally successful painter, explained this process of role adjustment:

> I used to get what I called "hotel disease" when I traveled with [my husband], being cooped up in a hotel in a foreign country. I'd attack it by setting myself something to do—like take riding lessons or finding dance facilities, something, no matter what. I was his secretary for two years. I finally refused to sign anything [with my married name]. He couldn't understand it. But I felt it was too humiliating to be a wife-slave. Eventually, I got him to hire a secretary. She works for both of us.
>
> I used to go to business lunches where the [art] prices are set, but I got sick of being ignored. I used to make scenes to get attention. Finally, I just stopped going.

This woman began a serious study of dance and later choreography. She now has an artist-identity of her own.

> Last year I earned only $128 in two nights of dancing. But I felt terrific this time. Like [my husband] and I were equal. I had a cast party the second night, like I always do. You're too keyed up to sleep or anything, and you want to be surrounded by people. And this time he helped me. He bought the cheese, and I ordered the beer.

The allocation of roles in a household with a successful artist is slow to change. Because money is available, role allocation usually is modified by shifting some of the wife's duties to paid personnel. Joan continued,

> I still answer the phone. There is a great deal of dealer traffic here. I have a part-time housekeeper, but I need more help, I still feel that I'm a woman and I have to take care of everybody. I help him entertain business associates. It's fun because I cook well, and then we eat simply the rest of the time. Child care is mostly mine. I do the bills, and run the furnace. The burden of role alteration is mine, really, and sometimes I find I am doing both the old and the new role obligations—cooking, child care, and the bills.

The efforts of the wives of artists to achieve expressive freedom may involve them in an extensive critique of marriage roles. The experience of Kelly, another SoHo wife, illustrates this possibility.

Kelly was an all-scholarship student who gave up early hopes of becoming a veterinarian for the immediate income she could get as a teacher. She and her husband had met and married while they were quite young, and she assumed the role of patron to his art career. Her satisfaction with a derivative identity did not last, however.

> The woman's role so often is simply to support the artist. That was my role. We've been married for ten years now. Women are economists, emotionally, and money-wise. They can't and they don't stay up drinking until four A.M. They're responsible. Since it's their way to control their artist-men, they even like being the responsible ones. You promote this dependency on you.... You go through a period of invisibility, providing for your husband's painting. Finally, it gets so that you just have to get out on your own. The more you get involved in things outside the couple, the less claustrophobic marriage is.

Kelly has quit teaching and for the past year has been taking courses in fiction writing. She has been aided in her turn toward an artistic career and in achieving an identity in the marriage equal to that of her husband by the fact that they decided to have no children.

Women Artists and Marriage Avoidance

Marriage and motherhood is considered problematic by single SoHo women artists. They conclude from the example of their married friends that were they to become wives they would have to assume most of the burden of running a more complicated household and responding to the needs of children. Their time in the studio would not have top priority and would not be considered uninterruptable. Unlike wives who work in offices, women artists working at home lack the external distancing mechanisms which would provide a separation of their parenting and painting. Male artists achieve occupational-role protection through their emphasis on their cultural prerogatives as males; women, by contrast, are disadvantaged by these same cultural assumptions. For this reason, women artists in SoHo have generally sought to avoid or to escape from marriage.

Jane is a determined photographer whose example will illustrate the dilemma offered by marriage. She came to SoHo with her husband, an artist, and bought space in one of the early artist cooperatives. She worked as a medical technician, and her husband taught art intermittently. When her husband was given a post as a university art professor, Jane was able to quit her job. She devoted all her time to renovating their living loft and his studio space. When the SoHo community mobilized to change the zoning and allow artists' residences, she threw herself into the campaign. These demands on her time intensified her role as a supportive figure for her husband's career but did not bring her any independent recognition. As a nonartist, she felt she was being treated as a nonentity. Out of self defense, she developed a longstanding involvement with photography into a serious art pursuit.

Her insistence on an equal and autonomous status as an artist was too much of a change for her marriage to accommodate. Still on good terms, she and her husband divorced and took up separate loft spaces. She refuses to even consider the possibility of another marriage. Her husband, missing the familial atmosphere, takes his evening meals with a family living next door.

"I did the consciousness-raising thing, like a lot of other women," said Jane. "We had a group from all over, including uptown people as well as some from SoHo. I had decided against kids long ago. My ego is too big. Unlike those other women in the group, as an artist I had a unique situation with men. I got bored with the meetings and finally I pulled my artist shit—'I have no more time for this talk; I've got to get back to my art!' " Art suits her ambition to be an independent and autonomous woman. "As a woman in the arts, I haven't encountered much negative feedback, at least not from other artists. In my business, I'm my own boss and I like it. I'm in control. I can even refuse a photography commission, and I sometimes do."

The data on SoHo artists in this study indicates that marriage has a differential effect, depending on sex. It acts as an aid to the achievement of the male's occupational goals, but it is an impediment to the occupational ambitions of the female. Many SoHo women artists have a realistic perception of the difficulties which they may experience in combining marriage with an art career. The result is deliberate marriage avoidance by many women artists. This is especially likely to be true of women whose occupational identity came at an early age. Kate is such an artist.

Kate is exceptionally successful in the arts, an achievement which is rare for a woman.[16] She paints with an individualistic style and vision which have received wide recognition, and there is a waiting list to purchase her paintings, which sell for $10,000 and up. She lectures on art on the nationwide university circuit and teaches an advanced class in painting at a Manhattan college. As Kate sees it, her commitment to being an artist came early enough in her life to preclude the more traditional roles for her as a woman, roles from which she always has felt it important to be emancipated.

At age seven I was drawing pictures all over my piano music. After a disastrous recital, my mother decided that maybe I was visual, so she shipped me off to art school every Saturday afternoon.... This was wonderful, except there were no classes for kids under fifteen, and I was eight. I tell ya, I learned how to draw. It took three years. The other kids were doing better than I was at first, and God forbid that this should be allowed to happen. I was a high achiever. At eight I had decided to be a painter.

Kate's decision to become a professional artist meant that she had to overcome the resistance of her family. Her mother had intended art to be an avocation for her, certainly not a career.[17]

After high school, and then art school, I had to confront the seriousness of my decision to be a painter. Everyone was saying, "You'll get married and move to the suburbs. You'll have kids." But here again I have a stubborn streak. I did just the opposite, I love to break the rules. I love the contrary.

For artists such as Kate, marriage and children are seen in opposition to a meaningful development of the self as a creative, autonomous person.

Kate works with a succession of young art students who act as her assistants. The pace and drive they are exposed to in Kate's studio— nine or more hours of work a day, six days a week—dissuade many of them from continuing their own careers as artists. Some of those that drop out of art are women assistants, and Kate can see only one likely result for them. "They're driving kids around in a station wagon right now, probably rapidly becoming suburban alcoholics," she speculated. For her, the alternative to a career in the arts is the suffocation of identity.

Single women artists set extremely demanding schedules for themselves and are among the most professionally focused of all artists in SoHo. While they remain intensely involved with others, their single status allows them to follow a pattern of elective sociability in which they retain control. A less successful but fully as determined woman artist explained the priority of career over marriage in different terms but with the same conclusion: "I prefer to live alone. Yes, I know the costs would be less if I lived with someone. I absolutely cannot live on my painting income. But living with someone else would take too much time. It would be too distracting. Chances are, he would not know art, and then where would I be?"

Child Rearing and Social Structure

With the arrival of the first children in SoHo, the subcommunity of parents was confronted with the need to neighbor. Children had to have playmates; parents had to have others with whom to exchange child-care lore and the services that lightened the child-care burden. Neighboring quickly formalized into dependable day-care arrangements.

The day-care group which started in the late fall of 1968 enrolled the very first SoHo children. "We had just discovered one another," explained a founder. "We met while walking around and saw that we all lived nearby." At first parents took turns providing child care in their own lofts. They kept finding additional parents, however, and soon a group of ten participating families was involved. Most of the children were two to three years old when, in 1970, the parents discovered that their improvised system was overloaded and inadequate to meet the more complex needs of growing children.

The group formally named itself the SoHo Children's Cooperative Playgroup and approached the New York Children's Aid Society for space. Children's Aid had a facility in Greenwich Village three blocks above SoHo, and the Playgroup operated from that location for a year. But parents found it was too far a walk for those who lived in the lower SoHo blocks near Canal Street. The following year, the Playgroup moved to a more centrally located space, but it was soon apparent that the group needed a permanent area of their own in which to store their accumulating supplies and where the children might be allowed to play freely with water and paints. This was impractical in a borrowed facility.

As participants increased, the Playgroup parents decided they could legitimately ask the city for space. There were, after all, no public parks or schools in SoHo. Parents reasoned that the recent legalization and rehabilitation promised to bring in added taxes. Beyond some additional sanitation pickups, the SoHo renovation had cost the city nothing. But before they went to the city, the Playgroup went to the SAA to present their problem. SAA president Charles Leslie and others dissuaded the parents from asking for resources from the city. The coordinating committee felt that the community should avoid actions that would cause the politicians to see the district as a fiscal liability and hence rescind the SoHo zoning decision. The Playgroup's problem was handled within the community itself. Four residents, including Leslie, had bought a building on Prince Street and were selling floors in this new cooperative to other artists. As sponsors, they gave the Playgroup a basement area in the building for use rent-free for five years.

The first parents to look at the basement described it as "horrendous," but as renovators themselves, they saw the potential of the space. At least it had windows and a water supply. In a few months, volunteer parent labor had cleaned it out, tiled the floor, installed sinks and bathrooms, and painted the room a cheerful color. Rummage sales and bake sales were held to pay for the materials and to equip the new schoolroom. For a time, the Playgroup took on the character of a community-sponsored institution, with many childless artists lending a hand. The parents felt the school was a community resource. They have estimated that since the space was fixed up in 1972, almost all the children in SoHo have used it at one time or another.

Children at the Playgroup are divided into two groups which both diminish age-grading and reflect growth differences in children. A morning group of 15 three to five year olds is followed at noon by a group of 15 one and a half to three year olds. Three volunteer parents work each shift, assisted in the last several years by one full-time licensed teacher. The parent participants are usually mothers, but a few fathers have been regular workers. They are the at-home artist husbands of wives who have office jobs. Men are more likely to share in the weekend major cleanup routines.

For the first three years of its existence, the Playgroup held regular fund-raising parties and ran a coffee and cookie concession working the Saturday gallery crowds. These events were the equivalent of suburban church or school socials. Said one participating mother, "There was a strong neighborhood spirit involved among donors, buyers, and onlookers. We had card tables with food and coffee, and there were kids all over running their tricycles into people's shins. We were—we *are,* a neighborhood." Now, however, as the parents' careers and incomes have gained ground, they have less time than money. They prefer to pay an increased tuition and to forego the uncertainties of cookie sales. SoHo sidewalks have gained in anonymity.

Playgroup parents and their children have formed a social network of their own in SoHo. The children in each cohort go on to grammar school together at either P.S. 41 or P.S. 3, where they remain classmates. The parents have continued to act in concert, setting up after-school programs in their lofts on the same rotation basis as they did while Playgroup participants. "Bruce is in a group of five or six kids that go to different parents' houses in the afternoon," said one mother. "I work. He has known those kids since they were all babies."

Several additional nursery school systems have evolved with the community. There are now two additional parent-initiated play-groups combining parent labor with licensed teachers. Two others are staffed entirely with paid teachers and are run as commercial enterprises. The original SoHo Children's Cooperative Playgroup, once with long waiting lists of children, now has vacancies and is but one choice among several for SoHo parents.

The new facilities offer a stratified range of child care, with the fully

professional nurseries making their appeal to a newer SoHo parent
population which has a higher income and is more likely to have both
parents employed outside the loft studio. In addition to offering a professionalized staff and elaborate equipment, the commercial nurseries
emphasize structured experience rather than free play. This is a departure from the philosophy of the parent-run playgroups, which had no
sense of a curriculum. One Playgroup mother said, ''We're generally
permissive. Kids do what they want, as long as they don't interfere with
other kids' play or wreck the place.'' Looking back critically on their
own childhoods, these parents are committed to removing repression
from the school experience. In the newer commercial facilities, teachers
can point professionally to lessons in which children learn colors and the
names of animals, and sit down for lunch at tables where they find their
places by identifying their namecards. The emphasis is still on play, for
these are preschoolers three to five years old, but it is play which teaches
rules and structure in a more deliberate way than the parent-volunteer
nurseries thought necessary.

The quick organization of the volunteer nurseries and their smooth
functioning was made possible by a shared cultural outlook on the part
of the parents. The task of the nursery school was seen as the fostering
of individualism through an emphasis on expressive activity. Paint, clay,
song, dance, and games were used to accomplish this objective. Social
experience was considered important for the development of inter-
personal skills; inhibiting rules were not. If children spontaneously exchanged clothes, insisted on playing in the nude on trips to the nearby
public park, or urinated in the sandbox, parents took this in stride. The
only harm that seemed to be done was that neighboring groups, in particular the Italian parents living near the park, strongly objected. It was
because they objected to this libertarian style of child rearing that Italian
parents never enrolled even their older preschool children in the SoHo
playgroups. Artist-parents were reluctant to repress any signs of individual preference. They assumed that when a child was personally
ready, he or she would quickly learn to eat neatly or to read painlessly.

The new professional nursery schools regard part of their job as mod-
ifying this permissive approach to child development. Their staffs are
practitioners of what they regard as a science. The teachers believe that
their schools have to correct deficiencies that exist in SoHo by virtue of
its being an adult community. In a minor way, then, the commercial
nurseries have to a degree imposed an external set of values on SoHo.
From their point of view, SoHo parents are still socially isolated, living
away from their own parents, to whom they otherwise might turn for
child-care advice. Jean Gollobin, head of the Children's Energy Center,
a commercial nursery, observed, ''The parents are often desperate.
They may be new to SoHo, and they don't know people. They're not

aware of the process of growth in their children or how to deal with them.'' In Gollobin's point of view, the establishment of a successful nursery has entailed the reeducation of SoHo parents.

> In the beginning I was really a group babysitter and charged very little. I didn't know how to treat the parents financially or in respect to discipline—when the children were to be picked up and when they were to be left off. They paid only when they came, and they did not always come. They expected the staff to wait if they were late in picking up their child, and they didn't call us even then.

Now, things are different. In a commercial nursery, parents pay a yearly fee of $2,000 or more for 42 weeks. In addition, they are required to volunteer for special trips or to donate special skills. The children arrive promptly, each with a lunch, and are picked up on time. The largest of SoHo's professional nurseries has a staff of nine which works with forty-five children in four groups. Most teachers, and all those hired in the last few years, are licensed. The clientele has also changed in the last few years. Said the head of one nursery,

> Our parents are more middle class and professional. They come from a wider stratum than the loft counterculture people we had at the beginning. My new clients ask about the insurance, the sprinklers, whereas the old ones were just grateful for a safe place for their children to be with other children, somewhere away from the paint and plaster dust of their lofts. And their frazzled nerves. Now, they are more regular, responsible, and noncountercultural.

The professional teachers see divorce as revealing a weakness in the community which calls for the therapeutic intervention of the schools. The commercial nursery schools have found that they have had to develop a counseling system to deal with the impact of divorce on the children. In a representative case, the teacher became aware of a divorce crisis in the home of one of her students. She sat down with the child, who was not yet reading, and composed a chart so the child would know that she belonged somewhere at the end of each school day. The parents were designated by two colors, the days of the week by five, and the teacher and the child together created a chart that would show which parent would be at the school at five o'clock and to which of their homes she was to be taken.

Teachers are ambivalent about divorce and the consequently entangled family relationships in which they observe the children enmeshed. In almost every case, the teachers are single women with an urban middle-class background themselves. They are drawn to the freedom they see in an art community and they identify with mothers who actively define their lives. But as one teacher expressed it, "My radicalism is inside." Outside, their job is to prepare the children to cope, and this involves them in counting the costs of other people's freedom. These costs are used to justify their interventionist role in family life. In a characteristic example, a teacher told of a little girl, two and a half years old, who had said to her mother, "Pack my bags, I'm going to live with daddy. He needs me more." The mother, reduced to tears, appealed to the nursery school teacher for advice. This teacher invited both parents to come into the school, where she sat between them with the child on her neutral lap. She explained a workable division of parenting to the mother and father, as well as the child's needs for security.

Single Parents

As it is for children everywhere, divorce is a challenge for SoHo children. But SoHo parents feel that it is a healthy challenge. Children generally alternate stays with each parent when both continue to reside in the area. The mother's home is regarded as their permanent residence, however, and most chldren "visit" with their divorced father on weekends. Some fathers also take the children one other night during the week, often only at the mother's insistence.

Parents in SoHo generally feel that it is best that their children learn to perceive them as adults, rather than simply as parents. Adults have interests and obligations set in a wider context than the person of the child. One mother explained what this means in the case of the single-parent home.

> It's good that the kids realize that I have a life of my own, and that certainly includes lovers. I'm not uncomfortable that the kids should meet my lover in the morning for breakfast. My daughter, who is ten, is somewhat sensitive on this, and tells these men right away that she has a wonderful daddy, and that he is an artist. This is just to let them know that she's not confusing them with the father role, and she's not necessarily impressed with them.

SoHo's child-care ideology emphasizes that the value of individual expression is important for child and adult alike. Children in single-parent homes are thus expected to be able to deal with a multiplicity of shifting family relationships with a complex cast of participants. One teacher, whose work has resulted in her knowing many SoHo families, summed it up this way: "Kids have to compete with their parents for time, for attention. This encourages their individuation and self-reliance—but perhaps it's self-reliance with nightmares."

Educational Militancy and Community Ideology

When SoHo children have completed preschool in the district, they are sorted into several grammar schools. A few from families with sufficient incomes go to private schools such as the nearby Grace Church School. None have gone on to the several Catholic parochial schools in adjacent neighborhoods. Most parents face a choice between two public schools, P.S. 41 and P.S. 3, both located ten blocks away in Greenwich Village.

P.S. 41 is well regarded academically in the community. It has an active core of involved parents from the Village and from SoHo and is known to offer a structured education based on mastery of reading and math. Classes and grades are conventionally arranged by age groups, and the curriculum is uniform and sequential. SoHo parents seeking a stable, structured education choose P.S. 41. Some of these are parents whose children had not done well in the open classrooms of P.S. 3. Others feel that their children need educational structure to compensate for a loosely organized home situation.

The large majority of SoHo parents, however, choose P.S. 3 for their children. This school originated during the teachers' strike of 1968. A group of P.S. 41 parents, a faction within the P.T.A. living in Greenwich Village, opposed the strike. The dissidents broke the locks on P.S. 3, a surplus school scheduled for demolition, demanded that it be reopened, and chose a staff from among substitute teachers. The Board of Education, taken aback but interested in creating pressure to end the strike, paid the staff. While the strike lasted, the parents got a taste of running a school; and when the strike ended, they demanded that P.S. 3 be retained as an annex of P.S. 41 in which experimental education could be carried out. The concerned parents shifted their own children to P.S. 3, children for the most part just entering the first grade. Parents who had moved to SoHo with school-age children took over several key leadership positions in the P.S. 3 parents' organization and directly affected its educational policy.

By 1970 the parents' committee constituted the administration of the P.S. 3 annex. They wrote a constitution and bylaws, and acted as a school board which made clear its intention to run P.S. 3 as an autonomous school. The parents appointed a group to interview all prospective teachers, and they debated school-policy questions. In June of 1971 parents restructured the school.

Initially, teachers responded positively to the chance to participate in an experiment in locally controlled and innovatively designed education. Recruitment for the start of classes in 1971 was no problem. Teachers accepted the jurisdiction of the parent-board, despite its extra-legal status. The central board, which had not given the parents any formal authorization to run a school, dealt with them through the legal fiction that they were an extension of P.S. 41.

The parents were highly critical of the usual performance of the city's schools, just as they were totally unimpressed with the claims to authority and expertise made by teachers and administrators. A teacher put in charge of P.S. 3 by the central board was not recognized by the parents and, after months of being circumvented and ignored, was withdrawn. The parents relied upon their own educational credentials and were very successful at developing alternative sources of support and legitimacy. Several of the Greenwich Village parents taught in the Education Department at the City University of New York. SoHo parents, with less formal credentials but with equal self-assurance, remembered their own years in public schools as a distasteful and repressive experience which they were determined not to inflict on their own children. They were sure they could run a school that children would want to come to, just as they were sure that bureaucrats at the central Board of Education could not.

The parents instituted a structure of organization that precluded professional teacher control. Their governing body, a school council, consisted of three teachers, three community people, and twelve parents. The council was chaired by the school's head teacher, who was an educational philosopher in the tradition of A. S. Neill. His attire of casual sandals and hippy beads convinced some observers that the parents had deliberately sought an administrator without ambition or a taste for power. The school was designed around a "charrette" structure in which parents and teachers codetermined school policy and interacted within each other's spheres. Under its new head teacher, the school secured a Ford Foundation grant at a time when the foundation was underwriting experiments in decentralized education in New York City. P.S. 3 also sought and received Rockefeller Brothers Fund money to make up for the inadequate budget which an alarmed central Board of Education had assigned the school. Instead of destroying the school, the budget cuts had succeeded in widening its base of legitimacy and deepening its parent involvement.

The parents adopted an open-classroom structure which mixed children of several ages together and submerged the importance of grades. Having a first-hand grasp of the grant structure in the world of the arts, the parents obtained additional grants from the New York State Council on the Arts to pay the salaries of dancers and visual artists in residence, most of whom were recruited from SoHo itself. Throughout the curriculum, the emphasis was on the individual development of each child in an environment that offered a diversity of stimulating projects. Ranking and the comparison of students with each other against a benchmark of expected skills was avoided. Children were urged to learn from and to teach each other, and different rates of progress were expected. This was the rationale for classrooms with children of mixed ages. A flood of parent volunteers served to make the classrooms and the special projects areas of the school into places where personal interest could take root in personal interaction. The authoritarian and central role of the teacher was deemphasized. One mother described the ambiance:

> Classroom activity tends to be geared to the older kids, and the youngest advance rapidly. They've had a lot of preschool experience, and they know a lot and are eager to be with older kids. There's not a lot of pressure on skills like reading. Our kids develop as independent thinkers. There's less cliquing than in other schools. It may be that we are producing a lot of kids that will not fit into the structures of society, since normal schools do teach more repressively. They stress lining up, and order. This kills curiosity and thinking. It may be all right if they don't fit in. We may be producing a lot of artists and creative people.

The central value in the school's philosophy is the encouragement of individualism. A second mother, also from SoHo, said, "We want to produce children who make new structures, not ones that fit into existing ones. This does not mean we want the children to be revolutionaries. Just people who are not merely rank and file." A teacher agreed: "P.S. 3 is really a school for kids with special needs. The kids are individuated, and their parents insist on this more than on any other cultural tenet."

The period 1969–71 was the high point of parent involvement and of their power over school policy. In subsequent years, the head teacher won appointment from the Board of Education, which he used to successfully insulate himself from parent recall. As the world of education normalized after the strike, the teachers grew more concerned with their professional perquisites of status and security. They have regained control of their classrooms, admitting only on their own terms the parents who had originally interviewed them for a position. Even the school secretary has asserted control of her office and has expelled the disruptive parents who at one point made it their clubhouse for educational politics. The commitment to an open-classroom structure at P.S. 3 has remained, but the participation of parents has fallen to an adjunct and support status.

The teachers' central complaint was that the parents had proved to be an antistructure. Said one staffer, "Some parents, N, for example [from SoHo], I couldn't have gotten along without. But most teachers threw them out. They so totally didn't believe in structure." The teachers saw themselves as having to provide the routine on which education was dependent, while the parents had concentrated on the dramatic and the spontaneous gesture.

By 1972 the parents had relinquished the daily operation of P.S. 3 to the paid staff and the teachers. Teachers were being hired according to city-wide seniority lists, no longer through a parent selection process. They were safe from the former threat of parent-initiated removal.

For SoHo parents, the educational issues in the P.S. 3 affair were ones of both broad ideology and the immediate welfare of their own children. When they lost administrative control to the bureaucratically persevering Board of Education and the teachers, the parents shifted their attention to providing enrichment services to the students. In these activities, they both reaffirmed their ideological opposition to bourgeois market values and used the school as the institutional peg around which they have continued to elaborate a SoHo parent and family subculture. One SoHo mother, active in P.S. 3 activities, explained,

> We try in the school to off-set the isolation and loneliness and competition that is created by the structure of society. This includes personal separation. Much of the thrust of my volunteer work is toward collective activity—mixing parents and children of different ages. They all bring different experiences.
>
> This year we sponsored a school fair. My part was to organize a fund raiser for Tommy's class. I rejected selling—making the children extensions of the commercial system, agents. Instead, the whole class and many of the mothers met in my loft, and we cut out fabric and drew patterns and had a quilting bee. People don't get together like they once did, helping each other. That's a real loss. The kids sewed, ironed, and drew the patterns. It came out beautiful. Rather than sell it to one rich person, the kids thought of raffling it off, which they did, for 25 cents a chance. They grossed $280. It was used to buy sports equipment for the class. Last weekend the class went to a Pennsylvania farm, a trip which I arranged. There were 23 kids and 8 adults. It rained all weekend, but there was a huge barn there. The kids dressed up in old stuff from the attic and put on skits. We need this community feeling. It's hard for parents to meet with each other, and the school only partially solves this.

Loft dwellers, especially families of single parents, use the parent activities at P.S. 3 as an extended support system to overcome the partial isolation of those with children in the adult community of SoHo.

These parents, as the teachers delight in pointing out, are also market-conscious. They are sophisticated consumers of education, and so long as the world and the educational system ranks their children, they want those children to be ranked first. In the open classrooms of P.S. 3, therefore, the parents hedge their bets on personal growth. Having lost control of teacher selection, the active and informed parents manipulate the placing of their children in certain classes. For the child with reading problems, parents want a specific teacher known to be able to achieve reading results. For children slow in math, a different teacher is considered to be the best choice. Usually, this means that the parents seek the more structured classrooms and the more disciplined teachers. The newer children, whose parents are not yet in on the informal rating system, settle for the teachers who are left over. When SoHo parents decide that the unique and irregular pace at which their child is developing constitutes a learning problem, they want better educational results. One teacher reported, "Some teachers here are known as 'structure teachers,' and strangely enough, these are the most popular. The philosophy of the school as a whole does not seem to matter; the individual classroom does."

There is no real paradox here, of course. As parents, artists seek to provide their children with the training and the environment which will allow them both to cope creatively with and to depart from what they consider to be an over-organized society.

Conclusion

In the occupational subculture of the SoHo community, marriage or couple relationships are dominated by the salience of the artist identity of one or both participants. Because work takes place in the living space, and because there are few formal organizational props to the artist identity, the domestic audience becomes crucial in the enactment of the artist status. This enactment involves eliciting the emotional and material sponsorship of the domestic partner for the other's artistic endeavor, and results in permanent or periodic exemptions from domestic responsibilities. At almost any point in a career, an artist can claim, "This is the time I must devote exclusively to my art, and nothing must be allowed to interefere." Role negotiation proceeds from that gambit.

Exemptions from domestic responsibilities must be continually renegotiated in the light of changing financial and reputational circumstances and to take into account the competitive demands of the other partner. The organization of domestic life around the primacy of the artistic career can be stable, even extending beyond the life of the artist, when, for example, the surviving partner inherits the obligations of managing the artistic estate so as to enhance the stature of the deceased. Whether a relationship is of long or short duration, the primacy of career imposes particular tensions upon it. Where both partners are artists, they must find a way to alternate the patron role in a dance which demands continual sensitivity and watchfulness if neither is to feel exploited and neglected. The coordination of roles is easier if the two artists work in different media whose exhibition, travel, and preparation schedules allow the interests of each to be advanced in succession. For most SoHo couples, only one partner has an artistic career, and that career dominates the attention of the relationship, leaving the burden of patronage with a nonartist.

While initially appealing, the role of being the systematic and dependable foundation for another's expressiveness can be difficult to sustain. It is initially attractive because the culture of the middle class holds the artist in esteem, particularly as a vehicle with which to associate rebellion. But the cultural emphasis in the SoHo community itself on expressiveness rather than on the context for expressiveness results in the domestic patron feeling inadequately compensated. Success entails an expansion of the audience for the artist without commensurate recognition for the nonartist supporter. The occupational dependency of the artist on the marriage partner lessens, while the nonartist's sense of unrecognized sacrifice increases. This dynamic leads to rebellion by the nonartist in the direction of an independent claim to an artistic status or a career, a claim which makes the nonartist unavailable as a support player. Protracted artistic failure also imposes a burden on the relationship. By calling into question the validity of the artist's talent, it questions the meaning of the supporter's sacrifice. With failure, the artist's dependency increases, as does the impatience and leverage of the nonartist. A breakup of the relationship at this point can trigger an abandonment of the artist identity by the partner who loses the last shred of an audience.

Because the assumptions of the middle class favor the centrality of the male's career in marriage, and because SoHo participates in these assumptions, women artists have a difficult time asserting the primacy of their occupational involvement in the context of marriage. Recognizing this, many have avoided marriage or couple relationships. When marriage is not avoided by these women, childbearing is. Bringing up children has the effect of reinforcing role divisions in which the woman acts as the domestic organizer for both children and husband, with the energies of the household going in large measure to sustain the male's career. For this reason, the presence of children in a household can speed up the process of dissatisfaction with marriage on the part of women, and their search for other avenues of individual expression.

The establishment of day-care cooperatives in SoHo and the campaign of parents to influence the policies of the nearby public schools has provided mothers with a chance to assert an independent status consistent with the subculture of the artist community. Parents, mostly mothers, support an educational philosophy which stresses the maturation of the child as a unique process, and which holds that schools should provide an enriched context of choice and stimulation, while

avoiding the promotion of overt competition along predetermined lines
of endeavor. In the later grades, there is some uneasiness with expressive education and parents begin to expect that as children "progress at
their own rates" they will simultaneously acquire the necessary functional and competitive skills. School volunteerism is also a field in which
some SoHo mothers can assert an ideology somewhat critical of SoHo,
one which favors community and nondirective empathy among children
and parents.

As they mature, children find that their own autonomy is in competition with that of their parents. They are not shielded from the effects of
the personal needs, desires, and satisfactions which their parents pursue
apart from their children, and children learn that they must compete with
other interests for the attention of their parents and negotiate a satisfac-
torily evolving role for themselves within the home.

''The Evolution of SoHo as a Real-Estate Market

For the first years of SoHo's legal existence, major real-estate developers treated the area as low-cost marginal land for which a better use was not immediately apparent. On the lookout for dramatic upgrading, they did not see any significance in nor seek to exploit SoHo's slowly developing cachet as an artist nieghborhood. The problem which SoHo residents faced during the early 1970s was to stop random proposals for the incompatible redevelopment of small segments of the district.

The effectiveness of the residents' opposition depended upon their continued ability to politicize the land market. They sought to defend the stock of loft buildings as the preserve of light industry and artists and to defeat attempts to treat the area as a commercial slum occupying a potentially valuable land bank. To counter the financial leverage and political contacts of developers, the SoHo community had to rely upon its ability to raise symbolic issues, to generate ideological sympathy, and to enlist the expertise of its allies in the art public.

As a community with an occupational culture and a cosmopolitan outlook, SoHo has had a problem sustaining the interest of its residents in local politics. Residents define normal politics in terms of ideas and ideologies which are usually relevant only in national contests. In the fall of 1972, for example, SoHo's approximately two thousand adult residents turned out to enthusiastically support the presidential campaign of George McGovern and raised more than $10,000 in a sale of donated art. On election day, the community registered approximately seven hundred votes, virtually every one for McGovern.[1] When city council seats were at stake or a borough president was running for office, most SoHo residents lapsed into the narrower concerns of occupation and family. They sought the privilege of ignoring the routine chores of political maintenance that were essential in a community with a small population situated on valuable and sought-after urban land. Ordinary politics was left to ten or twenty residents, led by a commercial artist and a journalist, who worked closely with residents from outside of SoHo, renters from new high-rise buildings and cooperative apartments nearer the financial district to the south. These activists, representative of a new urban middle class, founded a liberal Democratic clubhouse, which by 1976 had gained control of the district leadership in Lower Manhattan from the regular Democratic clubs whose base was the shrinking working-class Italian neighborhoods. Yet the new club, the Downtown Independent Democrats (DID), was frequently hard pressed to find artists willing to act as poll watchers in the district. Victory gave the DID the control of the patronage positions of paid election officials. Due to the lack of artist involvement, however, the DID found it had to rehire the corps of Italian housewives who had worked the elections for decades under the regular Democrats. As a result of its indifference to the routines of local politics and to the interests and concerns of neighboring communitites, SoHo could not always count on the consistent support of locally elected officials in its conflicts with developers.

In the postlegalization period, SoHo's problems have been to maintain its boundaries against a series of specific and limited development projects which would have allowed the conversion of manufacturing buildings without regard to the legal character of the area as a preserve of blue-collar employers and resident artists. Isolated development schemes have not provoked a SoHo-wide feeling of danger and mobilization as did the proposed highway construction and the zoning issue. Opposition to piecemeal development has fallen to a small group composed of veteran community leaders who see any project as a precedent for letting bulldozers overrun the entire district, those immediately adjacent to and liable to injury by the project, and lawyers and citizen activists from outside SoHo who have consistently allied themselves with the community.

The Battle of the Sports Palace

In the fall of 1972, as four important Madison Avenue art galleries—Castelli, Emmerick, Sonnabend, and Weber—prepared to move into a renovated paper warehouse on West Broadway (and thus transform SoHo into an art market of the first rank), a developer announced plans to build a twenty-one-story sports center on a parking lot on the southern edge of the district. The building was to have on its four levels tennis courts, garages, a hockey rink, steamrooms, and two regulation-sized basketball courts. The customers for whom the facility was designed were said to be health-minded "Wall Streeters" able to pay charges as high as $20 per hour for tennis-court use. Many SoHo residents saw the project as being a gymnasium for New York University, which lay just to the north of the district. In either case, nearby painters, who depended on natural light, were furious. Those immediately affected became a committed opposition. One resident said,

> I got into things down here with the sports-center affair. I was in the direct shadow of the thing. There would be no light past 11 A.M. in the summer in my loft, and none past 9 A.M. in the winter if the thing were built. We called it "the Slab." This was rank commercialism starting to destroy the whole area. When I moved in I saw this as a place for silence, contemplation—that's why we came. The artist needs quiet to collect his thoughts. And I always liked old buildings.

The artists in the vicinity of the project revitalized the SoHo Artists Association, circulated petitions, and spoke out at a new round of community meetings and public hearings. The developer was initially able to outflank the artists by getting support from the more numerous residents of the Italian South Village area, immediately to the west of SoHo. He offered their children $100,000 worth of free access to the facility. Under the leadership of the two Catholic churches in South Village, St. Anthony's and St. Alphonsus's, the Italians backed the plan. So did most of the area's elected officials, including Assemblyman Louis DeSalvio. The support of the South Village residents, plus DeSalvio's last minute conversion, was sufficient to muster a majority of votes for the project at the Board Two level. Support for the SAA's stand from the two local reform Democrat clubs was not equal to the ethnic opposition.

The Board Two defeat revealed that SoHo had been the object of resentment from the nearby Italian community all along. Social change in the SoHo district had not taken place without causing a sense of dislocation among the South Villagers. As late as 1969, clubs of Italian youth in the South Village had still expressed their territoriality, and the Italian-run taverns had posted signs reading "No Hippies Allowed." "I was walking up Thompson Street at 2 or 3 A.M. on a Saturday night, and I passed this social club," recalled one artist. "Someone yelled out, 'Get that fag in the white pants,' and they poured out after me and my friend Steve. They caught us on the corner of Prince and Sullivan and broke my nose. Steve creawled under a car but they dragged him out and beat him too."

Violence abated shortly after this time. Many Italian ethnics were leaving South Village tenements for suburban housing that symbolized both assimilation and status gain. With its population declining and ethnic businesses closing, the area was losing its sense of ethnic identity. New York University students found the valuable rent-controlled apartments of the area, which the Italians had formerly distributed among themselves, available to them for the first time. A series of friendly conversations between SAA officials, South Village leaders, and police representatives held in 1971 also helped to defuse the potential for violence.

But while demographic change made aggressive street behavior pointless, it did not resolve the displacement and discomfort felt by the members of the ethnic population who remained. The sports-center issue enlivened the embers of this resentment by seeming to juxtapose the interests of the two communities.

Beyond the use of a sports facility, issues of status were also involved in the dispute. "We could afford that price of recreation," said a South Village spokesman and longtime Board Two member. "We didn't want people to get the idea that the whole Italian middle class had fled to Staten Island. We didn't want to be seen as simply a poor community." The Italians in Little Italy, to the immediate east of SoHo, also approved the sports project for reasons of status. While they did expect some free use of the facilities for themselves, they were also upset by a recently released commercial film which depicted their neighborhood as poverty-stricken, riddled with criminal elements, and bereft of legitimate means of upward mobility.[2] A luxury sports facility in the immediate area would encourage quite a different image of Little Italy.

For their part, the artists were used to dealing with their Italian neighbors in stereotyped terms. Artists assumed South Villagers were not sympathetic to them or to their art. "God forbid that they should go into the galleries and see what's being done to the Virgin Mary," said one SAA official. "They'd kill us." The artists' feelings of avant-garde identity were heightened by their perception of their neighbors as being provincial. In the words of one artist, South Village was thought to be "a little Calabrian mountain top." Most of SoHo, when not buying their bread and sausage in South Village, ignored the ethnic community.

With the sports-center issue, SoHo encountered for the first time community groups with needs which were both complex and opposed to those of artists. And SoHo, the recipient of so much support from the middle class of Greenwich Village in the past, lost. At least, they lost in the first round held at the level of the community board and of local political maneuvering. The second round, held at the city's Board of Standards and Appeals, was also lost when that board granted the project the necessary enabling variances from height restrictions.

At this point, a volunteer attorney saved the issue for SoHo on legal and technical grounds. The lawyer, Charles Jurrist, had come to New York City in 1970 as a new law-school graduate and had taken a position on the staff of an important Wall Street firm. Such large firms, often called "law factories" because they employ as many as a hundred staff lawyers who toil in specialized areas of research and case preparation, were having some trouble attracting the best law-school graduates in the early 1970s. In response, these firms offered their recruits paid time to do more exciting and varied legal work in the public interest, so-called pro bono work.[3] Jurrist became involved in a pro bono program administered through Volunteer Lawyers for the Arts and eventually was put in touch with SoHo artists.[4]

As it had in the case with young city planners, the SoHo community was able to benefit from the longing of bureaucratized professionals for a cause. One of the artists who worked closely with Jurrist was a woman whose work he had long admired. Representing such clients proved to be both glamorous and culturally gratifying. As one artist explained, "Jurrist knew of D.W.'s work by reputation, and when they met he saw a culture super-hero. The result was a perfect working and social relationship."

Through Jurrist, the SoHo community was able to obtain excellent legal representation. With legal counsel to guide them, a group of six residents immediately affected by the sports center initiated a suit against the Board of Standards and Appeals (BSA). They charged that the board, in granting the variance for the building, had violated its own rules of procedure, especially by allowing construction which would alter the essential character of the SoHo neighborhood.[5]

The BSA, thrown on the defensive by the suit, sought a series of trial delays which postponed the start of construction for so long that the financial backers of the project finally pulled out, leaving the developer unable to proceed. The SAA had arranged to have representatives from the federal Environmental Protection Agency testify at the trial that auto pollution in the area of Canal Street was already at a nearly toxic level, and that the project would have to be supported by pollution-impact studies showing that its operation would not worsen the situation.

By June 1973, eight months after BSA approval, the sports center was so locked up in litigation that the sponsor withdrew his proposal. The site was reverted to use as a parking lot. Guided by their middle-class appreciation of the law as a complex political tool, and with the help of sophisticated legal counsel, SoHo had outmaneuvered a well-connected developer and survived the opposition of neighboring communities to the east and west. SoHo never again let itself be underrepresented on Community Board Two. It used its connections with the reform Democratic clubs in Lower Manhattan and Greenwich Village to gain renewed appointments for SoHo residents as board members. Through active work with Board Two, SoHo has subsequently been able to cooperate with the Italian South Village and to defuse much of its antagonism toward the artist community.

Landmark Designation

During the SoHo Artists Festival of May 1970, SAA officials were approached by Margot Gayle, head of an organization called the Friends of Cast-Iron Architecture. "We said she could distribute her literature, and instantly there materialized a card table, a carton of brochures, and a vase of artificial flowers," recalled a festival coordinator. From that time on, the SAA worked with this and other organizations to get SoHo's cast-iron buildings under the protection of a landmark's designation.

Official protection of landmarks in New York City was established in 1965 when the administration of Mayor Wagner responded to pressure from private preservationist groups who saw the last remnants of nineteenth-century New York disappearing under the bulldozer. The mayor appointed an eleven-member commission under the Landmarks Preservation Law and empowered it to protect both individual buildings and entire neighborhoods from changes that would destroy or reduce their architectural or historical distinction. The designation process proceeded rapidly so that by 1974, 439 individual properties and 25 historical districts had been designated landmarks, the districts containing about 8,500 structures.[6] A building given such a designation cannot be demolished until the city has had the chance to seek a new use or a new owner who will preserve its exterior. Exterior alterations require prior commission approval.

The artists in SoHo were not without an appreciation of the beauty and valuable record of architectural innovation which economic stagnation had preserved in the loft district around them. But they had an immediate, pragmatic reason to support a landmark designation. Such designation slowed the process of demolition by requiring public hearings and a one-year waiting period while the city had the chance to seek an alternative to the destruction of a building. This process meant that time would be available to politicize a proposed land-use change. The artists would be linked to a sizable constituency in the city-at-large that was organized to defend things of historical value in the urban environment. Since artist living-working quarters were, in every case, an alternative use for SoHo buildings, landmark designation in the district meant that razing and reconstruction could be prevented and the artists' grip on the area maintained.

For three years, SAA president Charles Leslie worked with the preservationist coalition which, along with many academically established architects and art historians, consisted of several special interest organizations, each with its own funds and membership.[7] A high level of self-conscious urbanity—the multitude of specialized civic constituencies capable of political action and public appeal—made this preservationist effort possible. Once again, SoHo artists were fortunate to be in a position to benefit from previously organized commitments to the cultural richness of the city.

Public hearings on the designation of portions of SoHo began in the summer of 1970. The Landmarks Preservation Commission (LPC), balancing competing political pressures, originally proposed to designate as landmarks only a few blocks where cast-iron buildings constituted almost a continuous frontage. Pressure from the preservationist constituency forced the commission to enlarge the scope of the proposal, however. In an effective educational effort among the city's growing middle class, the Friends of Cast-Iron Architecture mapped and publicized 120 cast-iron fronts in the SoHo district—36 of them exceptional—and noted 40 other noniron buildings of architectural distinction. They conducted walking tours through the lower Broadway area, typically drawing 150 participants on a Saturday in the spring and summer. Thus funds were raised and support recruited for the cause of cast-iron buildings and a district-wide landmark designation. For its part, the SAA helped house a team of art historians from Italy who spent the summer of 1971 tracing the origins of district buildings. Together with students from Pennsylvania State University, they produced much of the documentation which the LPC needed to carry its case before the Board of Estimate, the final decision-making body on matters of designation.

The major difficulty was that SoHo was a commercial and industrial district. Up until this time, no commercial district in the city, indeed in the world, had been named a historical landmark. Owners of commercial property opposed such a designation. While landmark status had been shown to increase the prestige and value of a residential area, such as Brooklyn Heights, its effect on commercial property was considered an unwanted constraint. The president of the Real Estate Board of New York considered the landmark law not merely undesirable, but unconstitutional, a case of a "clearly confiscatory law."[8] In their opposition, organized realtors demonstrated their incapacity to see that the city's renewal was dependent upon its environment as a living area as well as a working location. The middle class returning to the city from suburban simplicity were showing that they desired historical interest and depth in their surroundings.

While on record as being against the landmark concept, real-estate groups were preoccupied with downtown and midtown Manhattan office expansion and did not present an organized opposition to the SoHo landmark proposals. Again, the lack of a committed opposition allowed SoHo proponents to achieve a substantial victory. On August 14, 1973, twenty-six blocks of SoHo were named a historical district. The SAA Newsletter commented at the time, "The Historical District will prevent demolition of structures inside the area unless *no* use can be found—not

likely in a living-loft-hungry city—which should stop the high rise
speculators. Existing building exteriors may not be altered in ways that
do not conform to Commission guidelines, and this should be a brake to
honky-tonk."[9]

With the district's new historical status and the sophisticated legal
blockade against developers, SoHo had effectively been saved from
reversion to raw material for the siting of new projects. The residents
were to find it considerably more difficult, however, to obstruct realtors
who chose to work within the status of the district, exploiting rather than
opposing its residential direction and artistic cachet.

Merchandizing an Image: SoHo and the Press

During the politically precarious stages of SoHo's formation, the
city's newspapers played a benevolent and protective role. Staff reporters who specialized in art criticism and art-world social news comprised
a well-established link between the press and artists and gallery owners.
Such links, publicity assets for art sellers and sources of inside information for the journalists, were cultivated on a personal basis by both sides
and entailed nonspecific moral obligation. SAA activists considered
some reporters to be friends and allies from whom they could garner
advice and on whom they could count for favorable publicity. These
reporters came to know the community, and have remained in sympathy
with it. They comprised an essential link which enabled SoHo as a
community to moblize the art public into a supportive constituency.

As a suitable target for impressionistic urban journalism, SoHo came
to the attention of a second set of reporters. These reporters specialized
in mudraking and at first depicted SoHo as a David in a struggle against
the Goliaths wrecking the city—the highway builders, the obtuse bureaucrats among city planners, and the fast-buck developers. Through
the 1974 sports-center fight, SoHo was the beneficiary of this type of
journalism and enjoyed the support of these "advocate journalists."

As SoHo settled down politically, however, and its residents turned to
their work and their families, it lost its embattled status and its presumed
innocence in the eyes of these journalists. They seized upon a new
drama—the moral corruption of the community. The argument went, in
story after story in the press, that as loft living became respectable
for the general middle class, nonartists and quasi-artists had rushed into
SoHo, pushing loft prices up beyond the reach of deserving poor artists
and enabling early co-op "pioneers" to sell at outrageous profits. The
journalists wrote with the anger of betrayed acolytes. "SoHo is on its
way to becoming another Greenwich Village, possessing a tradition of
art but producing little worthwhile art, becoming a stage on which other

aspects of culture ape the visual art that inspired them," proclaimed a writer in the *New York Times* in 1975.[10] The artists themselves were depicted as unscrupulous as well as unproductive. A writer in the *Village Voice* said in 1974,

> Artists are hustlers too. One source waved a paint-splattered hand around his elegant and spacious loft and said snottily, "To make it down here you gotta have the bread. You get it any way you can. You steal it. You marry it. You inherit it. Or you talk your old man into a great real estate deal." More than line, form, color, revolution, Watergate, or sex, property is the SoHo passion.[11]

Some artists were accused of going into the business of sponsoring the sale of new co-ops.

> That many of these profiteers are artists, and that they had no entrepreneurial interests before SoHo was created, is one of the signal ironies of life in this district. What was mandated by the best minds in city government as a haven for beleaguered artists, has become a real estate boondoggle, attracting what the critic Lucy Lippard calls "a geography of boutiques, bars, and fancy food." And artists who can't afford the price are moving out.[12]

The badge of heroism, besides being shifted to "the best minds in city government," was bestowed on new bearers of the mystique of "the artist," alleged refugees from SoHo's greed, now found by the press to be living in new marginal neighborhoods. There, according to journalistic mythology, poverty and precarious existence stoked their creative fires.[13]

These journalists had determined that SoHo artists were no longer worthy of protection or forbearance. SoHo activists were surprised and disturbed at this loss of press protection. As residents saw it, the damage lay in the fact that nonartists, seeking a pleasant spot to live in the midst of a chic art market, would be legitimated and encouraged by this supposed exposure of real estate nihilism in SoHo's loft market.

A third set of reporters soon came to have an influence on SoHo. These were the journalist-photographer teams that descended on the community, beginning in 1974, to depict a new use of real estate. From that time, loft living was heavily marketed in the city's smart magazines and in the consumer and "living" columns of newspapers. Loft existence was portrayed as the new wave in urban experience. *New York Magazine* swept away all remnants of protective obscurity from SoHo with its cover story in May 1974 entitled "The Most Exciting Place to Live in the City." In twenty-seven pages, a half dozen reporters and photographers took readers on a tour, complete with a foldout map, of "high style lofts" and "where to eat, shop and live in the historic cast-iron district."[14]

Initially the writers of the feature had approached the SAA for help. Assuming as they had in the past that it was more prudent to try to manage the news about the community than to ignore the reporters, SAA officials supplied information they hoped would lead to a balanced and toned-down story. Artists spent hours detailing the social structure of the community, its origins, and its hard-working, middle-class character. The SAA provided access to the lofts of artists of all types, especially the modest lofts of the nonfamous, who comprised most the community. None of this material was used to present a rounded picture of the community. SoHo as "La Boheme," now old news, was replaced by "SoHo the Luxurious," as tale of consumer glamour. Page after page of color photos depicted luxury co-ops lofts and famous artists lounging in kitchens and living rooms. This feature was followed in a few months by another photo-essay which covered the overlooked area of SoHo bathrooms.[15]

From 1974 on, SoHo rapidly became a real-estate event as far as the press was concerned. In an effort to resist the embrace of its new admirers, the SAA declared, "We do live in a changing neighborhood. Like all neighborhoods in this city, it will always be changing. Whether it goes the way of the artists or the way of *New York Magazine* and the real estate interests, or the way of the developers depends on what we do about it."[16]

The press was marketing a new trend in urban living—the renovation of former industrial spaces in largely abandoned downtown areas of New York and other older cities. The phenomenon was larger than SoHo. Community meetings and efforts by the SAA to present the true profile of the SoHo community were beside the point. The middle class was being encouraged to reclaim its own impulses toward the creative through a share of the SoHo-style life.

In October 1973 a young publisher started a news weekly in SoHo, transforming the notion of "SoHo" into a nongeographic attitude. It featured "the outrageous" as a new fashion in dress, human relations, and recreation—a style which utilized art-gallery symbolism as a prop for a new consumer life-style. By 1978 this venture, the *SoHo Weekly News,* was in competition with the more political and literary Greenwich Village weekly, the *Village Voice,* and even with the *New York Yimes,* to see which paper could claim preeminence in the avalanche of new real-estate loft listings. The image of SoHo as a community of working artists was papered over with loft promotions.

The Failure of Enforcement: The Effort to Keep out
the "Art Life-Stylers"

In proposing the creation of a SoHo district, the City Planning Commission had argued that "joint living-working quarters are a special light manufacturing use" compatible with the existing zoning and that "residential use is to be permitted only in conjunction with artist work quarters."[17] The city had licensed an "administrative community"—a community legitimated by administrative and legislative decision.[18] The residential population, intended by the CPC to play the role, along with marginal industry, of place holders in a landbank reserved for corporate expansion, was given unquestionable legitimacy by legislative action.

The planners intended that SoHo observe set limits to its residential composition. To insure that only artists would occupy SoHo lofts for living purposes, the legislation provided that the Department of Cultural Affairs inquire into the credentials of potential residents, to certify those who were bona fide artists, and to refuse residential permission to the rest. As subsequent years have shown, the middle-class employment of art as the theme for a consumer life-style and their wish for residential proximity to working artists and an art-market milieu created pressure for nonartist residence in SoHo that neither the informal moral condemnation of the artist community nor the administrative efforts of gatekeepers have been able to withstand.

Certifying Artists

In the spring of 1971 the city's Department of Cultural Affairs (DCA) set up a committee to certify artists elegible to live in SoHo. Twenty people were selected by the DCA, five artist activists from SoHo itself, five artists from outside SoHo, and ten management people representing arts institutions. With the help of the SAA, notices were distributed explaining that certification was essential to keep out the "non-artists flocking into SoHo who are driving up rents and taking the legal space reserved for artists."[19] It was argued further that certification would be necessary in any event when the five-year moratorium with the city elapsed and inspectors would be sent into SoHo to see that building codes and occupancy restrictions were complied with.

The response from resident artists was not enthusiastic. By June 1972, after a year's effort, only 344 artists had been certified out of an estimated 2,000 artists in SoHo. Many artists had withdrawn into the immediate security of their lofts, for the moment free of inspectors, and doubted that the Department of Buildings would ever enforce certification. These artists felt, in addition, that the effort of certification was a needless questioning of their identity. "I know I'm an artist," said one SoHo resident, characteristically. "What do I need to have somebody else tell me I'm an artist for?"

The DCA responded to this reluctance by stressing in its application forms and announcements that the purpose of certification was "to evaluate the degree of your commitment to your work and your need for large space, not to make aesthetic judgments."[20] To many artists, this read like an invasion of privacy. They remained convinced that, until it seemed to be absolutely necessary, they were better off remaining uncontaminated by a bureaucratic process which they could easily evade. Confronted with the restraints of administrative regulation, artists chose to invoke occupational individualism rather than locality responsibility.

Committee members, activists in the struggle for artists' rights to live where they found space to work, were themselves sympathetic to the uncooperative artists. Despite their rational conviction that certification was needed, committee members performed their functions with considerable self-doubt. "We can understand artists refusing to cooperate with us, a city bureaucracy," said Claire Tankel, a DCA member in liaison with the committee. "It *is* presumptuous of us to claim to be designating individuals as 'artists.' We feel presumptuous certifying real artists. I mean, who are we in the city to say someone is an artist or not?"[21]

The only teeth the committee had were not its own but those of the Department of Buildings. It could turn over the names of uncertifiable residents and request an inspection and possible eviction. But the committee members were prevented from doing this. The consequences of authorizing and inviting this type of clearing action could easily result in widespread and uncontrolled evictions of artists and nonartists alike, as inspectors uncovered the building-code violations with which most loft dwellers lived out of economic necessity. "We do not blow the whistle on people wholesale by calling the Buildings Department or Con Ed because we are aware that many artists are living in SoHo illegally," explained Tankel. "They can't afford to bring their spaces up to code, and by forcing compliance, we would be bringing about a great hardship."[22]

From the beginning, the SoHo community itself has recognized a complex set of exceptions to its demand that every loft resident in the district be an artist. Some of the early residents, the "pioneers," were not practicing artists. They either had been artists or intended to become artists when their present jobs permitted. Because they worked hard in their cooperatives and in community affairs, they were accorded honorary artist status. A few of these, who had natural leadership ability but less-than-perfect credentials, became workhorses in SAA affairs. Other residents, architects in particular, were invaluable sources of aid in the zoning alteration struggle. Some nonartists had been divorced or widowed by their artist spouses. Other residents, businessmen, earned an exemption by assuming the administrative work in their otherwise all-artist coops. The functional and emotional interdependence of artists and nonartists was, in many respects, a strength of the community. In any case, it defied administrative separation.

For its part, the certification committee has a had a difficult time trying to establish criteria by which to draw a line between those who are certifiable and those whom commercialism, lack of commitment, or minimal need for space makes ineligible. The outrageous applications are easily dealt with. Said Tankel, in March 1977,

> I have never seen such fraud attempted as we have had recently. Lately there has been a flood of applications, and 1,100 are now certified. We have art collectors trying to get in, lawyers. They bring in the paintings of other people to set up when our committee visits their studios. One person we certified then turned around and told us his loft was available for commercial parties. We rescinded that certification.

The pseudoartists and the commercial artists provide the bottom line of uncertifiable applicants. A SoHo artist and commission member explained,

> We had one case of a designer of interiors who sent in a photo of what looked like a Lower East Side furniture-store interior. Then we had a guy who photographed an obscure and very poor art show—at the level of an old-people's-home exhibit—using really dim polaroid shots. It just happened that I had seen this work, but in a show which attributed it to somebody else. . . .
> We refuse only one percent of the applicants. These are the unvarnished fakes or those who don't qualify by occupation, like the interior decorator.

Above this line of clean distinctions, the ambiguities of the art world, the need of nearly all artists to have a nonart job or to do commercial work, and the reluctance of the committee to question the self-definition of artists make the job of certification a difficult one. The committee's bias is toward the inclusionary. Said Tankel,

> We have very loose, case-by-case standards. We just certified an art critic on the basis that she served the community as a whole. But we only certified her for her present space—she can't move to a larger one. We don't deal with the population of artists as such, only with those who come to us with their credentials. We look at the seriousness of their commitment to *creative* art.[23]

The SAA itself, charged by the CPC in 1971 with the task of helping to police the community against incursions by nonartists, is inhibited in exactly the same way as the certification committee. It lacks any enforcement tools other than a vague moral condemnation of illegal occupants, on the one hand, and, on the other, the ability to call in the Department of Buildings for what would be an uncontrolled search for code violations.

There is only one point at which the certification process has acted as a legal barrier. Artists' cooperatives seeking to legalize their status have been allowed to clear their buildings of violations and to file retroactive prospectuses with the state Attorney General.[24] Cooperatives taking this route have had the moral pressure generated by some of their members strengthened by the self-interest of all, and all the occupants have sought certification as artists.

However, the problem remains that legal cooperatives are only a small minority of all SoHo and NoHo buildings, the two areas having been made jointly subject to artist-only restrictions since 1976. A CPC study conducted in the fall of 1977 and issued in December revealed that, of 178 buildings that had been totally converted to residency in SoHo, only 7.3 percent were done legally and had been issued valid certificates of occupancy.[25] Of the 58 conversions in the adjacent loft district of NoHo, only 3.4 percent were legal. Thus roughly 94 percent of all the converted buildings in SoHo and NoHo have not been granted legal status, and their occupants have thus far been able to evade compliance with the artist certification program to which the legalized cooperatives have responded.

It appears, however, that many more residents will be seeking to gain valid certificates of occupancy, signifying that their buildings meet all zoning and building regulations, in order to avail themselves of a program of tax abatements offered by the city to legally converted loft buildings.[26] Under this program, too, checks are made for conformity with the artist-only restrictions. But once a building is granted tax abatement, no subsequent inspection is made to see that all residents are artists. Nine years after the establishment of SoHo, an administrative mechanism for monitoring the occupational qualification of residents still does not exist.

The Real-Estate Game: The Present Situation

Despite the inflation of the real-estate market, the publicity directed at the glamorous elite among loft dwellers, and the charges by journalists that the community has been corrupted by an influx of bankers and lawyers, SoHo remains in many respects a stable community. The foundation of continuity in SoHo consists of the early arrivals, renters with long leases and co-opers, who could never hope to establish themselves in new loft areas for the same housing costs they are paying in SoHo. Rather than fleeing the community, they have stayed.[27]

The change in the community is due to three factors. Some artists, giving up the attempt to establish themselves, take up new careers; and some, though not all, of these "lapsed" artists leave the community. This is the leakage factor. Other artists are notable successes and are thus freed from the constraints of having to stay in physical proximity to the market. Such artists leave SoHo for rural farmhouses, where their children can have horses, or for newer loft districts where they can have entire buildings to themselves. This can be seen as the evaporation factor.

Far more significant in numbers are the incoming residents who occupy newly converted buildings. This is the expansion factor in a district of increasing residential density. Most buy into cooperatives being developed by speculators. Because these residents are buying into the community at the top of the market, and because speculators are interested in sales rather than in conforming to artist-only restrictions, many of these new residents are not artists but young professionals.

Newly graduated art students are finding it more difficult, but certainly not impossible, to find space in SoHo. If they were to be shut out, the community would lose the new blood that presently makes it a creative center. At the present time, however, space reserved for artists remains available. Much of this is in rental units in artist cooperative buildings. The original generation of loft dwellers demanded entire floors of 2,500 to 4,000 square feet. As fuel oil and tax increases have driven up maintenance charges, these artists have learned that they can get along in less space. Many have subdivided their floors to create rental units of 1,200 to 2,000 square feet; house rules in all artist cooperatives have effectively reserved these units for artist tenants.

The Escalating Cost of Housing

When artists first moved into the South Houston Industrial District in the early 1960s, they paid as little as $60 to $90 a month to rent 2,500 to 3,600 square feet of unheated loft space in a "raw" condition, that is, just as the last industrial occupant had left it. These were the worst buildings; toilets were broken, the plaster water-damaged, window sills rotted out, the chutes used to connected one level with another left as irregular holes in the floors. Artists constituted a market below that of industry.

After legalization in 1971, however, prices began to rise throughout the district. As artists took over many of the least serviceable buildings, building owners came to realize that the new residential market was not one of last resort, but a preferred market which could be made to support rents equal to and above industrial rates. According to the experience of several realtors active in SoHo and as confirmed by newspaper advertisements, prices in the district escalated rapidly for a 2,500-square-foot loft (see table 1).

Table 1
Cost of SoHo Residential Loft Space

	Rental			Co-Op	
	"Raw"	Finished	"Fixture Fee" to Departing Tenant	"Raw"	Finished
1972	$225	$275–$325	$2,500–$3,000; up to $5,000, if superior, for a 5- to 8-year lease	$12,000	$35,000
1975	$350	$350–$425	$6,000 up to $10,000 for a 5-year lease	$18,000	$50,000 to $70,000
1980	$500	$700	$8,000 to $15,000 for a 2- to 5-year lease	$30,000 to $60,000	$80,000 to $130,000

"Fixture fees" are charged for finished or partially finished rental lofts and vary with the rent, the time left on the lease, and the imagination of the seller. The buyer expects to amortize the fee over the length of the lease and considers it to be additional rent, or hopes to pass it along to a subsequent renter of the space. Typical maintenance charges for co-op partners have risen from $225 per month in 1972 to $450 or more in 1980, depending on the type of mortgage, and are often increased in the short term to raise money for major repairs.

Loft Speculation

Prices in buildings coming onto the market have escalated through one of several variations on the game of loft-conversion speculation, as the following examples demonstrate:

The Free Conversion. This conversion is free, not to the tenant, but to the landlord. In this siutation a landlord of a building grants a seven- to ten-year lease to an artist who has renovation skills and some capital, but not enough money to purchase a loft in a cooperative building. The artist divides the loft in half, renovates both sides as living-working quarters, and occupies one unit while renting the other to a subtenant. For a great deal of work, considerable investment, and the assumption of all the risks of living in an illegally converted space, the tenant is able to defray his rent with income from the subtenant. Despite leases which grant the tenant ownership of the improvements, these occupants are at the mercy of landlords. As illegal occupants, they can be evicted, or less drastically, the landlord need not extend the lease on favorable terms. The building owner has exchanged commercial tenants paying, for example, $450 per month for 5,000 square feet for an artist paying $700 and renovating the space as well.

The "Ethical" Sponsor. This variant is applicable to several residents in SoHo who have legitimated themselves as friends of the community through service to the SAA or simply by long-time residence. It is usually architects who fall into this category, but lawyers who have gained an intimate knowledge of SoHo real estate as volunteer counsels to the community have also yielded to the temptation to play the real-estate game. In a few cases, so have artists.

Such a sponsor will locate a building owned, for example, by a machine-tool repair company moving to New Jersey. The sponsor acquired the building through a mortgage given by the former owner, upgrades the public systems in the building—the roof, boiler, major electric lines, and plumbing—and sells space to artists. One such building, assessed for $180,000, was purchased by the sponsor for $200,000 and sold to artists organized into a cooperative for $478,000. The sponsor's repairs cost approximately $60,000, and he handled the job of selling the spaces himself. The sponsor walked away with a considerable profit from a building which had not had its conversion legally recognized. Buyers benefit as well. For a purchase price of $20,000, renovation costs of $10,000, and special assessments for building improvements and legalization costs of $5,000, buyers have a 2,500 square foot space for which they will pay only $225 a month but which can sell (as of 1980) for $80,000. Why doesn't the sponsor comply with the law and assume the burden of obtaining a residential certificate of occupancy for the building? One such sponsor said,

> Once you get a certificate of occupancy you are in trouble. You don't need one, first of all. And it means your real-estate taxes will go up. And if the building doesn't qualify during the inspections, buyers are afraid they'll be kicked out. Getting variances costs a lot of money, both for physical changes and also legal expenses. And who's going to force you to get a certificate of occupancy anyway? After the scandal in the Buildings Department a few years ago, there's no more

inspectors. There're maybe 129 co-ops in SoHo, and only 10 have a certificate of occupancy. The Buildings Department can't even keep up with their own paperwork.[28]

The Buildings Department is, however, searching for illegally occupied buildings, and nervous occupants are seeking certificates of occupancy.[29]

The "Neighborhood-Buster". This individual is a sponsor of a building conversion who seeks to create near-luxury apartments for the general housing market. One such renovator owns a twelve-story industrial building on Broadway that has 10,000-square-foot floor areas. While he has owned the building for many years, since 1972 his industrial tenants have begun to move out. Half of his floors are now empty. His remaining tenants, dress companies and hat companies, employ as many as a hundred workers each. Despite twenty years of occupancy for some of these tenants, the building owner keeps them on three- to six-month leases. He wants to convert his building to "Class A" or conventional apartments, rather than to artist housing—if not the entire building, then at least half of it. Why not artist housing? "I am congenitally opposed to artist-only restrictions," he said. "I want this space for executives moving into New York and into an artist area. I don't want workshops there—I want tenants who will fix up the spaces, give them character, and stay five or ten years. I want people for whom money is no object, who want a new kind of life-style."

Through the efforts of SoHo representatives and members of the community board committed to enforcing the artist-only zoning in the area of the building, this owner, as were two others before him, was denied approval of the variances required to convert his building.

The CPC has been a particular help in situations where renovators request variances to exempt them from artist-only zoning restrictions. In one precedent-setting case, they submitted a detailed brief to the Board of Estimate appealing for a reversal of a variance granted by the Board of Standards and Appeals.[30] They argued at length that such a variance would "sharply alter the essential character of the neighborhood and will be detrimental to the public welfare of this city and state."

Due to close cooperation among the SAA, the liaison personnel from the CPC to the community, and Community Board Two, SoHo has been protected from frontal assaults on its identity as an artists' district from developers seeking legal variances. However, many developers do not take the legal route.

The Rational Sponsor. This sponsor is most likely to be an architect-lawyer team, able to handle all of the work of drawing up documents and selling spaces itself, building its fees into the sale price of the building. One such team recently sponsored the formation of a cooperative in an industrial building zoned for manufacturing uses and artist living-working quarters only. The building was assessed for $180,000. They paid $300,000, giving the original owner a handsome profit, but just a small part of the proceeds of the conversion. First, the new owners cleared the fully occupied building of its manufacturing tenants—makers of underwear, dresses, novelties, and musical supplies. Most of these companies, unable to find new space for the $420 per month they had been paying for 3,000 square feet, went out of business, and their employees lost their jobs. Next, the sponsors drew up documents creating a *non*residential cooperative, swept the loft spaces, and undertook to show and sell the floors. For this they charged $120,000, a cost that was passed on to the cooperative. Full 3,000-square-foot lofts sold for $60,000, with the occupants assuming all the costs of renovation and all the legal problems associated with illegal living in a building restricted by the zoning and by its certificate of occupancy to manufacturing uses. Spaces were sold irrespective of the occupation of the purchasers, most of whom were nonartists. When the last floor was sold, the building had cost the new tenants $999,000. The sponsors were able to realize a profit of $580,000 for two years possession of the building. Yet even with this rate of profit, well-informed buyers were grateful. Two years after purchase one said, "If I hadn't bought then I'd be out of luck. I certainly couldn't afford anything in today's market."

Conclusion

The modern city acquires a potential for liberating human personality from external restraints and for advancing cultural development partially because it is an abrasive environment. It does grind down the ascriptive ties of solidarity with kinship, ethnic group, and neighborhood with the relentlessness of competition and of marketplace rationality, and as Louis Wirth among others has pointed out, this erosion of social solidarity can reach a point where a chasm of depersonalization and moral drift opens up, frightening residents into the false refuge of a totalitarian coherence. [31] The city is able to support a release of creative potential in its residents, generating new forms of cultural synthesis, because it provides, in the midst of indeterminate order, a density and differentiation of interest groups. Through a potential to shift among interest groups and constituencies, the urban resident can hope to find a personal anchorage consistent with the self-determination of his identity. As Georg Simmel pointed out, the urban condition is one in which there is an absence of cultural determination combined with the possibility of elective social affiliation; this is what makes the city conducive to the self-determination of individual identity and the source of society's cultural innovation.[32]

If the city's openness to the culturally new in general and to the contributions of the artist in particular is to be sustained in what has become, on the one hand, a time of bureaucratic centralism and encroachment, and of market domination by fewer but more powerful actors, on the other hand, then cities must as a matter of deliberate policy strive to acquire the following characteristics:

First, there should be room for unanticipated developments in land use. Central urban planning should be revealed to be, at best, a conceit of clairvoyance and, at worst, an unjustified usurpation of the interests of some groups in favor of others. Legitimate planning activity should be limited so as to provide support for spontaneously generated patterns of land use which may arise from the activities of the occupants of that land. SoHo is, from a planning point of view, just such an unanticipated land use, one which grew out of a coincidence of a specific pattern of urban decay with the spatial needs of a developing and territorially concentrated interest group. SoHo reveals that one of the more important virtues of urban master plans is their incompleteness.

Second, the SoHo example suggests that status groupings—voluntary affiliations of those organized around a commitment to a common value and shared prestige order—will comprise an important source of new urban communities. These status communities are likely to seek the advantages of residential proximity for their members and spatial concentration for their institutions so as to facilitate their activities. Out of spatial needs, these new community forms will seek to acquire territorial niches within the metropolis. Because these communities of mutual interest are important contexts within which individuals are integrated into systems of social responsibility and productivity, these avocational or occupational communities deserve to be encouraged by cities seeking to limit the destructive consequences of anomic drift and urban pathology.

Third, the city should be prepared to accept and cooperate with a new method for the distribution of urban land, a method in which status communities politicize their claims to territory and appeal to the wider metropolitan audience for validation of those claims. This politicization is useful in promoting the internal organization of the status communities themselves and encourages them to base their claims to territory on their character as functional assets to the city as a whole. The challenge to the professional planner comes in trying to work with these status communities so as to erect systems of administrative accountability which insure that territorial enclaves remain protected from the free market in real estate while continuing to contribute to the needs of the entire city.

Neither goal will be easy to accomplish, and both will require that systems of administrative protection be altered to meet changing conditions. Status communities, as real-estate enclaves, should not be allowed to become simply guilds of the fortunate whose date of arrival alone entitles them to inclusion in a land-use shelter. Provision for the participation of new community members, either through expansion of the enclave or systematic turnover of residents, must be provided if the enclaves are to retain a legal and moral basis as serving a city-wide need through the provision of sanctuary to a functional category of citizens, rather than to specific individuals. If this can be administratively achieved, these new communities can become centers for city-wide participation and vitality.

The course of development taken by SoHo is informative of the prospects and problems associated with this new form of urban community, the territorial status community. The social interaction of SoHo residents with each other and with the wider city, a process through which they define the extent of their community, is multilayered and changes in emphasis with time. First, SoHo is by necessity a political community. It was through organizing themselves and their allies as a pressure group that residents were able to obtain the zoning changes and schedules of zoning enforcement which legitimated their occupancy in the loft district and which mapped SoHo as a unique housing monopoly of an occupational group. Political action has created both the external boundaries and the internal structure which enabled SoHo to act as a constituency for its own needs. Since political action has lost its urgency for most residents in recent years, owing to the end of the threat of demolition, the defense of the community has fallen to a system of administrative structures such as landmark district protections, the artist certification process, and community board participation in land-use determination. These structures are the routinized means by which the residents have continued to protect their tenancy and, in association with surrounding residential areas, to monitor city services and private or public development initiatives.

SoHo has been able to act successfully as a territorial status community before the wider metropolitan audience because it has been accepted as representing the housing interests of an occupational segment of the city with which many city officials and influential nonartists are in sympathy. Political concessions made to SoHo were concessions made to the city's artists as a category. Once SoHo residents raised the issue with the public, the city administration allowed itself to be persuaded that a "culture industry" is important for tourism and as an attraction to the corporation-headquarters sector with which planners had identified the future of Manhattan. The conviction that artists were essential to creating a stimulating environment became a persuasive ideology, cir-

culated by the media to the city as a whole, and important to legitimating
the sponsorship of the city government with the public. As the prime
proponents of that ideology, SoHo residents convinced one another that
it was worth undertaking the responsibilities of community leadership
and activism that exceeded mere self-interest. The transition of SoHo
into a legally recognized community was dependent upon the ability of
its residents to articulate their occupational interests as consistent with
the broader cultural perspective of nonartist supporters and with the
interests of artists in general.

Effective political action by the SoHo community, whether as legislative pressure, administrative innovation, or the mounting of a public
relations campaign, has depended upon the specific nature and
homogeneity of the residents' subculture. Residents were able to define
a common program of action because they shared the same occupational
goals and suffered the same occupational plight. The channels of their
territorial interaction were preformed through their organization as a
subculture around art-world institutions and the support networks
employed at the informal level which sustained their assaults on the art
market. Residents brought these patterns of social affiliation into the
district with them when they located in SoHo. As the artist population
increased there, it generated new cooperative institutions and new possibilities for network formation.

While patterns of social organization such as housing cooperatives,
child-care and educational arrangements, and even to some extent the
contemporary art market, have become centered in the SoHo district,
they have not become aligned with its boundaries. Because residents
have in their social networks and in the institutions of the urban status
community of art a basis for intimacy and occupational organization,
they can ignore the locality community without suffering social isolation. The priority of career in the lives of residents causes them to treat
local political mobilization as an exceptional condition, perhaps necessary from time to time, but more often a diversion from the true work of
their lives. Unless politically embattled, SoHo's spatial and social boundaries are invisible to its own residents. Personal interests are disengaged
from the territorial community as residents withdraw into the matrix of
career and the realm of the private. SoHo residents are able to choose
among the ways in which they can actualize community and interact
with others. However, the family and the support network are far more
salient for them personally than is the instrumental context of territoriality.

As the community has matured politically, the need to address problems on a territorial level has lost some of its urgency, and loft living
some of its expressive content. The conversion of factory space into
studios and the residential occupancy of an industrial area once con-

veyed an artistic designation. Now, such occupancy is a commonplace among the middle class in a number of older American cities. The pioneer period of intense mutual aid, when housing co-ops were economic lifeboats shipping water at every turn, has given way to settled occupancy, to bank financing, to an impersonal rota of duties for partners, and to a retreat into individual careers. Co-ops were always more an instrumentality than a mode of social affiliation desired as an end in itself. The intense cooperation of the building renovation period was not intended to become a way of life. The building facades which give SoHo an ecological distinctiveness are now historical relics under the custodial eye of their own interest group, both inside and outside of government; their very usefulness as a protective bulwark has externalized them in the eyes of their occupants. School and day-care systems for children, while continuing to involve residents as neighbors in mutual-aid relationships, have become formalized and less demanding of the parents' time. The pursuit by mothers of their own career identities has paved the way for commercial day-care operations with less client and cultural ties to the SoHo district. The ability of SoHo parents to transfer their cultural perspective to their children has diminished as parents have had to accommodate the claims of teachers to professional autonomy and their interests in a more structured and less individuated curriculum. Schools for older SoHo children are all out of the district, and parental ideology now constitutes the rationale for enrichment and volunteer involvement rather than the basis of the education program. In an adult-centered community such as SoHo, educational concern has been largely limited to those parents with school-age children, and this concern has united parents within school boundaries that ignore the demarcations of SoHo.

Thus, the web of relationships and shared beliefs generated by the residents of SoHo has shifted away from the spatial community in recent years. Without an agenda, the community does not assemble. Without new political campaigns, new arrivals are not integrated, and leaders remain unrecognized and hesitant in the absence of expressions of support. The administrative structures which have prevented the development of some crises have had the paradoxical effect of reducing the salience of territorial identity. Without contentious community meetings, spokespersons and representatives of the community lose their visibility and prestige. Caretaker functions, unacknowledged, cause leaders to become discouraged and cynical, and the context for the development of new leadership is absent.

If SoHo had remained attractive only to artists, the political capacity of the territorial community could be perceived as dormant rather than as doubtful. The problem now is that new residents include an increasing number of nonartists, as both a result and a cause of rising real-estate values. With nonartists quickening the competition for lofts, prices have escalated sharply. Both developers and owners of individual spaces have taken quick profits on their investments, at times helping nonartists to bluff and evade the artist certification process. Even those artists with relatively substantial and steady incomes, experienced college art teachers, for example, find that they have to spend more than 40 percent of their gross incomes to rent lofts priced at $600 and $700 a month, and that few suitable spaces can be had for less. When the artist can't pay the rent, the lawyer just out of law school and earning $30,000 a year in the financial district stands waiting. Those who rent or sell lofts, however committed to an ideal of artist occupancy in the district, find it difficult to avoid pricing to the top of the market if they come to feel that the community as a whole has lost interest in providing reasonably priced space to young and as yet unsuccessful artists.

SoHo has remained accessible to artists at the entry level of their careers only because they are willing to live in basements and in the smaller subdivided areas, often closer to 800 than to the legal minimum of 1200 square feet. The standard loft of the early 1970s, which had 2000 to 3000 square feet, is accessible to new arrivals only if they are willing to rent as groups, sharing kitchens and competing for easel space. The squeeze is on, and the gate to SoHo is closing for the young artist. Unless SoHo is able to reassert its ideological commitment to being a haven for those of the city's artists who cannot find working space on the open market, it will forfeit the public support on which it depends and cease to function as a protective setting for artistic innovation.

Action is necessary to affirmatively involve government and private sponsors in purchasing loft buildings which could be used to provide reasonably priced working and residential space for newer artists. Such a project, run as a public corporation under the management of the SoHo community association and others as public trustees, could issue artists nonrenewable leases for fixed periods of, say, five years. The initial renters, in consideration of their work in renovation of the units, might qualify for ten-year leases. In any case, these leases would not be transferable to other occupants but, upon vacancy or the termination of the lease period, would revert to the corporation for assignment to newer artists.

If positive action is not taken to sustain the mission of the SoHo community in the city as a whole, action which would involve the community in new channels of cooperation and normative self-regulation, the community will risk its future as an art center. Through an inner decay in which residents abandon their commitment to SoHo's artistic function, and through the occupation of newly converted buildings by nonartists, the district will lose its artist character and its ability to support the remaining artists with a dense subcultural environment. It will lose the residential depth that makes it exciting and convincing to buyers as a primary art market, and it will lose the distinct identity and difference that makes it attractive to restauranteurs and tourists. The tide of artistic, subcultural, and small business vitality could well recede from SoHo, leaving it an empty shell. Its artist certification process would unravel. Without effective residential defense and the support of political patrons outside the district, SoHo would inevitably lose its zoning protection. Without the overlapping protection of special occupational zoning and militant defense by residents, the district's landmark status would be far less tenable and individual buildings would fall to the effective challenges of developers. Rather quickly, SoHo would merge into a depleted urban landscape, partly as another upper-income residential district and partly as a site for commercial office expansion. The mission of sustaining artists and their functional contribution to the city would, to a significant extent, become an aberration of the past.

Appendix 1
Methods

This study is longitudinal, extending from the initial phases of artist residency in SoHo in the early 1960s to the culturally heterogeneous community of 1980. My familiarity with the community as a long-term participant and observer and my theoretical interests in community development and in occupational identity have enabled me to develop the occupational and residential typologies which guided this research.

I have worked as a printer and carpenter in the SoHo community since 1968 and have been active in two artist housing cooperatives. Since 1973 I have lived in the district. Beginning in 1975, I have had five years of participant-observer involvement in SoHo through membership in a political club in the area, involvement in the SoHo community civic association, and membership on the community board which represents the SoHo district.

I have relied most extensively on open-ended interviews, and those with whom I spoke were informants as much as they were subjects. Each interview followed a loose schedule and lasted about two hours. Some people were visited two or more times during the period of this study, 1976 to 1979. Pseudonyms or altered initials are used to protect the anonymity of all subjects except those who are public figures. Where reference to the specifics of personal background are appropriate, these specifics have been altered to obscure the identity, but not the social characteristics, of the subject.

Sixty-eight individuals were interviewed, forty-eight of whom were SoHo residents who worked in an art medium and considered themselves artists. The SoHo sample was predominantly male but included twelve women artists. They lived in households ranging from single-member through roomate arrangements, communal patterns, and marriages, both with and without children. The subjects included artists at all career stages and degrees of occupational recognition. Their ages ranged from twenty to the mid-sixties, but most were between their middle twenties and early forties. I sought out artists working in a variety of media. Most were painters and sculptors, but I spoke with dancers, novelists, film makers, video artists, and conceptual artists as well.

I interviewed twenty individuals who were not resident artists. This group included art dealers and the staffs in SoHo galleries, architects and craftspeople working and living in the community, nonartist spouses of artists, housing developers, artists living in surrounding areas, and nonresident planning and political activists. The total group of sixty-eight subjects included virtually all of the community activists in SoHo and those city officials, planning agency staff members, and citizen activists from outside SoHo who had played important roles in the movement for artists' housing and the legalization of SoHo for artist occupancy.

I have made use of existing community studies and urban planning literature where appropriate, and have analyzed public and private planning surveys of the district as a source of land-use data and as evidence of urban planning ideologies. In addition to interviewing participants in the process of community change, I studied the records of the community association and its publications, the public press, and art journals. I sought both the factual information and ideological content that had a bearing on SoHo's efforts to control its future and manage its public image.

Appendix 2
Tables

Table A1
Number of Employees in New York City in Apparel and Other
Textile Products (in Thousands)

1949	354.0
1958	276.9
1968	229.3
1974	162.6
1978	153.0

Source: U.S. Department of Labor, Bureau of Labor Statistics,
Employment and Earnings for States and Areas, 1934–1980, Bulletin 1370–13, p. 428.

Table A2
Number of Manufacturing Employees in the Borough of Manhattan (in Thousands)

1958	538.5
1959	534.5
1960	523.5
1961	504.0
1962	498.6
1963	479.3
1964	472.5
1965	469.2
1966	466.8
1967	460.9
1968	456.8
1969	447.5
1970	417.7
1971	382.4
1972	362.7
1973	345.7
1974	319.0
1975	294.0
1976	296.4

Source: U.S. Department of Labor Statistics, *Employment and Earnings for States and Areas, 1939–1980*, Bulletin 1370–13, p. 439.

Table A3

Office Space Completed in Downtown and Midtown Manhattan in Rentable Square Feet, by Year of Completion, 1950–1973

Completed	Downtown	Midtown
1950	206,000	3,227,000
1951	429,000	763,000
1952	– – –	995,000
1953	– – –	888,000
1954	– – –	2,299,000
1955	503,000	1,344,000
1956	– – –	3,875,000
1957	1,105,000	3,839,000
1958	1,400,000	3,401,000
1959	2,595,000	3,202,000
1960	900,000	3,591,000
1961	2,595,000	4,788,000
1962	1,150,000	2,796,000
1963	912,000	6,533,000
1964	110,000	4,888,000
1965	1,616,000	2,038,000
1966	1,000,000	800,000
1967	604,000	1,400,000
1968	3,329,000	3,568,000
1969	3,211,000	10,695,000
1970	3,980,000	4,617,000
1971	7,857,000	8,110,000
1972*	6,132,000	11,115,000
1973*	4,700,000	5,225,000

*The 1972 and 1973 figures are estimates.

Source: Regional Plan Association, *The Office Industry: Patterns of Growth and Location,* Prepared by Regina Belz Armstrong, edited by Boris Pushkarev. (Cambridge, Mass.: MIT Press, 1972), pp. 134–40.

Notes

Chapter One

1. For the plan to rationalize land use in Lower Manhattan see New York City Planning Commission, *Plan for the City of New York* 1:31; 4:9, 20–28.

2. The notion of the convertibility of class, status, and power is from Max Weber. *From Max Weber: Essays in Sociology,* ed. Hans Gerth and C. Wright Mills (New York: Oxford University Press, 1946), pp. 180–95.

3. The "factory showroom" has been a characteristic of Manhattan business enterprise since the nineteenth century. See, for example, Edgar M. Hoover and Raymond Vernon, *Anatomy of a Metropolis* (Garden City, N.Y.: Doubleday, Anchor Edition, 1962), p. 63.

4. *Plan,* 4:20–28.

5. Artists with appreciating housing investments but modest incomes would be a sub-category of what Herbert J. Gans calls the "trapped" segment of the inner-city population. Herbert J. Gans, "Urbanism and Suburbanism as Ways of Life," in *Readings in Urban Sociology,* ed. R. E. Pahl (Oxford: Pergamon Press, 1968), pp. 95–118.

6. Weber writes, "With some over-simplification, one might thus say that 'classes' are stratified according to their relations to the production and acquisition of goods; whereas 'status groups' are stratified according to the principles of their *consumption* of goods as represented by special styles of life." *From Max Weber,* p. 193. For a recent discussion of status communities see *Status Communities in Modern Society,* ed. Holger R. Stub (Hinsdale, Ill.: Dryden Press, 1972).

7. In this sense, artists can be considered intellectuals. "Only if intellectuals preserve critical intelligence, maintain some remoteness from day-to-day tasks, and cultivate concern with ultimate rather than with proximate values can they serve society fully," writes Lewis A. Coser, paraphrasing the position of David Riesman. Coser, *Men of Ideas* (New York: Free Press, 1965), p. 359.

8. For a discussion of the cultural contradictions of the middle class see J. R. Seeley, R. A. Sim and E. W. Loosely, *Crestwood Heights: A Study of the Culture of Suburban Life* (New York: John Wiley and Sons, 1956), pp. 378–403. For a discussion of the im-

plications of these contradictions for youth rebellion, see Joseph Bensman and Arthur J. Vidich, *The New American Society: The Revolution of the Middle Class*. (Chicago: Quadrangle Books, 1971), pp. 253–59.

9. For a discussion of alienation and occupational ideologies see Joseph Bensman and Robert Lilienfeld, *Craft and Consciousness: Occupational Technique and the Development of World Images* (New York: John Wiley and Sons, 1973).

10. *From Max Weber*, p. 342.

11. See Lewis Mumford, *The City in History: Its Origins, Its Transformations, and Its Prospects* (New York: Harcourt, Brace and World, 1961).

12. Joseph Bensman and Arthur Vidich, *Metropolitan Communities: New Forms of Urban Sub-Communities* (New York: Franklin Watts, 1975).

13. *From Max Weber*, pp. 186–87.

14. Joseph Bensman, "Status Communities in an Urban Society: The Musical Community," in *Status Communities in Modern Society*, ed. Holger R. Stub.

15. For discussions of earlier artists' communities in New York City, see Caroline F. Ware, *Greenwich Village, 1920–1930* (New York: Harper and Row, 1965); Albert Parry, *Garrets and Pretenders: A History of Bohemianism in America* (New York: Dover Publications, 1960); and Malcolm Cowley, *Exile's Return* (New York: Viking Press, 1934).

16. A. C. Spectorsky, *The Exurbanites* (Philadelphia: J. P. Lippincott, 1955); Seeley, et al., *Crestwood Heights*.

17. Bensman and Vidich, *New American Society*, pp. 236–59.

18. Mason Griff, "The Recruitment and Socialization of Artists," in *International Encyclopedia of the Social Sciences* 5 (1968): 447–54. .

Chapter Two

1. Mayor's Committee on Cultural Policy, *Report of the Mayor's Committee on Cultural Policy, October 15, 1974* (New York), p. 8. This report outlines the economic benefits of art and culture to the city's economy, and indicates that two-thirds of the galleries exclusively devoted to painting and sculpture and belonging to the nationwide Art Dealers Association of America are located in New York City.

2. *Gallery Guide*, the monthly listing of exhibits and the most ubiquitous advertising vehicle for the art market, showed these numbers in its May 1975 issue (vol. 5, no. 7). Published by Art Now, Inc., Kenilworth, New Jersey.

3. Richard Blodgett, "Making the Buyer Beg—And Other Tricks of the Art Trade," *New York Times*, October 26, 1975, sec. D, p. 1.

4. All quotations of SoHo residents are from my interview files. Subjects will be identified in the text by relevant personal and occupational characteristics where appropriate. They will remain otherwise anonymous. Subsequent quotations from interviews with SoHo residents will not be footnoted.

5. Bensman and Vidich, *New American Society*, ch. 7. According to the authors, the new middle class, a product of both the post–World War II economic boom and broadened access to college education in its skills and tastes, lacks a relevant past of its own upon which to model its life-style. I would argue that avant-garde art and its subculture provide one of the patterns through which a segment of this new middle class can individuate itself.

6. One SoHo poster outlet has a staff of twenty-two, more than that of any gallery for original art, and sales in the "low seven-figures." They have two branch operations. They started selling frames when they discovered that the posters cost far less than the frames. Rita Reif, "Art Posters Drawing in Profits," *New York Times*, May 24, 1976, p. 45.

7. "Market Research Report on Introductory Art History," March 15, 1972, prepared for McGraw-Hill College Textbook Division, cited in Patricia Hill, "Art History Textbooks: The Hidden Persuaders," *Art Forum* 16 (June 1976): 58–61.

8. The General Services Administration is the world's largest builder and landlord and since the administration of John Kennedy has sought to buy and commission art by American artists for the decoration of its buildings. The program languished until 1972, however, when a decision was made to utilize ½ of 1 percent of the construction costs to commission art for display in or around these buildings. By fiscal 1975 the GSA was spending over $2 million a year for art, much of it outdoor sculpture, a most recent example being Claes Oldenburg's *Batcolumn,* a 100-foot red baseball bat of metal grid construction for the Social Security Administration building in Chicago. See Jo Ann Lewis, "A Modern Medici for Public Art," *Art News* 76, no. 4 (April 1977): 37–40.

9. See Erving Goffman, *The Presentation of Self in Everyday Life* (Garden City, N.Y.: Doubleday, 1959) for a discussion of the uses of entrée to the backstage for performers cultivating an audience.

10. One buyer, hoping to acquire a work by Roy Lichtenstein, the well-known American pop artist, described a ceremony in which, after seven years of waiting and of buying lesser works from that artist's SoHo dealer, Leo Castelli, he was finally initiated as a major collector. The ceremony took place at Lichtenstein's studio in the Hamptons. Having brought the buyer into the presence of the artist he admired, Castelli asked him to choose from among several recently completed works. A selection of other than the "right" work for his particular collection, the client was led to believe, would mean failure in his test as a collector. The client carefully made his selection. After a pause, the artist and the dealer beamed their approval. Closing the $50,000 to $70,000 deal was then merely the psychological denouement of a moment of social solidarity. Blodgett, "Making the Buyer Beg."

11. Adam Zagorin, "Artists Operate Co-op Galleries," *Art Workers News,* March 1977, p. 6.

12. Ibid.

13. Leonard Sloane, "Collecting at the Chase: Fine Art Stands for Good Business," *Art News* 78, no. 5 (May 1979): 49.

14. Ibid.

15. Robert Metz, "The Corporation as Art Patron: A Growth Stock," *Art News,* 78, no. 5 (May 1979): 40–47.

16. Sohm was featured in December 1975 at the Institute for Art and Urban Resources, 108 Leonard Street, N.Y.C., in their series on contemporary art collectors.

17. Hill, "Art History Textbooks."

18. Grace Glueck, "Art People," *New York Times,* October 15, 1975, sec. C., p. 18.

19. When the Australian National Gallery in Canberra bought the American abstract expressionist artist Willem de Kooning's *Woman V* in 1974, and Jackson Pollock's *Blue Poles* for $2 million in 1972, there was criticism on both aesthetic and economic grounds. Critics felt such purchases were a mistake in priorities when people were starving around the world. *New York Times,* October 14, 1974, p. 16.

Closer to home, the General Services Administration expenditures for art dropped nearly 90 percent between fiscal 1976 and 1977 as a result of public pressure on Congress, and of Congress on the GSA, against George Sugerman's *People Sculpture* selected for Baltimore. See Lewis, "A Modern Medici."

20. Grace Glueck, "Art People," *New York Times,* May 14, 1974, p. 32.

21. Judith Cummings, "Record $3.28 Million paid for a Rembrandt," *New York Times,* Sept. 30, 1976.

22. Grace Glueck, "Art People," *New York Times,* May 14, 1974, p. 32.

23. D'Lynn Waldron, "A Billionaire Makes His Dream Come True," *New York Times,* November 3, 1974, p. 11.

24. Blodgett, "Making the Buyer Beg."

25. Ibid.

26. Carol Lawson, "The Bulls Return to the Art Market," *New York Times,* March 28, 1976, p. 33.

Chapter Three

1. Grace Glueck, "Only a Handful Will Make It," *New York Times,* March 3, 1974, Sec. C, p. 1.

2. Hilton Kramer, "Vollard: Dealer For the Demigods," *New York Times Magazine,* June 4, 1977, p. 82.

3. In the catalog to Impresario—Ambroise Vollard, Una E. Johnson writes of Vollard, "He was willing to follow the advice of the artists who were forging a new vision but who were generally ignored by many critics and dealers." *Ambroise Vollard, Editeur,* MOMA, June 1977, p. 19.

4. Louis K. Meisel, ed., *Photo-Realism 1973: The Stuart M. Speiser Collection* (New York: Eminent Publications, 1973).

5. Barbarale Diamonstein, in a discussion with Castelli and Lichtenstein, sheds light on the founding of the pop art movement and substantiates my thesis that in the contemporary competitive art market where there are substantial economic possibilities, it is the dealer who is pivotal in defining a "movement."

DIAMONSTEIN: How would you describe the Pop Art movement, Roy? And who made the movement? Did you ever expect the press to react to the artistic adventures of that group in the way that they did?

LICHTENSTEIN: No, I wouldn't have imagined anything like that. I was brought up in an era when very few serious American artists had any success with their art, and I was teaching and painting, and I expected to continue that way. So, I had no expectation that something like that would happen. In fact I though nobody would like the work. The only gallery that I thought would look at the work at all was Leo's or possibly Green Gallery. Most galleries, advanced galleries, seemed committed to Abstract Expressionism. I also didn't realize that other artists were doing a similar kind of work.

DIAMONSTEIN: Who helped it coalesce into a movement, and who made it?

LICHTENSTEIN: I think it began when Leo (there was also, of course Ivan Karp, Heana Sonnabend, and Dick Bellamy) saw within a three week period three artists doing somewhat similar things. Leo's description of me bringing my work to the gallery for the first time is about right. I left the paintings at the gallery and came back three weeks later and saw Warhol's work and heard about Rosenquist's. I think this was seen to be a movement by Leo, and there were other artists involved too: Oldenburg, Dine, Wesselman, and Segal to name some.

"Pop Art, Money, and the Present Scene: An Interview with Roy Lichtenstein and Leo Castelli," *Partisan Review* 45, no. 1 (1978): 84.

6. Richard Blodgett, "Making the Buyer Beg."

7. Grace Glueck, "How Do You Price Art Works? Let the Dealers Count the Ways," *New York Times,* January 30, 1976, p. 33.

8. Ibid.

9. Norma Skurka, "Museum At Home," *New York Times Magazine,* March 21, 1976, p. 73.

10. Harold Rosenberg, *The De-definition of Art* (New York: Macmillan Co., Collier Books, 1973), p. 12.

11. Ibid.

12. Richard A. Peterson, "The Production of Culture: A Prolegomenon," *American Behavioral Scientist,* 19, no. 6 (July/August 1976): 669–84.

Chapter Four

1. The data on the background of the SoHo artists interviewed for this study is not presented as a scientifically derived random sample of the whole SoHo population, still

less of the population of artists in general in America. It was gathered to facilitate the construction of a typology of artists and to analyze the SoHo community structure. However, because artists at all career stages, of various ages, of both sexes and of numerous styles were interviewed, including all the politically active artists, this group seems to be illustrative of the SoHo artist population. Moreover, because SoHo is the generative center of the New York market in contemporary art, and because the New York market is central to American art, this group of artists is also representative of artists in America.

In seeking to determine the class characteristics of the parents of the artists interviewed, I relied upon their reports of their parents' occupations. This seemed to me to be factual information, and was usually accompanied by other data on childhood which supported the data on parents' occupation. Of the forty-eight SoHo artists interviewed, data on the parents of four was not obtainable or not considered reliable. Of the forty-four remaining, class of origin was assigned on the basis of the highest occupation reported for either parent during the childhood of the artist. The breakdown is as follows:

(1) *Three* artists can be considered to have come from the upper class, in that their parents were high government officials or owned substantial businesses.

(2) *Eighteen* artists can be considered to have come from the professional sector of the middle class, consisting of the traditional professions, college professors, public school teachers, engineers, scientists, licensed accountants, and top business executives.

(3) *Seven* artists can be considered to have come from the small business sector of the middle class, which includes small manufacturers, store owners, wholesalers, importers, and farm owners.

(4) *Five* artists can be considered to have come from the middle-managerial sector of the middle class, including private and government managers, military officers, and sales representatives.

(5) *Three* artists can be considered to have come from the lower sector of the middle class, including lower-level office staff, salespersons in stores, and skilled technicians.

(6) *Eight* artists can be considered to have come from the working class. This group includes one fire fighter, two semi-skilled or unskilled laborers, one nonmanagerial restaurant employee, two industrial workers, and two skilled building trades workers.

Beyond the predominance of middle-class occupations in this group, thirty-three out of forty-four known occupations if we consider categories 2–5 to be middle class, two other observations seem significant. First, if we add categories 1–3 we have twenty-eight artists whose parents could claim independence on the basis of their professional status or the market yet who experienced an element of frustration because their clients, employers, or the market significantly invalidated their claims to autonomy. The more rationalized society becomes, the less those in such occupations are able to make good on their conception of themselves as autonomous. The artist occupations of at least some of their children suggests cultural continuity of the desire for autonomy, while the occupational situation is shifted to avoid the limiting conditions.

Second, if we consider categories 1 and 6, of the eleven artists whose childhood home life fell outside the middle class, four may have anticipated a middle-class status and culture. Shortly after these artists left home, two of the families in category 1 experienced a status decline to the middle class because of business bankruptcy in one case and illness and alcoholism in a second case. Both households reverted to middle-class jobs for support. Of those in category 6, two parents moved into the middle class, one as a store owner and one as a union official.

2. Mason Griff attributes the alienation of the artist to youthful encouragement followed by a sudden withdrawal of support when parents realize their children's avocational interests in art have become vocational interests. See "The Recruitment of the Artist," *The Arts in Society,* ed. Robert N. Wilson (Englewood Cliffs, N.J.: Prentice-Hall, 1964), p. 89.

3. Erving Goffman, *Stigma: Notes on the Management of Spoiled Identity* (Englewood Cliffs: Prentice-Hall, 1963).

4. U.S. Bureau of the Census, *Census of Population: 1970 Detailed Characteristics, New York, Final Report PC910–D34,* table 171.

5. Hall Winslow, *Artists in Metropolis* (New York: Pratt Institute, 1964).

6. Ibid., p. 22, 145. Winslow found that the median total income for eighty-eight fine artists registered with the New York Artists Tenants Association who responded to his questionnaire in 1963 was $5,200. Only 30 percent of this income was derived from art work.

7. Theodore Caplow classifies artists with a group of occupations that defy precise definition but are characterized by "the sharpest short run changes in income and prestige." Theodore Caplow, *The Sociology of Work* (New York: McGraw-Hill, 1954), p. 63.

8. The nineteenth-century French avant-garde was a rare instance of a movement of artists which sought to sweep away both existing culture and social institutions in the name of new chiliastic possibilities. Renato Poggioli, *The Theory of the Avant-Garde* (New York: Harper and Row, Icon Edition, 1971), p. 9.

9. Cowley, *Exile's Return.*

10. Ware, *Greenwich Village,* pp. 262–63.

11. The movement to elevate the status of craft to that of another fine art with its own distinctive materials has been led by the American Crafts Council and its journal, *American Craft.* In the spring of 1979, the name of the magazine, its format, and philosophy were changed to promote the new trend. Full-page glossy color photos of finished objects replaced the how-to-make-it emphasis of the earlier journal. In place of an essay on glazes, the new journal has picture articles entitled "Celebration of Clay" or "A New Language in Metal." Letters to the editor suggest the enthusiasm with which the change in the magazine has been received. To quote one letter, "*American Craft* is now the type of magazine which all segments of the craft world, including collectors, would be likely to subscribe to. It has the kind of aesthetic and professional appeal necessary to attract potential collectors. This is a valuable step. If a magazine speaks almost exclusively to those already involved in craft, as I believe *Craft Horizons* did, it is preaching to the saved...." *American Craft* (August/September, 1979), p. 79.

12. Painters in other cultures have long been familiar with ritual methods of material preparation and their alchemical use in composing the artist's mind and revealing the inner nature of reality. A text on the shelves of many SoHo artists interviewed that discusses painting as a religious ritual is Mai-mai Sze's *The Way of Chinese Painting* (New York: Random House, Vintage Books, 1959). See, in particular, pp. 64–84.

Chapter Five

1. Poggioli, *The Theory of the Avant-Garde,* p. 82.

2. Ibid., p. 179.

3. Damages and fines in the case totaled $9,252,000 against the executors, among them, Frank Lloyd and Mr. Lloyd's Marlborough Galleries. Damages included a fine of $3.3 million against Lloyd and his galleries. Lloyd and his appraiser from the Saidenberg Gallery are fellow members of the Art Dealer's Association of America, formed to uphold ethical standards in the art market. The judge in the case condemned the appraisal as being inadequate. Edith Evans Asbury, "Rothko Executors Ousted; Penalties Put at $9 million," *New York Times,* December 19, 1975, p. 1.

4. Roy Bongartz, "Writers, Composers and Actors Collect Royalties, Why Not Artists?", *New York Times,* February 2, 1975, Sec. C, p. 1.

5. Ibid., p. 25.

6. Brenda Price, "An Artists' Gallery Guide," *The Feminist Art Journal,* 5 (Spring 1976): 21–26. Thirty galleries were surveyed, and twenty had taken in no new "unreferred" artists in 1975.

7. For a discussion of bohemianism in Greenwich Village, see Parry, *Garrets and Pretenders*. For a discussion of the Black Mountain School see Martin Duberman, *Black Mountain* (Garden City, N.Y.: Doubleday, Anchor Press, 1973).

8. César Graña, *Modernity and its Discontents: French Society and the French Man of Letters in the 19th Century* (New York: Harper and Row, Harper Torchbooks, 1967), pp. 72, 78.

9. For a discussion and analysis of the everyday "life world" and the potential of fine art to explore the assumptions of that life world, see Alfred Schutz, *On Phenomenology and Social Relations,* ed. Helmut R. Wagner (Chicago: University of Chicago Press, 1970).

Chapter Six

1. Joseph Bensman, "Status Communities in an Urban Society: The Musical Community," in *Status Communities in Modern Society,* ed. Stub.

2. See Anselm Strauss, "The Art School and Its Students: A Study and an Interpretation," in *The Sociology of Art and Literature: A Reader,* ed. Milton C. Albrecht et al. (New York: Praeger Publishers, 1970), p. 168.

3. See Griff, "The Recruitment and Socialization of Artists."

4. Judith Adler, "Occupational Aesthetic and Occupational Subculture: The Shaping of Artistic Practice within a Work System" (unpublished paper); see also her *Artists in Offices* (New Brunswick, N.J.: Transaction Books, 1979).

5. See Bernard Rosenberg and Norris Fliegel, "Dealers and Museums," in Albrecht et al., ed., *The Sociology of Art and Literature: A Reader,* p. 478.

6. See Rosenberg and Fliegel, "Dealers," p. 475.

7. Such an event was sponsored by the Association of Artist-Run Galleries and the New Alliance for Artists in New York. See pamphlet entitled "Artists' Day, 1976: An Assembling of Artists' Works," ed. Jerry Herman (New York: Association of Artist-Run Galleries n.d.). This protest resulted in 500 jobs for artists. Edward Ranzal, "U.S. to Provide Work for Artists," *New York Tiems,* October 22, 1977, p. 24.

8. Alan Toffler, *The Culture Consumers* (New York: St. Martin's Press, 1964), pp. 24–41.

9. For a useful typology of types of informal networks and circles, including those in science as well as the arts, see Charles Kadushin, "Networks and Circles in the Production of Culture," *American Behavioral Scientist* 19, no. 6 (July/August 1976): 769–84. Kadushin's "movement circles" in the arts stress a conception of art innovation which is more in opposition to a definitive establishment and is less an incremental and rationalized feature of the avant-garde, as is the case in SoHo. For a further comparative discussion of networks in science and the arts see Diana Crane, *Invisible Colleges* (Chicago: University of Chicago Press, 1972).

Chapter Seven

1. See map, p. x.

2. This account is based on D. T. Valentine, *Manual of the Corporation of the City of New York* (New York: City of New York, 1860, 1865, 1868, 1869). See the 1865 edition, pp. 509–655, for a valuable history of lower Broadway from colonial days to 1865.

3. Bayrd Still, *Mirror for Gotham* (New York: New York University Press, 1956), p. 85. By 1835 the whole of Manhattan was laid out in building lots in a "rage of speculation" far in excess of population requirements. The bubble burst in 1837, leading to a serious business collapse.

4. "Even the permanent residents—if anything was permanent in this fast-expanding city—resided in hotels and boarding houses to an extent not customary elsewhere" (Ibid.,

pp. 90–91). Boarding houses served poor immigrants as well as whole families of "quality folk."

5. Valentine, *Manual* (1868), p. 216.

6. Landmarks Preservation Commission, *SoHo—Cast Iron Historic District Designation Report* (New York: City of New York, 1973), p. 6.

7. Ibid., p. 142.

8. Still, *Mirror for Gotham*, pp. 126–27.

9. Valentine, *Manual* (1868), p. 216.

10. Landmarks Preservation Commission, *SoHo—Cast Iron*, p. 6.

11. Jacob Knickerbocker, *Then and Now*, quoted in Hoover and Vernon, *Anatomy*, p. 75.

12. *Directory to the Seraglios in New York, Phila., Boston & All the Principle Cities in the Union, Edited and Compiled by a "Free Love Yer"* (New York: Printed and published for the trade, 1859). Available at the New York Historical Society.

13. Valentine, *Manual* (1862), p. 405; *Manual* (1868), p. 216.

14. Robert Murray Haig, *Regional Survey of New York and Its Environs*, vol. 1 (New York: Regional Plan of New York, 1928), p. 81.

15. Margot Gayle and Edmund V. Gillon, Jr., *Cast-Iron Architecture in New York* (New York: Dover Publications, 1974), p. v. Their study includes a comprehensive discussion of cast iron as a building material and its architectural styles.

16. Chester Rapkin, *South Houston Industrial Area* (New York: City of New York, 1963), pp. 133–47.

17. Gayle and Gillon, *Cast-Iron Architecture*, p. ix.

18. Ibid., pp. viii–ix.

19. Hoover and Vernon, *Anatomy*, p. 63.

20. Haig, *Regional Survey*, p. 72.

21. Hoover and Vernon, *Anatomy*, p. 65.

22. Haig, *Regional Survey*, diagram 25, p. 86.

23. Ibid., p. 99.

24. Rapkin, *South Houston*, p. 145.

25. Hoover and Vernon, *Anatomy*, pp. 23–27.

26. Haig, *Regional Survey*, p. 60.

27. Rapkin, *South Houston*, p. 12.

28. The New York City Planning Commission circulated a survey of the SoHo area informally. Results of the survey are summarized in *Plan*, 1:67–72.

29. Herschel B. Chipp, ed., *Theories of Modern Art* (Berkeley: University of California Press, 1968), pp. 501–20. According to Chipp, the prewar influx of European artists was second in importance to American art only to the 1913 Armory Show of international modern art.

30. Winslow, *Artists*, p. 13.

31. Ibid., p. 30.

32. Ibid., p. 21.

33. During the 1950s, for example, a block of studios at 43–55 West Tenth Street in Manhattan was razed. At one time these buildings contained living and working spaces for forty artists and two architects.

34. Winslow, *Artists*, p. 113.

35. Rapkin, *South Houston*, table 2, p. 225.

36. Ibid., p. 298.

37. Allan M. Siegal, "Millions Spent Yearly in Unlicensed Plumbing Jobs," *New York Times*, May 6, 1974, p. 32.

38. Rapkin, *South Houston*, p. 156. Of thirty fires in the South Houston District reported to the Fire Department from 1960 to 1961, none were caused by artists.

39. Richards, interview.

40. Susan Goodman, "1000 Artists at City Hall Picket for Their Lofts," *Village Voice*, April 9, 1964, p. 1.

41. Winslow, *Artists*, table 19, p. 135.

42. Richards, interview.

Chapter Eight

1. For a full discussion of redevelopment in Lower Manhattan, see Maynard T. Robinson, "Rebuilding Lower Manhattan, 1955–1974," (Ph.D. dissertation, City University of New York, 1977).

2. Hugh R. Pomeroy and S. J. Schulman, *Program Study for the New York State Chamber of Commerce Committee on Lower Manhattan Redevelopment* (New York: Downtown Lower-Manhattan Association, 1957); Downtown–Lower Manhattan Association, *Lower Manhattan, Recommended Land Use, Redeveloped Areas, Traffic Improvements, 1st Report* (New York, 1958).

3. The Lower Manhattan Plan was reaffirmed in 1969 by the New York City Planning Commission. See *Plan*, 1:31; 4:9, 20–28.

4. The commission argues: "One of the biggest obstacles to the orderly growth of the national center is the difficulty developers have in assembling a large tract. . . . We believe that the national center functions are so basic to the City's welfare that the City should be able to complete assemblage for private and nonprofit developers, even if the existing use conforms to the zoning and is not a nuisance. . . . In the arsenal of existing tools, there are some whose potential for shaping development the City has only recently begun to exploit. One that can be useful in parts of the expanding business district is the City's power of condemnation for unassisted urban revewal. Other tools include: remapping, height and setback variations, street closing" (Ibid., 1:34).

5. Ibid., p. 22.

6. *New York Times*, June 29, 1977, sec. B, p. 18.

7. U.S., Department of Labor, *Employment and Earnings for States and Areas, 1939–1974*, bulletin 1370-12 (1975), p. 513.

8. Rapkin, *South Houston*, p. 225.

9. *Plan*, 1:72.

10. From 1969 to 1976, manufacturing jobs in Manhattan fell from 447,500 to 290,800. Data obtained from the New York State Department of Labor, Division of Research and Statistics.

11. I. D. Robbins, *The Wastelands of New York City, a Preliminary Inquiry into the Nature of Commercial Slum Areas, Their Potential for Housing and Business Development* (New York: The City Club of New York, 1962).

12. Ibid., p. 11.

13. Ibid., p. 5.

14. I. D. Robbins, "Planners?" May 21, 1964 (A privately distributed sixteen-page analysis of the Rapkin Report on the South Houston Industrial Area, available at the Municipal Reference Library, New York City).

15. Rapkin, *South Houston*, pp. 285–87.

16. Herbert J. Gans, *The Urban Villagers* (New York: Free Press, 1962).

17. Robert Goodman, *After the Planners* (New York: Simon and Schuster, 1971), pp. 64–5.

18. Gans, *Villagers*, p. 318.

19. Robbins, *Wastelands*, p. 5.

20. Ibid.

21. Rapkin, *South Houston*, p. 12.

22. "Contrary to the prevailing impression, the South Houston Industrial Area is de-

voted principally to production activities and not to storage. In the most part, firms are flourishing establishments that provide employment for almost 13,600 persons, pay prevailing wages, and reveal a high degree of stability and solvency'' (Ibid., pp. 282–83).

23. Ibid., p. 39.

24. Ibid., pp. 188, 283, 285–97.

25. Ibid., pp. 282–83, 290–94.

26. Ibid., pp. 293–94. "In the majority of instances, the new rents would be in excess of the operational savings that the present firms can realize by virtue of an upgrading of their quarters. Many firms . . . would be compelled to leave their present accommodations. . . . If it should occur . . . it would reduce one of the great advantages of rehabilitation, which is to minimize relocation of establishments."

27. Ibid., p. 229.

28. Ibid., p. 298.

29. Jane Jacobs, *The Death and Life of Great American Cities* (New York: Random House Vintage Books, 1961), pp. 187–99.

30. Ibid., pp. 196–97.

31. Rapkin, *South Houston*, table 16, p. 53.

32. Ibid., p. 53.

33. Ibid., p. 18.

34. Robbins, "Planners?" p. 7.

35. *Plan*, 1:46.

36. In keeping with the intention of this study to preserve the anonymity of interview subjects, the names and some biographical details have been altered. See appendix I.

37. *New York Times*, November 13, 1959, p. 1.

38. *New York Times*, February 4, 1960, p. 1.

39. *New York Times*, February 1, 1960, p. 7.

40. *New York Times*, February 27, 1961, p. 1.

41. *New York Times*, April 18, 1963, p. 1.

42. Downtown–Lower Manhattan Association, *Lower Manhattan Expressway* (New York, 1964), pp. 8–9.

43. The organizations supporting the coalition supporting the expressway are listed in *Lower Manhattan Expressway*, p. 25.

44. *Lower Manhattan Expressway*, pp. 5, 17–18.

45. Robert Moses did this at several points where the momentum behind the construction of the expressway faltered, starting when local opposition first developed. *New York Times*, August 24, 1960, p. 1.

46. Donald Elliott, interview, October 20, 1974. Elliott was chairman of the City Planning Commission from November 1966 to February 1973.

47. *New York Times*, February 14, 1965, p. 1.

48. Rachele Wall, interview, August 17, 1977. Sections of this letter were reprinted in *New York Times*, March 25, 1965, p. 1. Louis DeSalvio was identified as "the assemblyman," although he denied the charges.

49. *New York Times*, May 27, 1966, p. 1.

50. *New York Times*, April 18, 1968, p. 1.

51. The Committee of Sponsors listed on the letterhead of the Artists Against the Expressway included William Agee, John Bennett, Leo Castelli, Richard Feigan, Arnold Glimcher, Don Judd, Roy Lichtenstein, Lucy Lippard, Robert Murry, Louise Nevelson, Barnett Newman, Ken Noland, Bob Rauschenberg, and Frank Stella.

52. Letter from Robert Motherwell to Richard Feigan in the files of the Artists Against the Expressway.

53. Letter in the files of Artists Against the Expressway.

54. *New York Times*, June 30, 1969, p. 1.

55. Wall, interview, August 17, 1977.
56. Ibid.
57. Ibid.
58. *New York Times,* June 30, 1969, p. 1.
59. Wall, interview, August 17, 1977.
60. *New York Times,* July 17, 1969, p. 1.
61. *New York Times,* August 21, 1969, p. 1.

Chapter Nine

1. Rachele Wall, interview, August 17, 1977.
2. Ibid.
3. Ibid.
4. New York State Multiple Dwelling Law, Article 7-B (1964), chap. 939, sec. 276.
5. George Maciunas, "Information Bulletin, Fluxhouse Cooperatives," New York, 1966. (Photocopied.)
6. *New York Times,* October 9, 1966, p. 68.
7. George Maciunas, "Fluxhouse Newsletter Number 3, September 12, 1966," New York. (Photocopied.)
8. Letter, Howard M. Squadron to J. M. Kaplan, July 12, 1968. Files of George Maciunas.
9. *New York Times,* August 8, 1967, p. 41; George Maciunas, "Fluxhouse Newsletter Number 14, August 12, 1967," New York. (Photocopied.)
10. *New York Times,* December 19, 1963, p. 1.
11. Shael Shapiro, interview, February 14, 1975.
12. George Maciunas, "Fluxhouse Newsletter, June 22, 1968."
13. George Maciunas, "Last Newsletter from George Maciunas, to Fluxhouse II & III, December 21, 1967, Not Applicable to Fluxhouse I," New York. (Photocopied.)
14. *SoHo Artists Association Newsletter,* October 20, 1970.
15. SoHo Artists Association, "Statement of the South Houston Artists Association," New York, May 1970. (Photocopied.)
16. *SoHo Artists Association Newsletter,* September 21, 1970.
17. *SoHo Artists Association News Bulletin,* November 1970.
18. John Rex and Robert Moore, *Race, Community, and Conflict: A Study of Sparkbrook* (London: Oxford University Press, 1967). In the analysis of Rex and Moore, the struggle over access to housing is the central process of the city as a social unit. "Being a member of one or another of these [five housing] classes is of first importance in determining a man's associations, his interests, his life style, and his position in the urban social structure" (p. 36). I would argue that the SoHo community *as a whole* acted as a housing class at times in its struggle to allow artists *alone* to reside in this manufacturing area, but that internal community divisions were significantly less deep and cannot meaningfully be termed housing class divisions. See also R. E. Pahl, *Patterns of Urban Life* (Oxford: Pergamon Press, 1968).
19. Quotations from staff members of the City Planning Commission are from my interviews. They will remain anonymous. Subsequent quotations from interviews with staff members will not be footnoted.
20. Urban Underground, *The Urban Underground Resurfaces: Statements of the Urban Underground, a Part of the Movement for a Democratic Society, at a Public Hearing of the New York City Planning Commission, February 19, 1969* (New York, 1969), p. 13.
21. At the base of the socialization of the children of the middle class lies an ideological tension. On the one hand, the wellbeing and growth of the unique individual to full poten-

tial is held to be the goal in living. But on the other hand, instrumentally effective conformity to given institutional goals, especially materialism, is held to be a sign of maturity. See Seeley et al., *Crestwood Heights,* pp. 378–406.

22. Donald H. Elliott, interview, October 20, 1974.

23. In her statement before the New York City Planning Commission on the SoHo proposals, Freedman urged that areas above and below SoHo, known as NoHo and Tribeca, be considered for artists housing and that four blocks set aside by planners along Canal Street be returned to the 43-block SoHo zoning area as originally proposed. Statement of Doris C. Freedman, chairman, Citizens for Artists Housing, before the New York City Planning Commission on CP-21256 and CP-21260, "Artists Housing in SoHo," January 6, 1971.

24. SoHo Artists Association, "A White Paper on the Need to Legitimize Artists' Studio-Residences in the South Houston Area," New York, 1970, p. 2. (Photocopied.)

25. Ibid., p. 3.

26. SoHo Artists Association, "Statement, May 1970," p. 1.

27. SoHo Artists Association, "White Paper," p. 2.

28. *Plan,* 1:74.

29. SoHo Artists Association, "Statement, May 1970," pp. 3–4.

30. Ibid., p. 2.

31. The artist survey figures for 1968 through 1970 were summarized as an unpublished document, "SoHo Survey, 1970," available at the City Planning Commission.

32. Ibid.

33. Ibid.

34. See *SoHo Artists Association Newsletter,* October 1970, for a report and summary of the arguments.

35. Ibid., p. 3.

36. Grace Glueck, "Neighborhoods: SoHo is Artists' Last Resort," *New York Times,* May 11, 1970, p. 37.

37. *Life,* March 27, 1970, pp. 61–65.

38. See for example, Grace Glueck, "Neighborhoods," and Ron Rosenbaum, "SoHo in New York: A Fight for Survival," *Village Voice,* November 6, 1970, p. 1.

39. Elliott, interview.

40. *SoHo Artists Association Newsletter,* February 10, 1976, p. 2.

Chapter Ten

1. SoHo has never supported the type of family-oriented community press described by Janowitz as supplying "content relevant for families grappling with the problems of child-rearing." See Morris Janowitz, *The Community Press in an Urban Setting* (Chicago: University of Chicago Press, 1967), p. 113.

2. The first generation of SoHo children appeared with the Fluxhouse Cooperatives. In 1969 the sixty-one units of the first six cooperatives contained 115 persons, 27 of whom were children. Fourteen were infants or below school age; the oldest child was in junior high school. While fourteen families had children, nine with one child each, thirty units were occupied by a single person. (Fluxhouse documents.)

3. A jazz saxophonist, a resident since 1968 in one cooperative otherwise occupied by visual artists, created an acoustical and, consequently, a social problem which served to warn subsequent co-ops against mixing musicians with visual artists.

4. See, for example, Talcott Parsons and Robert Bales, *The Family: Socialization and Interaction Process* (Glencoe, Ill.: Free Press, 1955), esp. chap. 1; and Richard Sennett, *Families against the City: Middle Class Homes of Industrial Chicago, 1972–1890* (New York Random House, 1970).

5. Grandparents also use their relationships with their grandchildren to underscore their disapproval of their children's artist identities. One mother, who reported that she and her artist husband lived in dungarees for months at a time in their loft, found that her mother began sending the granddaughter frilly dresses.

6. The Crestwood Heights study of middle-class suburbia found that in the dual value system held by the community, men tended to see persons in instrumental terms, while it was "the women's unequivocal view that mere things are for the sake of their effect on the production and refinement of personality" (Seeley et al., *Crestwood Heights,* p. 391). In SoHo, this cultural dichotomy takes the form of women becoming instrumental to a symbolic and expressive activity which, by the dominant assumption, is male.

7. Since the 1920s, when Americans traveled to Europe to seek the social freedom necessary for an artistic career, fine arts has continued to be in important respects a remittance occupation. See Cowley, *Exile's Return.*

8. Graña, *Modernity and Its Discontents,* pp. 81–84.

9. See C. Wright Mills, *White Collar: The American Middle Classes* (New York: Oxford University Press, 1951), pp. 112–60.

10. Artists who shift from fine to commercial art may be said to exhibit ambivalence toward their occupational stigma, in Goffman's terminology. See Goffman, *Stigma,* pp. 106–8.

11. Ware found in the "experimental family" pattern among Greenwich Village residents of the 1920s that, while women assumed previously male roles as providers, men seldom took responsibility for household chores. "The practical effect in the homes observed, however, and in those reported upon by teachers in progressive and nursery schools, was that the women went out to earn more often than the men took the responsibility for tending the baby and washing the dishes. The burden and responsibilities of the woman are often increased to the point where the entire home rested on her shoulders." See Ware, *Greenwich Village,* p. 410.

12. See Graña, *Modernity and Its Discontents,* for the reflective nature of the bohemian stance in relation to the bourgeoisie.

13. The "bohemian" response to failure allows the artist to participate in the culture of Romanticism more popular with previous generations. Cowley held this culture to contain among its tenets "world-weariness and 'the horror of daily life,' " by which he meant that "between the creative person and the surrounding society there is always an unresolved tension. . . . Daily life, therefore, is a constant denial and an intolerable burden." (*Exile's Return,* p. 61.)

14. SoHo artists still tell apocryphal stories about earlier generations of more bohemian artists in which their antics are revealed as pitiable and a caricature of the bourgeoisie. One such tale concerns Jackson Pollock, who is said to have arrived at a party given in his honor by wealthy Southampton collectors very late and very drunk. He staggered through the crowd over to the fireplace and urinated. After a moment's pause, the guests applauded. The artist who told this story added that such behavior was disgusting, particularly on the part of the patrons.

15. This school is housed in a church in the nearby Italian neighborhood, where it was established by SoHo parents. It has no religious identity, and Italian parents do not participate because they do not approve of family outsiders taking care of their three- and four-year-old children.

16. According to the National Endowment for the Arts, *Minorities and Women in the Arts, 1970* (Washington, D.C., 1978), female painters and sculptors over age 30 who worked forty weeks or more in 1969 and were in the same occupation in 1965 and 1970 had median incomes of $5,670, compared with $11,130 for males in the same category (p. 23). Among those similarly established in the arts, taken together, 9 percent of males earned in excess of $25,000 in 1970, while only 1½ percent of women reached this level (p. 14).

17. Griff's study of art students indicates that parents never thought of the talents of

their art-inclined children "in terms of a future vocation, but only as a hobby. This idea changes radically when the child suddenly declares that he wishes to make painting his life's profession and ends in precipitating a family crisis. . . . The entire family turns on the would-be artist in an effort to alter his plans." See Mason Griff, "The Recruitment of the Artist," in Wilson, *The Arts in Society*, p. 81.

Chapter Eleven

1. Figures compiled by the Downtown Independent Democrats and published in the *SoHo Newsletter*, January 13, 1973, p. 2.

2. The movie was *Mean Streets*, directed by Martin Scorsese and released in 1972.

3. For a discussion of the pro bono program see Marna S. Tucker, "Pro Bono ABA," *Verdicts on Lawyers*, ed. Ralph Nader and Mark Green (New York: Crowell Co., 1976), pp. 20–32.

4. Volunteer Lawyers for the Arts was a New York program set up in 1968 to provide free legal counsel to artists and art organizations.

5. Requirements for a variance from the zoning restrictions are set forth in section 72-21 of the Zoning Resolution of the City of New York. They include five requirements which must all be met for a justified variance, including the restriction that the variance in use not alter the essential character of the surrounding area or be detrimental to the public welfare.

6. Joseph P. Fried, "Preservation of City Landmarks Buildings," *New York Times*, October 12, 1974, p. 34.

7. These include the Historical Districts Council, the Municipal Arts Society, the American Institute of Architecture, the Victorian Society in America, and the Landmarks Preservation Commission itself.

8. Fried, "Preservation of Landmarks." In 1978, the U.S. Supreme Court upheld the constitutionality of New York's landmarks preservation laws in a case which sustained the City's right to limit office construction proposed for Grand Central Station, a designated "landmark."

9. SoHo Artists Association, *SoHo Newsletter*, no. 33, June 1, 1973, p. 2.

10. Fred Ferretti, "SoHo Grows Up and Grows Rich and Chic," *New York Times*, October 12, 1975, sec. 2, p. 32.

11. Anna Mayo, "The Artistoids of SoHo," *Village Voice*, May 16, 1974, p. 14.

12. Richard Goldstein, "SoHo Loft for Sale: Artists Need Not Apply," *Village Voice*, March 21, 1977, p. 22.

13. See, for example, Dee Wedemeyer, "Life Another Way; They Do without for the Sake of Art," *New York Times*, November 12, 1976, sec. B, p. 5.

14. "Special SoHo Section," *New York Magazine*, May 20, 1974, pp. 52–78.

15. Nancy Newhouse, "In the Lav of Luxury: Great New York Bathrooms," *New York Magazine*, September 30, 1974, p. 43.

16. *SoHo Newsletter*, no. 36, June 7, 1974, p. 1. This quotation was preceded by a two page attack on the *New York Magazine* article.

17. New York City Planning Commission "Appellant's Brief," Board of Estimate of the City of New York, Calendar no. 337, April 20, 1977, p. 6.

18. Bensman and Vidich, *Metropolitan Communities*, pp. 227–28.

19. "Artists Certification? Why Bother?" a handbill distributed by the Artists Certification Committee, Department of Cultural Affairs, City of New York, 1972.

20. "Artists Certification," an application form distributed by the Department of Cultural Affairs, City of New York, 1972.

21. Interview with Claire Tankel, Representative of the Department of Cultural Affairs, the City of New York, on the Artists Certification Committee, March 2, 1977.

22. Ibid.

23. Tankel interview.

24. "Lefkowitz Ruling 'Legalizes' Co-op Apartment Ownership in SoHo Area," news release, Office of Attorney General Louis J. Lefkowitz, Two World Trade Center, New York City, May 28, 1975.

25. There are 680 industrial buildings in SoHo and NoHo, taken together. Of these, 336 buildings have been converted into residential uses. In SoHo, 92.7 percent of the conversions are illegal in some respects, and in NoHo, 96.6 of the conversions are illegal. See Department of City Planning, *Residential Re-Use of Non-Residential Buildings in Manhattan* (New York: City of New York, 1977), tables 3 and 4.

26. In 1975 the J-51 program of tax benefits for the renovation of property was expanded to include incentives for the conversion of nonresidential buildings to residential use, effective September 1977. This program is governed by section J-51-2.5 of New York City's Administrative Code, originally passed in 1955. It exempts from real property taxes for a period of twelve years any increase in the assessed valuation of a building attributable to alteration or conversion. Also, up to 90 percent of the costs of the renovation may be abated over a period of between nine and twenty years. Buildings are checked to see that all residents are artists only during a two-year period prior to and including the day on which tax abatement in granted. To date only six buildings in SoHo have availed themselves of J-51 benefits, but the programs' application to loft buildings is new. (Ibid., pp. 39–40.)

27. In November of 1973 the editor of SAA's *SoHo Newsletter* conducted a survey of 23 rental buildings and 13 co-ops, each of which had been established before 1970 and some as early as 1968. Of 105 units in rental buildings, 62 remained occupied by the artists who had originally converted them at least three years before. Of 125 co-op units, 104 were occupied by their original owners. (SoHo Artists Association, *SoHo Newsletter,* no. 36, June 7, 1974, p. 3.)

My own survey in 1978 of seventy-four co-op units in nine artists' cooperatives, eight of which were established before 1970 and one in 1973, revealed only nineteen turnovers, two to nonartists. Eight units had been added to these co-ops through the subdivision of floors. Most were rented out, but some were occupied by divorced husbands or wives who simply could not afford to establish separate studios. Artists seem exceedingly reluctant to leave SoHo, and therefore the co-op population is particularly stable.

28. The quotations from this real-estate operator are taken from my files. The identity of this real-estate operator will remain anonymous, and quotations from subsequent real-estate operators will not be footnoted.

29. Beginning June 1977, after several years of requests from the SoHo Artists Association, the Artist Certification Committee, Community Board Two, and the Department of Cultural Affairs, the Department of Buildings issued a directive requiring inspectors to check the artist certification of occupants in SoHo and NoHo. "When such certification is not readily available at the premises for all occupied dwelling units, a violation shall be issued for the unlawful occupancy or use of the appropriate parts of the building." Directive 3 of 1977, Irving E. Minkin, P.E., Director of Operations, Housing and Development Administration, Department of Buildings, the City of New York, June 13, 1977.

30. City Planning Commission, "Appellant's Brief."

31. See in particular Louis Wirth's essay "Urbanism as a Way of Life," in *Louis Wirth: On Cities and Social Life,* ed. Albert J. Reiss, Jr. (Chicago: University of Chicago Press, 1964), pp. 60–83.

32. See "The Web of Group-Affiliation," in *Conflict and the Web of Group-Affiliation, Georg Simmel* (New York: Free Press, 1955), pp. 125–95, esp. p. 130.

Index

Abstract expressionism, 3, 15, 38, 49, 65, 88, 93, 107
Abstract illusionism, 40
Abzug, Bella, 185
A.I.R. (Artists In Residency) program, 124–25, 126, 177
American Crafts Council, 256n
Andre, Carl, 83
Apparel industry, 116, 117, 137, 247
Architects, real-estate speculation by, 235, 237
Architects and Engineers Against the Expressway, 145, 149
Art: and critics' function, 50, 90–91; movements in, dealer support for, 24, 31–41, 94; and religion, 9, 69–70. *See also* Abstract expressionism; Avant-garde art; Photo realism
Art, audience for: and artist's role, 6; and status community, 11, 101–2, 187; and successful artists, 93–95. *See also* Art buyers; Art collectors
Art, career in: early motivation, 53–54; and market pressures, 23–24, 58–59, 78, 80, 100, 192–93; messianic character of, 8–9, 67–68, 70; and middle-class values, 5–8, 12–13, 54–57, 71, 101–2, 174, 192, 193, 196; and parental pressure, 54–57, 64; and sideline careers, 7, 58–59, 87, 98, 196; and status awareness, 47–48, 84–85, 86, 87. *See also* Dealers; Galleries, Status community; Successful artists; Unsuccessful artists
Art, innovation in: as central artistic value, 76–77, 79, 84, 93, 107; and dealers, 24, 31–41, 94; and market pressures, 78–79
Art buyers: and cooperative galleries, 22; new class of, 16–17, 25–30, 31; popularity of photo realism with, 90; prints and drawings, 18–19; studio visits by, 19–21. *See also* Art collectors; Art market

Art collectors, 11, 41, 45, 78, 145; dealers as, 38–39, 42–43; and
    status, 25–26; wealthy, 28–29. *See also* Art buyers; Art market
Art Dealer's Association of America, 256n
Art Forum, 90, 91
Article 7-B, 126, 155, 185–86
Art in America, 39
Artist Rights Association, 83
Artists Against the Expressway (AAE), 144–45, 146, 148, 149,
    150, 162, 175
Artists' Day, 24–25
Artist Tenants Association, 119, 124–26, 168, 177; Committee for
    Artists Housing, 124
Art magazines, 39
Art market: barter trade, 49; and corporations, 7, 8, 25–26; ex-
    pansion, 15–16, 191–92; New York, 15–16, 107; prices, 20,
    27–29; and scarcity, 84; speculation, 19, 29, 38–39, 43, 48,
    80–81, 85; traditional, compared to avant-garde, 16, 26, 27, 28.
    See also Art buyers; Art collectors; Dealers; Galleries
Art of This Century Gallery, 118
Art schools, 98, 99, 192. *See also* Schools; Teaching as sideline
    career
Art studios, 19–21, 119. *See also* Loft buildings
Association of Artist-Run Galleries, 257n
Auction 393, 16
Australian National Gallery, 253n
Avant-garde art, 4, 68–69, 76, 91; and artist myth, 5–6; and crit-
    ics, 27; and new buyers, 25–27, 30. *See also* Art, innovation in

Ballard, William F., 125
Barker, Paul, 171, 172
Bayard, Nicholas, 111
Becker, Leon, 175
Bennett, John, 144
Bensman, Joseph, 10, 12, 97, 252n
Black Mountain School, 92
Bogardus, James, 114
Bohemianism, 8, 12, 57, 67, 192, 196–97; rejection of, in new art,
    92–93. *See also* Art, career in
Borewitz, Ruben, 83
Boston, West End redevelopment, 133
Building inspectors and codes, 2, 122, 126, 135, 161–62, 163, 167,
    230, 236. *See also* New York City Buildings Department
Buffet, Bernard, 19

Caplow, Theodore, 256n
Castelli, Leo, 16, 29, 38–39, 41, 148, 177, 220, 253n, 254n
Celebrity artists, 50, 51, 83–84
Central Trades and Labor Council, 140
Certification of artists, 66, 155, 186, 202, 229–30, 242
Chase Manhattan Bank, 26, 60, 129, 130, 140
Chelsea Girls, The (Warhol), 50
Child care, 199–202, 204, 205, 207–11, 217; cooperative groups,
    199–200, 207–11, 217. *See also* Schools

Children: and divorce, 210–11; obstacles to having, 190–92
Children's Energy Center, 209
Chipp, Herschel B., 258n
Christo, 83
Circle Gallery, 19
Citizens for Artists Housing (CAH), 154, 155, 177
City Club of New York, 131–32, 137
Citywide Coalition Against the Lower Manhattan Expressway, 141–43, 146, 147, 148, 150, 163
Classical art, 76. *Sea also* Art market
Collectibles market, 42–43
Commercial art and artists, 59, 63, 196, 231
Community Board Two, 164, 170, 174, 221, 223, 236–37, 265n
Conceptual art, 93, 95, 107
Contracts for artists, 83–84
Cooper, Paula, 16, 177
Cooperative child-care groups, 199–200, 207–10, 217
Cooperative galleries, 22–25, 61, 78, 144
Cooperatives, housing, 2, 180, 187–88, 227, 232, 241; children in, 190, 191; costs, 233, 234; Fluxhouse program, 155–61, 162, 166, 262n; Greenwich Village, 153–55; and renters, 166–70. *See also* Building inspectors and codes; Loft buildings
Cooper Union, 99
Copyright Act, 83
Corporate sponsorship of arts, 7, 8, 25–26
Coser, Lewis A., 251n
Cowley, Malcolm, 263n
Craft Horizons, 256n
Craftspeople, 68–69
Crestwood Heights study, 263n
Critics, 22, 77–78, 98, 145; as aesthetic intermediaries, 50, 90–91, 100–101; as tastemakers, compared to dealers, 27, 31, 33–40 passim. 45, 50, 51

Davidson, Joan, 177
Dealers: as collectors, 38–39, 42–43; committed to artwork, not artist, 44–45; cultivation of buyers by, 41–44; market pressure on artists, 23–24, 78–79, 100; services to artists, 46–48, 73–74, 75; situational trust relationship, 79–84; support and promotion of new art and artists, 6, 31–41, 48, 50–51, 61, 85, 100. *See also* Art market; Galleries
Democratic party, 147, 150, 175, 220, 221
DeSalvio, Louis, 139, 141, 142, 221
DeSapio, Carmine, 147
Diamonstein, Barbarale, 254n
DiBiumo, Dr. Giuseppe Panza, 29
Divorce, 210, 211
Douglas, Paul, 141
Downtown Independent Democrats (DID), 220
Downtown-Lower Manhattan Association (DLMA), 129–30, 132, 140
Drawings, market for, 18–19
Drexler, Arthur, 149

Elliott, Donald, 140, 168, 169–70, 172, 176–77, 182, 184
Emmerick, Andre, 91
Emmerick Gallery, 220
Environmental Protection Administration (EPA), 146–47, 223
Ethical sponsors, 235–36

Federal Housing Administration, 157
Feigen, Richard L., 15–16, 143, 144
Felt, Mrs. Irving Mitchell, 177
Fitch, James Marston, 148–49
Fixture fees, 234
Fleishman, Larry, 41
Fluxhouse cooperatives, 155–61, 162, 166, 262n
Fluxhouse Newsletter, 159
Ford Foundation, 213
Free conversions, 235
Freedman, Doris C., 177–78, 185
Friends of Cast-Iron Architecture, 164, 224, 225

Galleries, 11, 21, 31–51, 58, 68, 125; artist-run cooperative, 22–25,
     61, 78, 144; exhibitions, 35–36; growth of, 3, 15–16, 118, 192;
     presentation in, 16–18; prints and drawings, 18–19. *See also* Art
     market; Dealers
Gallery Guide, 252n
Gans, Herbert J., 251n
Geldzahler, Henry, 149, 156
General Services Administration, 19, 253n
Getty, J. Paul, 28
Gift-donation system, 44
Glueck, Grace, 22–23, 150, 183–84
Goffman, Erving, 20, 57
Gollobin, Jean, 209–10
Goodman, Roy, 186
Government and Arts, 7, 8, 24
Grace Church School, 212
Grana, Cesar, 92–93
Greenberg, Clement, 91
Greenwich Village, 92, 106, 119, 124, 174, 175, 194, 222, 223,
     226–27; and antiexpressway coalition, 139, 142, 147, 148, 151;
     family in, 263n; housing cooperatives, 153, 154–55, 157;
     schools, 207, 212, 213
Greitzer, Carol, 155
Griff, Mason, 12, 255n. 263n
Grooms, Red, 27
Guggenheim, Peggy, 118

Haake, Hans, 83
Halliwell, Noah, 173–74
Hammer, Armand, 28
Haughwout, E. V., 113
Hechshir, Mrs. August, 177
Heller report, 147
Hofmann, Hans, 118

Homosexuality, 198–99
Housing classes, 170, 188. *See also* Status communities

Incubator areas, 136–37, 176
Industry, 120, 121; and SoHo artists, 179–80. *See also* Manufacturing
Iran, art show in, 79
Italian ethnics, 139, 151, 209, 220, 221–22, 223

Jack, Hulan, 139
Jacobs, Jane, 136, 139, 142, 148, 154
Javitts, Marion, 148, 177
J. M. Kaplan Fund, 154, 156, 157
Johns, Jasper, 38, 39
Johnson, Dorothy, 138, 142, 143, 148
Johnson, Sam, 138, 143, 144
Johnson, Una E., 254n
Journalists, 51, 182–83, 226–28. *See also* Media
Judd, Don, 148
Jurrist, Charles, 222–23

Kadushin, Charles, 257n
Kaplan, Jack, 154, 156
Kaplan, Sam, 142
Karnheim, Carol, 146, 147
Karp, Ivan, 35, 42–43, 90
Kennedy Galleries, 41
Knickerbocker, Jacob, 113–14
Koch, Edward, 84, 147
Kooning, Willem de, 253n
Kramer, Hilton, 33–34, 101

LaTour, Georges de, 28
Lavender Mist (Pollock), 28
Lawyers, 223; real estate speculation by, 235, 237
Lehman, Maxwell, 125
Leslie, Charles, 207
Lewis, Mike, 170–71, 175, 176, 178, 180
LeWitt, Sol, 83
Liberal party, 150, 175–76
Lichtenstein, Roy, 38, 177, 253n, 254n
Life magazine, 102, 183
Lindsay, John, 142, 145–46, 147, 150, 158, 172, 175–76, 177, 184
Lippard, Lucy, 227
List, Mrs. Albert A., 177
Little Italy, 139, 148, 222
Lloyd, Frank, 81
Loft buildings, 9–10, 17, 21, 132, 180; architecture, 114–15, 148, 149; and art lifestylers, 227–28; availability to artists, 242; converted by artists, 118–21; demolition of, in Lower Manhattan, 130–31; illegally occupied by artists, 2, 66, 121–23, 144, 161, 190, 232, 235–36; landlords, 2, 121, 126, 235, 236, 237; and Rapkin report, 134–35; rents, 15, 132, 135–36, 168, 233–34,

242. *See also* Building inspectors and codes; Cooperatives, housing
Loosley, E. W., 12
Los Angeles County Museum, 28
Lower Manhattan Expressway proposal, 132–33, 138–51, 157–58, 161, 175, 177
Lower Manhattan Plan, 129–33, 137. *See also* New York City Planning Commission
Ludwig, Peter, 29

M-1 zones, 125, 156
M15-A and M15-B areas, 181
McGovern, George, 219
Maciunas, George, 155–61, 162
Mahl, Olga, 185
Manufacturing, 4, 114, 248; and incubator theory, 136–37; loss of, 115–18, 130–31, 134–35, 137, 180. *See also* Industry
Marlborough Gallery, 81
Marriage roles: and artist myth, 192–93, 216–17; and successful artists, 66, 195–97, 200, 201–2, 203, 217; and unsuccessful artists, 64, 195–97, 200, 201–2, 203, 217; and women artists, 204–6. *See also* Wives
Mass culture, and art, 8–9, 91–92, 93, 94
Mayor's Committee on Cultural Policy, 252n
Media, 34, 83, 185. *See also* Journalists
Meisel, Louis K., 36–37, 90
Metropolitan Museum of Art, 28
MICOVE, 131–33, 137
Middle class, 4–5, 13, 67, 152, 228, 229, 254n. *See also* Art, career in
Minimal art, 93
Minorities in SoHo, 133, 134, 137
Moore, Robert, 170
Moorman, Charlotte, 27
Moses, Robert, 132, 139, 141
Motherwell, Robert, 144
Movement circles, 257n
Multiple-dwelling laws, 125, 126, 155, 185–86
Museum of Modern Art, 33, 39, 118, 125, 149
Museum of Non-Objective Painting, 118
Museums, 6, 11, 37, 41, 44, 118, 125, 145; and status community, 98–100; as tastemakers, 31, 33, 34, 38, 39, 40, 45

National Endowment for the Arts, 263n
National Foundation for the Arts, 156, 157
National Gallery of Art, 19, 28
"Neighborhood busters," 236–37
New Alliance for Artists, 257n
New Democratic Coalition, 150
Newman, Barnett, 149–50
New realism. *See* Photo realism
New York City: Administrative Code, 265n; Board of Education, 212–13, 214, 215; Board of Estimate, 130, 140, 141, 142, 185,

225, 236; Board of Standards and Appeals, 157, 222, 223, 236; Buildings Depàrtment, 124, 126, 155, 157, 161, 162, 170, 175–76, 186, 229, 230, 232, 236, 265n; Community Board Two, 164, 170, 174, 221, 223, 236–37, 265n; Cultural Affairs Department, 179, 186, 202, 229, 230, 265n; Fire Department, 123–24, 167, 186; Planning Commission, 21, 117, 125, 129–30, 131, 134, 136, 137, 139, 140, 144, 168–85 passim, 229, 232, 237; Planning Department, 130, 137, 175–76
New York Magazine, 227–28
New York Standard Metropolitan Statistical Area (SMSA), 58
New York State Council on the Arts, 213
New York Times, 22, 33, 39–40, 101, 142, 150, 182–83, 226–27, 228
New York University, 221, 222
Nichols, Mary Perot, 142
NoHo area, 181, 232, 265n
Norton Simon Museum of Art, 28

O'Dwyer, Paul, 125
O. K. Harris Gallery, 35, 90
Oldenburg, Claes, 38, 253n

Parke-Bernet Gallery, 29
Parry, Albert, 12
Parry, Malcolm, 12
Pendleton, Judy, 83–84
Pennsylvania Railroad, 116
Perlmutter, Robert, 176
Peterson, Richard, 51
Photo realism, 27, 35, 37, 65, 76, 81, 88, 89; accessibility of, 90–91; commercial imagery in, 91–92, 93, 94–95; and creativity, 77–78
Plan for New York City, 130–31
Poggioli, Renato, 76, 77
Political activism, 187–88, 189–90, 219–20, 239
Pollock, Jackson, 28, 196, 253n, 263n
Pollution, 141, 146, 148, 223
Pool, Alicia, 172–74
Pop art, 38–39, 92, 254n
Popular art, 8–9
Posters, market for, 18–19
Prints, market for, 18–19

Race, Community, and Conflict: A Study of Sparkbrook (Rex and Moore), 261n
Rapkin, Chester, 134, 172, 176
Rapkin report, 134–37, 178–80
Rational sponsors, 237
Rauschenberg, Robert, 38, 83, 144, 148, 177
Real-estate market in SoHo, 4–5, 227–37, 242
Realism. *See* Photo realism
Reform Democrats, 150
Religion, and art, 9, 69–70

Rent control, 168
Rex, John, 170
Richards, Ruth, 125, 126
Robbins, I. D., 132, 137
Rockefeller, David, 26, 130, 140, 149–50
Rockefeller Brothers Fund, 213
Rockefeller Institute, 146
Rosenberg, Harold, 50
Rothko, Mark, 81
Royalties, 83–84
Ryder, Albert, 70

Saidamon-Eristoff, Constantine, 148
St. Alphonsus's Church, 221
St. Anthony's Church, 221
St. Nicholas Hotel, 113
Schools: cooperative child-care groups, 199–200, 207–10, 217;
    nursery, 199, 203, 207–10; public grammar, parental involve-
    ment in, 212–16, 217–18, 241. *See also* Art schools
Scientists' Committee for Public Information, 146, 149
Scull, Robert C., 29, 83, 177
Seely, J. R., 12
Sex mores, 198–99
Shapiro, Shael, 157–58, 185, 186
Sim, R., 12
Simmel, Georg, 238
Simon, Norton, 28
Snodderly, Max, 149
Social class origins of artists, 254n
Social networks, 11, 102–10; mutual aid in, 102–3, 109–10; and
    peer criticism, 103–4, 109. *See also* Status communities
Sohm, Hanns, 26–27
SoHo Artists Association (SAA), 21, 189–90, 235, 236–37; and
    artist certification, 228, 229, 230, 232; and artist residency le-
    galization drive, 163–85 passim; Coordinating Committee,
    163–66, 173, 189; and journalists, 102, 226, 228; newsletter,
    168–69, 190, 224–25; organized, 163; and preservationist coali-
    tion, 224, 225; Renters Committee, 167–68; and sports center
    proposal, 221, 222, 223; White Paper, 178–79
SoHo Artists Festival, 21, 183–84, 189, 224
SoHo Children's Cooperative Playgroup, 207, 208, 209
SoHo (South Houston) Industrial District: early history, 111–15;
    entertainment areas, 3–4, 18; fire in, 123–24; name first used, 1,
    163; nonartists in, 3–5, 18, 102, 106, 226, 227, 229, 230–32, 241,
    242, 243; settled by artists, 2, 117–18. *See also* Loft buildings;
    Manufacturing
SoHo Weekly News, 228
Solomon R. Guggenheim Museum, 33, 118, 125
Sonnabend Gallery, 220
South Village, 221–22, 223
Spectorsky, A. C., 12
Speiser, Stuart, 37
Sports center proposal, 220–23, 226

Status communities, 10–12, 97–102, 151, 170, 202; and urban
    planning, 238–40. *See also* Social networks
Stella, Frank, 144
Steward, A. T., 112
Stipends, 49
Successful artists, 11, 57–58, 73–93, 101; and dealers, 73–84, 105;
    hostile to commercial success, 79–80; number of, 58, 73, 99;
    and status, 84–85, 86–87, 102, 104; work methods of, 87–90.
    See also Art, career in; Marriage roles
Surrealists, 118

Taft Museum, 40
Tankel, Claire, 230, 231
Tax benefits: donations, 44; renovation, 232
Teachers' strike of 1968, 212, 214
Teaching as sideline career, 11, 31, 60, 63, 87, 98, 99–100, 192
Ten Downtown show, 22
Tenement apartments, 119, 120
Textile industry, 117, 137, 247
Thaw (Rauschenberg), 83
Title I legislation, 133
Tribeca area, 181

United States Supreme Court, 264n
Unsuccessful artists, 53–72, 86, 87; and art role as master iden-
    tity, 62–64, 71–72, 195, 196; marginal existence of, 64–67. *See
    also* Art, career in; Marriage roles
Urban planning, requirements for, 237–43
Urban Underground, 171–72

Van Arsdale, Harry, 140
Vidich, Arthur, 10, 12, 252n
Vietnam Moratorium Weekend, 183–84
Village Independent Democrats, 147
Village Voice, 142, 147, 182, 227, 228
Vollard, Ambroise, 254n
Volunteer Lawyers for the Arts, 185, 223

Wagner, Robert F., 124, 126, 132, 133, 137, 139, 141, 154, 155
Wall, Rachele, 141–42, 146, 150, 153–54
Ware, Caroline, 12, 263n
Warehousemen's Union, 176
Warhol, Andy, 38, 50, 83
Wastelands of New York City, The, 132
Weber, Max, 5, 9, 10
Weber Gallery, 220
Whitney Museum of American Art, 33, 60, 100, 149
Wholesale industries, 113–14, 180
Wiegand, Ingrid, 178
Wiegand, Robert, 182–83, 185
Winslow, Hall, 256n
Wirth, Louis, 237–38

Wives: child care and, 200; desire for career by, 202–4. *See also* Marriage roles
Women artists, 201, 203, 204–6
Woods, Shadrach, 148
Woods, William, 148–49

Zoning laws, 125–26, 127, 155, 156, 229; and legalization, 161–86